From the Ground Up

Creating a Culture of Inquiry

From the Ground Up

Creating a Culture of Inquiry

EDITED BY

Heidi Mills and Amy Donnelly

Contributing authors in order of appearance

Heidi Mills, Harvey A. Allen, Cara Hartley, Caitlin Watts, Kala Belcher,
DeNeal Cotton, Deanna Spoonemore, Amanda Hassen, Sarah Earle,
Julie Riley Waugh, Louise B. Jennings, Michele Shamlin, Tim O'Keefe,
Rick DuVall, Dori Gilbert, Jennifer Barnes, Susanne Pender, Amy Novak,
Cynthia Colbert, Amy Donnelly, Richard E. Ishler, and Debra Hamm

HEINEMANN
Portsmouth, NH

Heinemann

A division of Reed Elsevier Inc.

361 Hanover Street

Portsmouth, NH 03801–3912

www.heinemann.com

Offices and agents throughout the world

Library of Congress Cataloging-in-Publication Data

From the ground up : creating a culture of inquiry / edited by Heidi Mills and Amy Donnelly.

    p.   cm.

Includes bibliographical references.

ISBN 0-325-00267-3 (alk. paper)

    1. Center for Inquiry (Elementary school : Columbia, S.C.)   I. Mills, Heidi.   II. Donnelly, Amy.

LD7501.C67 F76 2001

372.9757′71—dc21

                        00–049891

Editor: William Varner

Production: Sonja S. Chapman

Cover design: Jenny Jensen Greenleaf

Manufacturing: Deanna Richardson

Printed in the United States of America on acid-free paper

05 04 03 02 01 DA 1 2 3 4 5

*To the children and parents at the Center for Inquiry.
The children have shown us the power of inquiry and the value of
an intimate learning community. The parents' trust in us throughout
this journey is humbling and sincerely appreciated.*

Contents

Acknowledgments

We must begin by thanking the family members and friends of the Center for Inquiry faculty and university partners. You know who you are. You have stood by us throughout this amazing yet exhausting and often stressful journey. You celebrated our accomplishments; you offered manual labor when opening and closing the school; you helped edit our work; you attended family picnics and fabulous fund-raisers; you held our hands when we needed you and you blew kisses when we needed time to work alone; you smiled when we were in our glory supporting our students' accomplishments; you worried about us when we became too obsessed with our work; and you dried our tears of joy and exhaustion. This is one of those moments when words are not enough to express our sincere appreciation. We know you know.

We are also appreciative of Drs. Stephen Hefner and Debra Hamm and the Board of Trustees in Richland District Two for supporting this collaborative venture. Bringing two institutions with different cultures and demands together is much more complex than we imagined. We will always be grateful for the leadership in Richland District Two, for without it, our school would not have been born or nurtured. We would also like to thank Jo Hecker for her work in sustaining the Center. Finally, we want to welcome Lyn Zalusky Mueller as the new lead teacher. She has been a supportive parent and a member of our professional thought collective for years; now we are looking forward to living and learning with her daily.

We are grateful for the contributions from teachers who did not contribute to this book but who graced us with their presence and moved on to make a difference elsewhere. Thank you Jane Ness, Tammy Ballard, Diana Stout, and Monica Faller. We are delighted to welcome Brent Petersen to the Center as a new faculty member. Parents, children, and his colleagues are thrilled about his appointment in the fourth- and fifth-grade loop.

We simply smile when we think of Jaretta Belcher, Judi Beacham, Angie DeBeaugrine, Sherry Grosso, and Linda Thompson. They have all touched the Center through their good work and devotion to the philosophy of the school.

The children love them, the parents love them, and we do too. We have tremendous respect for the ways in which they have complemented and extended our work. They are essential members of the Center for Inquiry family.

There are many, many people at the University of South Carolina who have also made a difference at the Center. Generally the USC College of Education faculty, administrators, support staff, and graduate students contributed to the success of the collaborative. The MAT students from Elementary Education helped us start and sustain the school. They all touched the school in their own special ways and we want them to know how much their devotion to the Center and the profession has made a difference, and gives us hope for the future of our profession. Specifically, we would like to express gratitude to Richard Ishler, Harvey Allen, Fred Medway, Christine Ebert, Irma Van Scoy, Tommie Toner, Carol Flake, Teri Kuhs, Wendy Valerio, Steve Mattison, Chris Beckam, Robert Johnson, Dan Barron, Pat Price, Gloria Price, Joyce Crosby, Sandi Bressette, Tom Benson, Sherrill Jaco, and Kay Ratcliff. We must say that Susi Long is voted our greatest admirer from USC. Her care, concern, and thorough feedback have been great sources of comfort and inspiration.

We have the good fortune of many supporters within the state of South Carolina as well. We have grown from the feedback they have given from their visits throughout the years and consider our professional relationships with John Kelley, Rhonda Corley, and Anita McLeod a blessing.

It was Karen Smith, Jerome Harste, Brenda Power, Ruth Hubbard, Shelley Harwayne, Carolyn Burke, Judith Linfors, Ralph Peterson, Bruce Novak, Bill Ayers, and Diane Stephens who offered incredible inspiration, insight, and support at the national level. While they acknowledged the value of our work, they also asked the hard questions that pushed us into new uncharted territory. They are among our greatest distant teachers. They live the model of inquiry we cherish.

And then we have the folks at Heinemann. It never ceased to amaze us when Bill Varner and Eric Chalek gave us suggestions. It was more than the fact that they were right and their ideas gave the text more power. It was as if they had been living and learning along side us at the Center. They seemed to know what we really valued and what we needed to share with others in the world with similar professional dreams. We would also like to extend a sincere word of thanks to Leigh Peake and Hillary VanDeusen who extended the initial invitation to pursue this project. Leigh and Hillary instinctively "knew" we had some important stories to tell, and we are pleased they accessed Bill and Eric to make it possible.

Finally, we would like to formally acknowledge the educators everywhere who blazed the trail we have followed. To the educators who dare to do what is right for children and who teach in thoughtful, caring ways. To those educators who do not simply turn the page and do what comes next. To the teachers who see teaching as a way of life, not simply a job. To those who see the beauty, dignity, intelligence, and diversity in every child. You are a gift to the Center for Inquiry in Richland District Two, the profession at large, and humanity. Thank you.

Foreword

Whenever I browse the NCTE convention catalogue and spot Heidi Mills' name, along with her colleagues from the Center for Inquiry, I automatically note the time and date of their presentation and make sure to arrive early to get a front row seat. Their presentations are always rich in content, inspirational in spirit, and filled with surprising voices. I was delighted to discover that the same qualities appear in their new book, *From the Ground Up: Creating a Culture of Inquiry.*

As the founding principal of a New York City public school, I so appreciate the authors' attempts to capture the essence of a school they began from scratch, a school whose community members, both child and adult, have learned to look at the world through the lens of inquiry. This book, a veritable videotape album documenting the sights and sounds of the Center for Inquiry, is after all, educators who are invested in the inquiry stance. It is also a book for all educators who have dreamed of starting their own school. Additionally, it is a book for parents who want to expand the world of possibility for their children's education and for their own involvement in the day-to-day life of the schools their children attend.

Readers will take many notes on the chapters of this book. They will underline passages, highlight sections, and write in the margins on such diverse topics as the meaning and habits of inquiry, community building rituals, the how-to of student-generated expert projects, the priority status given to the roles of teacher-research, demonstration, reflection, apprenticeship, the taking of multiple perspectives, and celebrations. In addition, readers will appreciate appendices filled with practical resources, transcripts of actual teaching-learning moments, and samples of student writing studded throughout the text. Readers will become familiar with such Center interactions and practices as the "Friendship Circle," "Classroom Explorations," "Journals of Ordinary Thoughts," and "Wonder Why Walls."

Additionally, readers will delight in hearing from such diverse participants as a student-teacher, several university faculty including an arts educator and a school ethnographer, a wide range of dedicated and reflective classroom teachers including a middle school teacher turned kindergarten teacher, the school's accomplished principal Amy Donnelly, and fifth graders with thoughts on what is essential at their new school. No doubt, readers will find themselves doing as I did and jotting down many quotable lines. I loved thanking educators who "do not simply turn the page and do what comes next," the goal of "subordinating the teaching process to the learning process," and children learning to "speak into the silence." I especially loved hearing the description of the "... traditional 2-by-4-by-6 approach to education—those being the two covers of a textbook, the four walls of a classroom, and the six instructional periods of the school day."

Then, too, readers will be uplifted by the reality of a successful school-university collaboration, the full participation of parents, the insightful student comments and questions related to their personal inquiries, the role of the visual arts, the Center's devotion to democracy and social action, and an incredibly honest epilogue that suggests perseverance in the face of the many harsh realities and obstacles that educators everywhere are confronting.

Here's to all the people represented in *From the Ground Up: Creating a Culture of Inquiry.* Thank you for sharing the story of your school, an ever-growing and dynamic work in progress. May many more educators throughout our country be inspired to begin their own school of choice and may the contents of this book be a warm wind that spreads across the land, carrying with it the camaraderie, dedication, honesty, and expertise of our colleagues from South Carolina.

—*Shelley Harwayne*

Preface
The Dream

HEIDI MILLS

Nothing happens unless first a dream . . . .

—CARL SANDBURG

It all started as a dream. The dream of starting a school that would truly nourish everyone who lived and learned there; a school that would touch those who simply entered as visitors; a school where best practice would be the norm rather than the exception; a school where preservice and inservice teachers, university partners, children, and parents would all cocreate the community and curriculum and, in so doing, foster democracy within, across, and outside of the classrooms.

I suspect many educators have had similar dreams. I also suspect that many have created incredible spaces for teachers and children to grow. It was the Manhattan New School that made a genuine difference in our vision and consequent journey. Because Shelley Harwayne, JoAnne Hindley, Jerry Harste, Chris Leeland, Bill Ayers, and their colleagues have so generously shared their successes and struggles with us and others across the country, we are now able to enter the professional conversation about starting schools. This is our story, a story we hope will inform and inspire others to make their professional dreams come true.

Like all good stories, the complexity of the events and depth of the characters make the plot seem simply elegant on one hand and incredibly dense on the other. In many ways, the vision we have created for this book is as demanding as the school itself. We want readers to vicariously experience the power and potential of the moment-by-moment interactions within and across classrooms. We want readers to understand the practical and political insights that made a difference as we ventured into unknown territory. We want readers to learn from a diverse range of perspectives—those that inform and transform our thinking daily. We want readers to appreciate inquiry as a stance we take on learning, learners, the nature of knowledge, and schooling. We want readers to feel the sense of urgency that we did when we finally committed to the project.

The Center for Inquiry in Columbia, South Carolina, is a place where we implement, challenge, build upon, and rethink our assumptions about teaching and learning almost daily. We have grown in ways we could have never anticipated because we have found that when you start a school, every assumption you have ever held is put to the test. When given the freedom to operationalize your beliefs, talk only gets you so far. No excuses; it's about your real values; it's about what really matters—period!

The teachers who live and breathe the model of inquiry that many in our field simply talk about have become my most important mentors. I imagine their voices, passions, and questions will touch you, too. But before you enter their classrooms, eavesdrop on our teacher study group conversations, or consider the impact of their teaching through a range of perspectives from our children to our college dean, it is important to share the critical incidents that made a difference as we embarked upon this adventure.

Finding Our Way

> Never doubt that a small group of thoughtful, committed people can change the world. Indeed, it is the only thing that has.
>
> —*Margaret Mead*

It all started years ago in Columbia, South Carolina, classroom teachers and university colleagues met monthly on Sunday afternoons for teacher support group meetings. We talked and talked and talked. We laughed and cried together. It was in the comfort and privacy of our intimate group of colleagues that we learned the value of professional conversations. After sharing good books, profound articles, successful strategies, and burning questions with colleagues who shared our expertise and spirit, we all made our way back into the real world of public and higher education. While we worked in various settings and found tremendous pleasure in our children and university students, we always felt as if there could be more. The *could be more* slowly turned into *should be more.* The more we met in our teacher support group, the more we grew.

Before we knew it, we were in the midst of intensive study group meetings supported by Eisenhower Grant funds to foster our thinking and strengthen our inquiry into an expanded vision of literacy that included mathematics. One day after an especially stimulating Eisenhower session, we suddenly found ourselves asking, "Wouldn't it be nice if we could work in a site where we could challenge and support one another; a site where our ways of teaching would be expected and common across all classrooms; a place where inquiry would pervade the lives of all of the children and adults who entered; a place where children could receive theoretically congruent instruction over time; a place where the university and public school could truly teach and learn from each other in transformative ways?"

In the meantime, Richard Ishler, the dean of the USC College of Education, had been promoting professional development school partnerships. Many of us joined his efforts as we embraced cross-institutional collaboration. (See Chapter 13 for a complete description of the professional development school movement by Richard Ishler and Harvey Allen.) It soon became clear that the mission of initiating and sustaining genuine change in existing schools was more complex than many of us anticipated. I became more and more uncomfortable with the fact that many teachers in the PDS sites felt as if we were imposing rather than supporting change. I also noticed that some of the most committed and dynamic PDS teachers were being ousted by their colleagues because of the positive attention they were receiving from the university. I found myself longing for the opportunity to promote real change. I honestly admired those who were patient enough to accept and celebrate small steps. However, I personally didn't believe I would live long enough to make a real difference through the structures that were in place. I think my impatience originally came from my father, but it was the thoughtfulness of a few teachers that took my breath away and left me longing for more. I believed it was possible in South Carolina, given the university commitment to collaboration, PDS relationships that had been established with local school districts, and the expertise in the local teaching force.

Working Within the System

A critical mass of amazing teachers created a multiage team at one PDS site. They were among the most involved in our teacher support group meetings as well. We worked together intensively and extensively. They looked to one another and distant teachers like Shelly Harwayne, Jerry Harste, and Deborah Meier for both validation and new challenges. After reading *Lasting Impressions* by Shelley Harwayne (1992) together, I noticed how energized they were by the Manhattan New School. The PDS teachers had given so much to our university students by welcoming them into their classrooms that I wrote a PDS Seed Grant proposal for them to visit the school. Amy Donnelly, a USC faculty member who had been instrumental in the success of the PDS work and who had administrative experience, joined teachers Dori Gilbert and Rick DuVall on the trip to New York. Upon their return, Amy called and said, "I feel confident and competent enough to create our own school!" And so it goes . . . a small group of committed individuals changed the world as we knew it in Columbia, South Carolina. Traditional barriers would soon be dismantled; new questions would be asked of the profession and of ourselves; new relationships would be forged, and parents would be given the chance to choose their children's school; the student population would be as diverse as the Columbia area, not simply the neighborhood surrounding the school; narrative progress reports and student-led conferences would replace grades and unit tests; classroom teachers would create curriculum with and for children; and finally, teachers and university colleagues would inquire side by side and, in so doing, bring democracy in public education to life.

What Is Inquiry?

As we began the journey together, we all came to realize that the phrase "our actions reflect our beliefs" would make all the difference in the world. In fact, that notion is one that still unites and challenges us as we work with children, families, and district and university administrators. We constantly examine our actions in light of our beliefs and question whether or not our beliefs accurately reflect our actions. We embrace Short and Burke's thinking: "We believe that curriculum involves putting into action a system of beliefs. Therefore, when we engage in inquiry about curriculum, we examine beliefs as well as our actions in the classroom" (1996, 97). While we will foreground our theoretical perspective here so that readers might use it as a touchstone when reading our stories about life, learning, growth, and change throughout the Center, it is important to be very open and honest about the fact that we have learned as much from investigating our practices as we have from interrogating theory. Carole Edelsky puts the relationship between beliefs and practices into perspective beautifully. When discussing what she learned when working in Karen Smith's classroom, she notes, "I can theorize from practice but I can't imagine practice from theory."

The definition of inquiry that follows currently frames and informs our work. However, given the transformative nature of inquiry, our definition will have evolved by the time this book is in print. To date, this thinking reflects what has united our school philosophically and what will push us into new uncharted waters in the future.

Our Definition of Inquiry

Inquiry is a philosophical stance rather than a set of strategies, activities, or a particular teaching method. As such, inquiry promotes intentional and thoughtful learning for teachers and children. Our classrooms are united philosophically, yet each classroom community is unique because the teachers know it is their right and responsibility to collaborate with children when making the theory their own in their own ways. At the Center for Inquiry, we operationalize an inquiry stance moment by moment, day in and day out, with the children, parents, university partners, and administrators. It is a way of living and learning together; a way of viewing and learning about the amazing world in which we live; a way of honoring and learning from the diversity that is humanity; a way of being true to ourselves, our children, and the profession; a way of fostering genuine professional development; and, most importantly, a way of respecting, building upon, and supporting all learners, tall and small.

Through weekly curricular conversations, we have inquired into and documented the assumptions that underpin the development of practical theory at the Center. The following lists reveal what matters most as we create curriculum with and for children.

Assumptions About Learners and Learning

- Children are sense makers by nature.
- Growth and change is not linear and sequential, but rich, complex, and recursive.
- Children learn by generating new hypotheses, by taking risks, and by reflecting on their accomplishments as well as their miscues.
- Children engage in genuine inquiry when they are invited to pose and investigate questions or issues they find compelling. These questions or issues could be completely self-initiated or related to a class theme or concept.
- Learning is propelled through reflexivity. When learners intentionally and systematically study themselves, they outgrow themselves as learners.

Assumptions About Teachers and Teaching

- Teachers devise learning experiences that promote an understanding and appreciation of the role of mentors in learning.
- Teachers function as mentors and use an apprenticeship model when devising learning invitations and responding to student work. Responsive teaching occurs when the curricular framework reflects the ways in which learning occurs within and across disciplines in the world.
- Teachers focus on the skillfulness of inquiry by helping children learn how to use primary and secondary sources and by illustrating the importance of learning from the process and products or artifacts.

- Teachers devote large blocks of time to reading, writing, and math workshops across grade levels.
- Teachers are natural researchers and use insights from intentional and systematic kid watching to make informed instructional decisions.

Assumptions About Curriculum and Evaluation

- Curriculum is created with and for children. A sense of wonder and thoughtfulness about knowledge, the learning process, and our world is fostered and negotiated in predictable and democratic ways.
- Teachers create space in the curriculum for children to learn how to think and share thoughts and insights like readers, writers, mathematicians, scientists, historians, artists, musicians, dancers, and so on.
- While workshops are necessarily unique across classrooms and disciplines, they all involve the following: (1) *demonstration*—strategy lessons and mini-lessons; (2) *engagement*—living the process (doing what readers, writers, and mathematicians do); (3) *reflection*—reflecting as individuals and/or groups on the content, skills, strategies, and concepts under investigation; and (4) *celebration*—public recognition for growth and change.
- Teaching through broad concepts unites learners and disciplines. Interdisciplinary ties are made visible and all voices and perspectives contribute to the depth and breadth of the class thought collective.
- Evaluation promotes growth, understanding, and new actions for teachers as well as children. To do so, we must carefully document and report patterns in children's thinking and behavior for the purposes of informing and transforming our curriculum and parents' appreciation of their children's growth.

Assumptions About Thought and Language

- Although questions promote a sense of wonder and often frame investigations, genuine inquiry is grounded in authentic conversations.
- Curiosity is nurtured when children share hunches, personal connections, and anomalies.
- New thoughts are generated when all participants in the classroom laugh, pose and answer questions, debate, listen, search, describe, teach, negotiate, and hypothesize together.
- Individual insights and strategies become part of the class thought collective through formal and informal conversations.

Assumptions About Sign Systems and Knowledge Domains

- Language, mathematics, art, music, and movement are communication systems that were created by humans to construct, interpret, and share meaning.
- All sign systems are similar to language in that they have cue systems such as symbols, syntax, and semantics.
- Each sign system offers learners a unique perspective on the world. The communication and learning potential in the classroom is enhanced through access to multiple sign systems.
- Sign systems are used as tools for learning when inquiring into knowledge domains such as science, history, sociology, anthropology, and so on.
- Students learn about language and mathematics during workshops, and they learn through language and mathematics during interdisciplinary focus studies and expert projects on topics in the physical and social sciences.

Assumptions About Democracy and Community

- All participants in the classroom function as teachers and learners, meaning that choice, ownership, and conversation are at the heart of learning rituals and the general curricular framework.
- All voices are heard, respected, and valued.
- Strong classroom communities promote collaboration, which in turn enhances academic rigor, independence, confidence, and competence.
- Time and space must be made in the daily life of the classroom for teachers and children to develop intimate relationships. Teachers and children learn to care for and respect one another once they learn about one anothers' passions, fears, histories, and expertise.
- You can have democracy without community, but it is impossible to have community without democracy.

Assumptions About Schooling and Society

- Teachers and learners strive to take action on new knowledge.
- Teachers and learners regularly ask how they can make the world a better place by developing and using new knowledge.
- Teachers and administrators benefit from asking the same questions of themselves that they ask of their students.

- Collaborative strategies that nurture teachers and learners create hopeful opportunities for the profession, our democracy, and humanity.

—Mills with CFI faculty, university partners,
and our distant teacher/professional mentors 1996–1999

Multiple Perspectives on the Center for Inquiry

The chapters that follow chronicle the conception and evolution of the Center for Inquiry during its first three years. We are in the midst of our fourth year, and it has not been an easy one. Since most of the chapters were written during our third year and were simply revised during the fourth, we have decided that we must write an epilogue to be truthful to our readers and ourselves. The epilogue includes the struggles that have emerged as a result of the standards movement, new questions and insights about power and control, and questions about maintaining the integrity of the philosophy over time. Each chapter is written from the unique perspective of a critical CFI team member. While essential insights about inquiry-based curricula and starting small public schools of choice are woven throughout each piece, Chapter 12 is written by Amy Donnelly, the former principal, to capture and interpret fundamental issues that made a difference during the first three years.

The first chapter "From the Dewey School to the Center: One Hundred Years of Inquiry," is written by Harvey Allen, who was our associate dean at USC when we embarked on this venture. Harvey has been devoted to the success of our school and has been instrumental in making the cross-institutional collaboration work. He portrays the negotiation from a simple promise to the creation and implementation of a model school.

The second chapter, "Critical Incidents Throughout the Beginning of Our Journey," by Heidi Mills, portrays the inside story. In the beginning it was Amy Donnelly, principal/USC faculty member; Debra Hamm, chief academic advisor for Richland District Two; Heidi Mills, curriculum and research specialist/USC faculty member; and Robin Cox, elementary teacher, who together learned how to negotiate their way from the initial proposal to the opening of a university–public school partnership. Since that time, Robin Cox has had two children of her own. She has been supporting us from the comfort and privacy of her home, where she has embarked upon her own personal inquiry about supporting the growth of infants and toddlers. Lessons that were learned along the way are woven throughout the chapter. Additionally, original artifacts that made a difference such as the curricular and assessment frameworks are included as demonstrations for others who are interested in taking similar steps in their own communities. (See the appendices for more artifacts, including the proposal for the Center presented to the Richland District Two School Board and teacher interview materials.)

The third chapter, "It's Our School" is written by members of Julie Riley Waugh's fifth-grade class. They embarked upon a mission to understand and share significant features of our school with readers and school visitors. Their chapter reveals inquiry in action. The children's voices come through loud and clear. The intentional and systematic nature of a rigorous inquiry-based curriculum comes through as well. The Center was created to support learning and learners, plain and simple. This chapter reveals what children value most within such a context.

The fourth chapter, "Inquiry for Professional Development and Continual School Renewal" is by Louise Jennings, assistant professor at USC and the Center ethnographer. Louise demonstrates fundamental features of inquiry within classrooms and throughout our professional development conversations. Her chapter serves as an anchor in the book, as it shows how inquiry both informs and transforms teachers, children, parents, and university partners.

The fifth chapter, "Creating Curriculum with and for Children" by Michele Shamlin, demonstrates how the essence of thinking, communicating, and living the lives of natural inquirers permeates everything children do in kindergarten. As a teacher-researcher, Michele wrote a chapter rich with classroom examples and insights about practical theory.

The sixth chapter, titled "Giving Children Voice: Daily Rituals That Support Learning Through Conversations," by Tim O'Keefe, vividly illustrates how instructional strategies devised to encourage children to share mathematical, scientific, and linguistic perspectives on the world also promote democracy in the classroom. As a teacher-researcher, Tim captures and illuminates essential features of the processes and products in his second-grade classroom and how he extends such work into the children's homes.

The seventh chapter, "Becoming Reading Researchers" by Julie Riley Waugh, chronicles the evolution of a unit of study in which math is the primary tool for learning. In so doing, Julie and her fourth graders use mathematical investigations to reflect upon and analyze themselves and the class as readers. New actions are taken up by individuals and the whole group after they decide to intentionally and systematically outgrow their current reading habits.

The eighth chapter, titled "Refining and Expanding Our Notions of Inquiry, Talk, and Classroom Community," by Rick DuVall, shows what inquiry looks like and sounds like, as Rick and his students investigate ways of knowing and interacting when creating community in their fourth-grade classroom. Rick was one of the original teachers at the Center and his perspective on curriculum and community now pervade classrooms throughout the school.

The ninth chapter, "Inquiry into Family Partnerships," by Dori Gilbert, Jennifer Barnes, Susanne Pender, and Heidi Mills, is a lovely account of the ways in which the teachers collaborate with the Center families. Their chapter is filled with artifacts that tell the story of life and learning within the walls of Center classrooms and beyond. The artifacts also unveil the thoughtful ways in which the teachers communicate with parents responsively. Finally, the communication strategies reveal how parents, teachers, and university partners all inform and transform one another throughout the year.

The tenth chapter, titled "Putting the Pieces Together," is written by Amy Novak. Amy was one of our first MAT interns from USC, and her chapter illuminates the power and potential of the Center as a demonstration site. She shows how the lessons learned at the Center live on in different settings. Amy's chapter is especially telling for those who are wondering about the value of internship placements in settings such as the Center for Inquiry.

The eleventh chapter, "Visual Arts as Inquiry in Elementary Education," is written by Cynthia Colbert, professor of art at USC and the lead art teacher at the Center. Cynthia's chapter reveals critical insights into university-public school collaboration. Additionally, she chronicles her journey as a full professor reentering the world of elementary school after nineteen years. She has made a significant difference at the Center and her unique perspectives on art education and university–public school collaboration provide an important lens for those interested in the arts as well as those who want to unite university professors with public schools in meaningful, lasting ways.

The twelfth chapter, titled "Living the Model," is written by Amy Donnelly, founding principal and USC faculty member for the first three years. As the lead administrator, Amy highlights the processes and products that were crucial to the success of the Center. She features the establishment of the Parent Advisory Board, the creation of the Center bylaws, the evolution of the CFI Volunteer Committee, examples of successful fund-raising efforts, demonstrations of Professional Development School Network collaborative efforts, standardized test score data, and the Center for Inquiry Review Board Report conducted by Karen Smith, elementary director of the National Council of Teachers of English. After birthing the Center and giving it life for three years via a joint appointment across institutions, she returned to the university and is now telling the story so that others might unite institutions for the sake of our children, our future, and our democracy.

The thirteenth chapter, "The Center for Inquiry as a Professional Development School," by Richard Ishler and Harvey Allen, foregrounds the importance of the professional development school movement in initiating and sustaining progressive schools. This chapter is especially important because it was written by our dean and associate dean at USC. Both authors worked on behalf of the Center for the first three years. They both embrace cross-institutional collaboration and are invested in the PDS activities.

The Epilogue, by Heidi Mills with Amy Donnelly, and the faculty illuminates how good work is difficult and often involves compromises. It describes how the faculty has responded to new demands placed on teachers by the standards movement. It also shows how important it is to pose new questions in response to external demands. It is the questions we ask of ourselves that determine the path we take as teachers and learners. It is all about inquiry.

References

Darling-Hammond, L. 1997. *The Right to Learn: A Blueprint for Creating Schools That Work.* San Francisco, CA: Jossey-Bass.

Edelsky, C. 1998. *Personal Communication with Karen Smith.* Urbana, IL: National Council of Teachers of English.

Harwayne, S. 1992. *Lasting Impressions: Weaving Literature into Writing Workshop.* Portsmouth, NH: Heinemann.

Short, K., and C. Burke. 1996. "Examining Our Beliefs and Practices Through Inquiry." *Language Arts* 73: 97–104.

1

From the Dewey School to the Center
One Hundred Years of Inquiry

HARVEY A. ALLEN

The Promise

The USC Professional Development School Network was well established in 1995 when Amy Donnelly, Heidi Mills, and a cadre of committed educators approached the administration of Richland School District Two with the idea of developing a small public elementary school organized around an inquiry-based approach to teaching and learning. While it is not totally surprising that two teacher educators might dream about organizing a school dedicated to inquiry learning, it is rather remarkable that they would actually work to make that dream a reality. Even more remarkable than the fact that these two visionaries might move from their comfortable niches as college professors to engage in the risk-taking behavior of promoting and organizing a school is that they could find a school district amenable to such a proposal, given the current environment in which public schools function. While colleges and universities are recently adjusting to tighter budgets, performance indicators, and demands for accountability, the public schools have existed in a climate of test scores, performance indicators, standards, and external accountability for years. For the administrative leadership of Richland School District Two to be interested in an inquiry-based school in the prescribed and monitored context of schoolkeeping in the mid-1990s is noteworthy. However, it is not entirely surprising that Richland School District Two would be interested in the proposal because, over the years, the district had achieved a reputation for putting the needs of children first and for actively promoting the personal and professional development of its teachers. A succession of strong superintendents, dynamic school principals and administrators, and competent and committed teachers, in concert with effective school board members and

1

involved parents, had worked to place the district's schools in the forefront of South Carolina's schools. From the USC side, Amy and Heidi enjoyed the support of College of Education administrators and faculty deeply committed to Professional Development Schools and other initiatives to promote partnerships and collaborations that would enhance the learning opportunities for schoolchildren, USC students, and professional educators. The promise of an exciting innovation had been evoked. Making the school happen would call for the collaborative efforts of educational leaders in the school district and the university.

Making the Promise a Reality

The process of creating a school from the ground up is an undertaking of monumental proportions and, consequently, it is seldom done. It is one thing for a school district to build a new elementary school to relieve overcrowding or to serve a bustling new housing community and yet another for a school district to collaborate with a college to create a new school of choice for a specific population of children. There was a sense of historical significance as planning for the Center for Inquiry commenced in 1995, since one hundred years earlier, John Dewey was planning his own school for inquiry in the form of a laboratory school at the University of Chicago. This soon to be heralded Laboratory School opened for instruction in 1896 on the campus of the University of Chicago. The Center for Inquiry opened in 1996 at Summit Parkway Middle School. The Center for Inquiry, which opened in Richland School District Two in Columbia, South Carolina, would pick up on the thread that runs true through American education by connecting an innovative school from our cherished past to one in a promising present. Professor Dewey and his colleagues formulated a school to promote best teaching and learning in the pedagogical context of a living, learning laboratory. The proposed Center for Inquiry would extend the laboratory setting from the university campus to the more realistic public school setting through the Professional Development School Network. A really great educational idea never really dies; vestiges of the Dewey Laboratory School were given new life in the Center for Inquiry.

The first step in the process of gaining approval for the school from the representative trustee boards of Richland School District Two and the University of South Carolina was to formulate a position paper delineating the advantages of a school exemplifying a culture of inquiry. A team of educational leaders, teachers, and administrators representing the school district, university, and community was formed to develop a workable plan for a public school of choice, namely, a center for inquiry.

The position paper that was developed to explain the purpose and functions, focusing on inquiry approaches, primarily addressed the two issues of curriculum and the interactions of students and teachers with the curriculum. The first issue dealt with what the curriculum would be and how the curriculum would be delivered. The second question addressed who the students and teachers would be and how the students, teachers, and significant others would function in an inquiry-based learning community.

The curriculum proposal for the Center would reflect all of the characteristics of an inquiry-based philosophy. The guiding philosophy of the curriculum was that students and teachers deserved better learning opportunities than those afforded to them by the traditional 2-by-4-by-6 approach to education—those being the two covers of a textbook, the four walls of a classroom, and the six instructional periods of the school day. The curriculum would be collaborative in nature, would integrate curricular areas, would connect academic subjects to meaningful real-life situations, would be learner-centered, and would function as a true learning community where all participants exist simultaneously as teachers and learners. The underlying principle was that all participants, including parents, children, teachers, and administrators, would collaborate to construct a learner-centered curriculum. The curriculum dimension of the Center for Inquiry would be strengthened by the collaboration that would necessarily result from the designation of the Center as a USC Professional Development School site in conjunction with Richland School District Two. The notion that the Center would be a PDS site was in the forefront of all of the envisioning and planning for the Center for Inquiry.

In addressing the question of who the students would be, it was determined that the school would strive to serve a population representative of the Columbia Northeast community and would capitalize on the opportunities presented by such a diverse population. Provisions for a diverse student and faculty population regarding age, ethnic, cultural, and economic backgrounds would ensure that the classrooms would be rich, interesting places to live and learn. A guiding principle giving direction and dimension to the teaching and learning situation was that teachers and administrators would function as researchers to examine how and what the students were learning. The concept of teacher as researcher would be utilized in the school to facilitate the learning process, to create rich, compelling learning opportunities, and to assess student performance in a variety of ways ranging from traditional standardized assessments to alternative methods. The alternative assessments would emphasize that the best measure of a child's work is a collection of representative samples of the child's work. For the Center of Inquiry to achieve any degree of success and acceptance with the parents, administration, faculty in other schools, and the school board, the students would be expected to attain or exceed the achievement and intelligence scores obtained by students in other elementary schools in the district. As a Professional Development School, the university–school district partnership would maximize learning opportunities for students, teachers, interns, and parents. A goal of the school would be to subordinate the teaching process to the learning process. Many educators have contended that in many cases, teaching does not directly result in effective student learning. However, the teacher as a person is essential to the facilitation of meaningful learning. Teachers in the Center for Inquiry would be less concerned with formal instruction and more directed toward enabling learning to happen.

The final component of the position paper that was prepared to delineate the advantages of a school focused on an inquiry-based approach to learning was to place the Center for Inquiry in the mainstream of local, state, and national initiatives for school improvement and educational reform. One of the telling points to recommend the Center was the impressive body of research on the strengths of small schools. The small schools research pointed to the advantages to be gained from a small elementary school of choice consisting of one classroom at each grade level, K–5. The Center would capitalize on the optimum size of the student population to get all of the people actively involved in a child's education—teachers, administrators, parents, and the students themselves. The teachers in the Center would be thoroughly steeped in content areas, knowledgeable in educational research, and capable of translating content mastery and knowledge of research into coherent curriculum and instruction. The needs, interests, and abilities of students would be accommodated in developmentally appropriate and responsive ways, to the end that students would begin to take responsibility for and ownership of their learning. Either by design or default, parents are the most important teachers their children will ever have. Parents would be encouraged to function as helping teachers at home and to become partners in the education of their children. Additionally, parents would be utilized throughout the school according to their areas of expertise. While the focus of the Center would emphasize the specific learning opportunities of the students in the school, requisite state and national initiatives such as Goals 2000, National Council / Association content standards, South Carolina Frameworks, South Carolina statewide testing programs, and Richland Two SQE requirements would be incorporated into the comprehensive program of the Center. The noted humorist Mark Twain once remarked, "I have never let my schooling interfere with my education" (Ryan and Cooper, 1984, 141). By that he meant that the school as an institution imposed rituals, bells and whistles, hoops and regimens that subverted rather than facilitated education. As the concept of the Center for Inquiry evolved, it was envisioned as a place where children would come first and where children and teachers would learn together. The Center for Inquiry, a daring new approach to a place called school, would be a school in the truest sense of the word.

Heidi Mills and Amy Donnelly gained the endorsement of Stephen Hefner, Superintendent of Richland School District Two, and Debra Hamm, Chief Academic Officer. The next step in making the promise of a center for inquiry a reality was to present the proposal to the Richland School District Two Board of Trustees for approval. Once approval could be secured from the school board, the Center for Inquiry could begin operation.

The topic of the Center for Inquiry caused a lively debate among the members of the Board of Trustees. There was much discussion concerning the relative merits of such a small school of choice. Concerns such as the economic feasibility, equity issues, the university's role in the school, transportation issues, and myriad other problems were discussed. A few board members were very concerned that the students in the Center would be detrimental to the achievement test profile for the district. Whether reading and mathematics would be high priorities in the instructional program was questioned. The availability of art, music, physical education, the Alert program, and programs for special-needs students was questioned. One of the overriding concerns was that the school would become too expensive. Richland Two administrators assured the Board of Trustees that no additional funds would be spent on the school above that allocated on a per pupil basis for every child in the district. The deciding factor, notwithstanding that the proposal for the Center was brilliantly crafted, was that the Center for Inquiry would be a Professional Development School site for the College of Education of the University of South Carolina. The collaboration among the University of South Carolina, Richland School District Two, other educational entities, and the Northeast Columbia community was instrumental in gaining the approval of the Richland Two Board of Trustees. What had started as an inquiry into the possibility of creating a new school had evolved into a promising concept and was now to become a reality.

Reference

Ryan, K., and J. Cooper. 1984. *Those Who Can, Teach,* 4th ed. Boston, MA: Houghton Mifflin Company.

2

Critical Incidents Throughout the Beginning of Our Journey

HEIDI MILLS

Until one is committed, there is hesitance, the chance to draw back, always ineffectiveness. Concerning all acts of initiative (and creation), there is one elementary truth, the ignorance of which kills countless ideas and splendid plans: that the moment one definitely commits oneself, then Providence moves too.

All sorts of things occur that would never otherwise have occurred. A whole stream of events issues from the decision, raising in one's favor all manner of unforeseen incidents and meetings and material assistance, which no man could have dreamed would have come his way.

— SCOTTISH HIMALAYAN EXPEDITION

Making the Investment

Once several teachers, two university faculty members, and the district's chief academic officer made the commitment to start a school, amazing things happened. In fact, we have learned to trust the process in ways we had never imagined before. Sometimes it was a challenge to relax and trust as we encountered a number of serious obstacles. However, each and every challenge presented opportunities to learn from someone or something and, most importantly, every problem revealed new possibilities. Some of our colleagues do not want to believe it, but it is true. The pattern defies natural coincidences. The right people, ideas, and materials always emerged at just the right time and we have learned the value of believing it into being.

6

I do not want to imply that we simply took a back seat and let it all evolve. Quite the contrary; we have worked harder than ever to create and sustain the school. We honestly believe this is the most challenging yet the most satisfying work of our careers. We have simply learned when to push and when to trust. Debra Meier's work with a small school in Harlem (1995) inspired and informed our decisions. In short, she helped us learn to stay focused on what mattered most (Stephens 1990). The previous chapter chronicled the inception of the Center from the associate dean's perspective. This chapter reveals the inside story and, as such, addresses many of the important steps that were taken as we were learning to negotiate our way.

Considering the Audience: It's About Seeking to Understand

We learned long ago that writers attend to their audience (Calkins and Harwayne 1991; Harwayne 1992; Power and Hubbard 1996; Short, Harste, and Burke 1996). While we understood this notion theoretically, it took Debra Hamm, our district office mentor, to help us learn how to communicate with the school board. As we were learning how to transform our original proposal into a document that the school board would consider seriously, we began to realize why many ventures such as ours don't ever become actualized.

Our original proposal was written for insiders (see Appendix A, p. 223). While we had a difficult time seeing this at first, when we look back, it is crystal clear. School board members ask very different questions than many of us. We seek to understand those questions so we may answer them effectively.

We laugh out loud now when we think about how pleased we were with our vision and our capacity to capture it so succinctly in the original proposal we submitted to the district office. We were so fortunate that the superintendent and his chief academic officer knew and respected us as professionals and were willing to take the time necessary to help us reshape the proposal for an outside audience. They knew we would find ourselves among people in power who truly wanted to know, who truly wanted to support our efforts, if only they could envision what we meant. They knew that parents and school board members would ask questions like the following:

What would our school day look like?

What would our classrooms sound like?

How big would the school be?

What materials would be used?

What qualifications would teachers need?

What would the adult-child ratio be?

Would it be more expensive than traditional programs?

Would the arts be included?

What did we really mean by inquiry?

What does looping mean?

So one of the first steps involved a series of revisions of the original proposal. Debra Hamm took the lead in finalizing the draft. Debra, Richland District Two's chief academic officer, understood our vision and had the capacity to transform it on paper into a plan that others would understand and accept (Appendix B, p. 231). She and Harvey Allen, our associate dean, presented it to the school board, and we are grateful. While we are confident we could do a better job now, we are equally sure that we would not have succeeded then, as we did not know how to communicate effectively within the school board culture.

Holding the Vision: It's About People, Not Programs

After receiving approval from the school board by a single vote, we began the work of actualizing the vision. We had to work fast to select teachers, create and mail a brochure to all elementary families in the district, and conduct orientations. Once again we found ourselves promoting the school to people who were not in our thought collective. They pushed us to drop the jargon and simply describe what we wanted and how our Center might be different from the typical schools in the area.

The Center for Inquiry brochure was mailed to all families in the Richland District Two area with a cover letter announcing the two school orientations. In the meantime, Amy Donnelly, the principal, worked with district office personnel to create the teacher interview protocol.

We had been working hard to communicate our agenda clearly and succinctly to outsiders and it had come time to once again use the language of the profession to push ourselves and to select teachers who were on the cutting edge. We created a context to explore the applicants' knowledge of theory as well as their appreciation of the role that theory plays in the classroom and professional conversations. We knew that it would be essential to hire teachers who embraced inquiry both as a guiding philosophy for creating curriculum and as a way of thinking and being in general. We wanted to recruit teachers who lived the model personally and professionally. If we could do so, we were confident that inquiry would pervade life and learning at the Center.

The interview questions and format (see Appendix C, p. 237) made a difference because they helped differentiate good elementary teachers who were solid leaders in their schools from those who truly embraced inquiry and had the potential to become national leaders through their teacher research. A review of the interview protocol and common questions reveals the fact that philosophical congruence was the characteristic we valued most. As candidates responded to questions posed by the interview team, they were rated in terms of their ability to do the following:

articulate how children learn

define inquiry-based instruction

describe characteristics of an inquiry-based philosophy

give examples that demonstrate theory as practice

describe the significance and possibilities related to a faculty united by a common philosophy

describe how theory is developed

In addition to asking them questions, we also invited the teachers to show us how they make instructional decisions and how they assess growth and change using data from their own classrooms. Their stories and artifacts unveiled what mattered most to the candidates and helped the principal and the others on the interview team make the first hiring decisions.

Teacher beliefs continue to be the central criteria when hiring teachers to this day. In fact, Susanne Murray was recently hired, and her résumé reflects the qualities we look for in our teachers (see Figure 2–1, p. 10). Susanne's vision and commitment is theoretically congruent with ours. This doesn't mean that we are looking for clones; rather, we are seeking out partners whose work will complement and extend what we have started. From our perspective, it is absolutely about making the theory our own in our own ways. It is about learning through our teaching and sharing what we learn through our teaching demonstrations.

If You Build It, They Will Come

It was astonishing! We knew we had much to offer parents, children, and the profession at large, but deep down inside we all wondered whether or not we would be embraced by the community. We knew that we had hired some of the strongest teachers in the district—country, actually—and that their reputations would make a significant difference. Still, we were surprised by the degree to which parents truly wanted the choice and voice that our Center

Susanne Murray

Professional Goals and Beliefs

The recent years have been a time of amazing growth for me within my chosen profession. I have uncovered a powerful ally in the concept of inquiry, and it has evolved into a new form of thought process. The verification of this partnership has led the way to a shift of direction and control of curriculum in my classroom. I have accepted my role as a learner with my students and am constantly reevaluating my own beliefs and values.

My goal as a teacher-researcher is to observe the students and identify what I need to do to foster excitement and curiosity, which will lead to new learning. As I embrace it myself through meaningful, collaborative, and reflective inquires I will devise new invitations based on my students' needs and interests.

I have heard it said that teaching is not magic, but it can be magical. I believe that living life as an inquirer will allow my students and myself to experience those enchanted moments in our classroom and in the world around us. I want to invite children to uncover the life they want to really live and help them become the people they really want to be.

Professional Development
- Member of National Council Teachers of English (NCTE)
- Member of S.C. Council of Teachers of English (SCCTE)
- Member of Midlands Writing Project
- Presenter at the Young Writer's Conference, 1997 Topic: "Using Literature Circles in the Classroom"
- Director of Center for Inquiry's After School Program 1996-1998
- Director of the Midlands Writing Project Young Adults Writing Camp 1998

Educational Experiences

B.S. in Elementary Education, Minor: Child Psychology
Illinois State University

M.Ed. in Elementary Education, August 1998
University of South Carolina

Teaching Experience

5th Grade	Clinical experience (December, 1991)
	Wheeling School District #21
3rd Grade	St. Norbert's School (1992–1993)
	Northbrook, IL
4th Grade	Joseph Pleviak School (1993–1994)
	Lake Villa School District # 41
8th Grade	W. A. Perry Middle School (1994–1995)
	Richland School District One
	Emphasis: Language/Reading
8th Grade	Summit Parkway Middle School (1996–1998)
	Richland School District Two
	Emphasis: Reading/Social Studies
5th Grade	Self-Contained Classroom/Team Teaching (1996–1997)
6th Grade	Reading Exploratory/Language (1997–1998)
8th Grade	Reading Exploratory

Figure 2–1. *Susanne Murray's Résumé.*

would promote. We held two parent orientations and both were standing-room-only in a middle school cafeteria that easily seats three hundred. First-grade teacher Dori Gilbert described the event this way:

> Upon the commencement, Dr. Donnelly, the Principal of the Center for Inquiry, began creating relationships instantly within our learning community by asking the audience to imagine a school where "everybody knows your child's name and your child's strengths. . . ." Smiles stretched across the faces in the audience as they nodded in silent approval of the opening statement. Our dream was becoming a reality. Then Dr. Mills shared a montage of videotapes of children engaged in inquiry based activities. The videos of the new teachers (Michele Shamlin, Dori Gilbert, Tim O'Keefe, Diana Stout, Rick DuVall and Tammi Ballard) provided a demonstration of classroom communities in action, where children learn to think and work as readers, writers, mathematicians, scientists, historians, artists and musicians. It provided a glimpse of what living and learning might look like during a day at the Center. (1996, 65)

We were careful to show, not simply tell. We were also careful to share genuine feedback from children and parents with whom we had worked in the past. Their voices came through loud and clear and they clearly made a difference. Sara Sharnoff, one of Tim O'Keefe's students at Lonnie B. Nelson Elementary, captured the spirit of the orientation by reading her reflection on her second-grade experience (see Figure 2–2, p. 12).

> I've been coming a long way this year. I've developed into a wonderful author, writer, and friend maker. I barely knew anybody. But I managed to make some friends. I've been here 180 days and stayed with the same people. We all had a lot in common. Our classroom is empty now, but I can remember the colorful pictures by my classmates hanging on the wall. School is not about homework and tests. It's about learning about people and what they are learning. It's about their lives and what they have experienced. It's about their stories and their tales, and their vacations and trips. It's about giggling and talking and something we definitely need, a chance to be children.

Parents obviously wanted what Sara had experienced for their own children. They came and then they applied. We had three times as many applicants as slots our first year. Such numbers challenge media reports advocating parent's desire for back to the basics schools. We used a stratified random lottery when selecting our student population and, in so doing, created the community based on planned diversity. The applications were coded for gender,

Sara   6/2/94

I've been coming a long way
this year. I've developed into
a wonderful another, writer, and
a friendmaker. I barely knew
enyboby. But I managed to
make some friends. I've been
here 180 days, and stayed with
the same people. We all had a
lot in comen! Our classroom is
emty now, but, I can remember
the colorful pithures by my
classmakes hanging on the wall.
School is not homework and
tests. It's about learning abaut
people and what there tearning.
It's about there lives and
what they have exspereansed.
It's about there stories and
there tails, and there vacations
and trips. It's about gigling
and talking and something we
dephenly need. A chance to
be childen.

Figure 2–2. *Sara's Reflection on Second Grade.*

Total School Population

	Kinder- garten	First Grade	Second Grade	Third Grade	Fourth Grade	Fifth Grade	Total School
Black	33%	25%	50%	28%	38%	25%	33%
White	62%	75%	45%	72%	62%	75%	65%
Other	5%		5%				
Boys	52%	50%	55%	55%	48%	45%	51%
Girls	48%	50%	45%	45%	52%	55%	49%
Free	7%						
Reduced	2%						

Gifted and Talented based on grades 2–5   35%

Figure 2–3. *Center for Inquiry School Statistics for 1996.*

ethnicity, academic aptitude, and economic background, and the final pool reflected the diversity inherent in the Columbia area (see Figure 2–3).

Now for the Real Building

We were all so invested in building our own learning community that we agreed to use the group of portable classrooms behind Summit Parkway Middle School without even visiting the site. Our first visit could best be described as devastating. The group of portables looked more like an abandoned army barracks than a school. It's not that we wanted a traditional school look, in fact, we wanted the Center to look and feel like a village or summer camp, but not a military one.

Based on our prior experiences building productive learning environments within individual classrooms, we knew that the context would make a difference in establishing a sense of community in the school. So, we rolled up our sleeves and truly accessed our imaginations to begin the physical transformation. Richland District Two had the foresight to allocate some start-up money in the budget and gave us the freedom to decide what we wanted to do with it. We chose several areas of focus: paint, awnings, landscaping, and an outdoor arena for whole-school gatherings.

We still have tremendous facility needs, yet we have fallen in love with our island behind the middle school. We have created an inviting and comfortable context with very little money. We have grown to love our portable classrooms and fondly refer to them as class cottages. Our outdoor arena has been instrumental in fostering a sense of community throughout the school as we begin and end each week together at the arena.

Creating Curriculum and Assessment Frameworks

After establishing our student population and initiating the changes to be made in the physical context, we began imagining and planning curriculum together as a faculty. Since we were starting from scratch, we vacillated between elation and terror throughout our initial meetings. To be perfectly honest, we were overwhelmed! Amy Donnelly and Jane Ness, our first administrative assistant, created learning engagements that would help us personally experience the power and potential of inquiry. We told our own stories, shared our burning questions, responded to powerful literature, and so on. However, even though we were a group of educators who loved theory and treasured opportunities to think together, we constantly found ourselves returning, sometimes crashing, to the ground to make very necessary and immediate decisions. Our questions quickly changed:

From: What are our beliefs about curriculum? Who owns curriculum and how is it best negotiated?
To: How might a curricular framework support curriculum development across classrooms without restricting the ways in which we create curriculum within classrooms?

From: What is kid watching and how might it inform curriculum?
To: What should our progress reports look like? How and when should we offer student-led conferences?

From: Why are we here and how might our collective efforts make a genuine difference?
To: What message do we want to send through our mission statement? How might we create a mission statement that captures a living philosophy?

It is difficult to determine the exact order of events that followed as we worked on curriculum, assessment, and philosophy concurrently. However, for purposes of clarity, we will present our final-draft thinking in each area separately.

Our Mission: The Essence of Imagination

What we can easily see is only a small percentage of what is possible. Imagination is having the vision to see what is just below the surface; to picture that which is essential, but invisible to the eye.

—author unknown

We loved the idea of mission and in fact felt that the Center itself was created through a mission that reflected our vision of what was possible rather than what was typical in public schooling. While many of us had achieved remarkable things within our own classrooms, we now began envisioning what our new school might be by imagining first and then taking action to realize the imagined potential. Our imagining involved much more than simple dreaming. Our vision was clearly grounded in theory and inquiry-based practices. We had simply come to the point in our mission to begin committing the vision to paper for ourselves and the families with whom we would soon work.

MISSION STATEMENT: FIRST DRAFT

The Center for Inquiry is about making classrooms exciting places for teachers and children to be. It is about sustaining children's successful learning strategies that they bring with them. It is about helping all children become thoughtful, intelligent people who care about others and who delight in learning. It is about helping preservice and inservice teachers recognize what is possible in elementary education. It is about genuine collaboration with families, the university, and the community. Put simply, it's about good teaching. It is also about developing habits of the mind and heart through living and learning at the Center for Inquiry. Habits that all participants, tall and small, elementary students, graduate students, parents, teachers, and administrators employ such as inquiry, imagination, perseverance, appreciation, confidence, reflection, joy, responsibility, respect, collaboration, and humility for the purposes of creating a more caring, more equitable, and more knowledgeable and democratic world.

We wanted to portray the focus on learning and learners, the collaborative nature of the venture across institutions, the role of preservice and inservice teachers, the fact that everyone would live the model of inquiry, and the fact that we valued inquiry as a driving force in perpetuating democracy within and outside of the school (Short, Harste, and Burke 1996). We would soon learn that this statement was much too lengthy to pass for the official district mission statement, but it certainly met our initial needs, and as we used it as our frame of reference when making decisions regarding our curricular framework and the progress report template. In other words, the mission statement served as our philosophical conscience throughout our curricular conversations our first summer together.

The Usefulness of a Curricular Framework

As soon as we started making schoolwide decisions, it became apparent that we had attracted teachers who were quite empowered and accustomed to autonomy. The teachers we had brought together were pioneers, and history has demonstrated over and over that pioneering spirits value freedom and reject constraints. We wanted our school to foster the strong sense of agency that they brought to it, yet we knew we needed some consensus regarding general frameworks for curriculum and evaluation if we were going to function as a cohesive unit.

We knew that the framework had to emerge from curricular conversations so that the teachers would have ownership. We also knew that we needed to invite new teachers in on the conversations that had been occurring for years among the teachers who were part of the original proposal. So we all brought professional literature that we valued to the group and read and talked. We read and talked together for days. As we did, we noted the features of teaching, learning, and curriculum that struck a chord or resonated with what mattered most to us all. I took thorough notes and passed them out to the group for analysis. We basically analyzed the conversations and generated a framework that would support curriculum development within and across classrooms without cramping anyone's individual style.

We all believed that we needed to provide children opportunities to learn about reading, writing, and mathematics in addition to using reading, writing, and mathematics as tools for learning (Short, Harste, and Burke 1996). Figure 2–4 (see p. 17) reflects essential features of reading, writing, and math workshops across grade levels. Although each content area features unique skills, concepts, and learning strategies, the workshop framework permeates the curriculum. As such, the workshop framework involves demonstration, engagement, reflection, and celebration.

We all agreed that it would be essential to create formal demonstration lessons that would highlight skills, strategies, content, or concepts within the context of meaningful learning situations. We would strive to show how to apply the ideas and why the issues matter. Through demonstrations, the teachers planned to weave the district and national standards in with the needs and interests of the class. While we all agreed that predictable, focused

Creating Curriculum at the Center for Inquiry
Richland District Two and USC: A Small School Partnership

Learning to Think and Work Like Readers, Writers, Mathematicians, Scientists, and
Historians

An Apprenticeship Model

- Understanding and promoting the role of mentors in learning
- Focusing on the skillfulness of inquiry by helping children learn how to use
  primary and secondary sources and by illustrating the importance of learning
  from the process and products/artifacts
- Incorporating the following features of our workshops across communication
  systems and grade levels:
    Demonstration—using strategy lessons, conducting mini lessons, focusing
    on why and how
    Engagement—living the process
    Reflection—reflecting as individuals and/or groups on the content, skills,
    strategies, and concepts
    Celebration—giving public recognition for growth and change

Our students learn about language and mathematics during workshops. They learn
through language and mathematics during interdisciplinary focus studies and expert
projects on topics in the physical and social sciences. Additionally, art, music, and
movement are accessed as tools for learning and communication during focus study
projects.

Figure 2–4. *Workshop Framework.*

demonstration lessons would be central to the curricular framework, individual teachers would determine the time and place in the daily forecast (daily
schedule) when such lessons would occur.

 We all agreed that it would be essential to create opportunities for
the children to *be*—live, learn, think as—readers, writers, mathematicians,
scientists, and historians (Kirby and Kuykendall 1991). To do so, teachers
planned significant blocks of time each day for genuine reading, writing,
mathematical, scientific, and historical explorations.

 We all agreed that it would be essential to provide daily reflection sessions within our curricular framework. Many of us had witnessed the power
of reflection through class strategy-sharing sessions during which the children highlighted strategies that helped them construct or revise their thinking. We planned for the teachers to build formal reflection time into the fabric of each day. In so doing, we predicted that our students would take an

active role in and gain control over their own learning while also supporting their young colleagues.

Finally, we all believed that it was essential to celebrate children's growth and change through exhibits and/or performances. By providing the time and space in the curriculum for learning celebrations, we would validate and extend the children's thinking and work. Additionally, their knowledge and strategies would be made available as process and product demonstrations for the class and/or school.

Finding and Reporting What We Value

While we all took quite different paths, we all had come to a point at which we knew it was unfathomable to think about curriculum and evaluation as separate entities. Kid watching, as originally framed by Yetta Goodman (1978) and developed by Tim O'Keefe, one of our teachers, had the greatest influence on our thinking about evaluation (O'Keefe 1996). Figure 2–5 (see p. 19) portrays fundamental features of kid watching that underpinned our evaluation conversations.

It would take years for many of us to actualize the depth and breadth of kid watching as Tim had demonstrated it, yet we knew we wanted kid watching to be both the anchor and springboard for capturing and reporting our children's growth and change. We knew we wanted an open-ended structure that would help us better understand and value our children's learning. We knew we wanted our curricular decisions to grow out of our kid-watching observations. We knew we wanted an evaluation device that would be theoretically congruent with our beliefs about teaching and learning. We knew a great deal of work had been done in authentic assessment, so we began with what was already established.

We considered the *Work Sampling System* (Jablon et al. 1994). We reviewed *The American Literacy Profiles* (Griffin, Burrill, and Smith 1995) and *Windows into Literacy* (Rhodes and Shanklin 1993). While each document had strengths and held tremendous promise as a primary resource, once again we felt the need to select a document that would clearly complement our work in curriculum. As we reviewed published evaluation devices, we discussed how the medium was the message. We found that some devices revealed certain things while they concealed others. We wanted an instrument that would portray the intimacy we valued in a clear, focused way. After exhaustive reviews, we came to the realization that we would need to create a document that would meet our particular needs.

One evening after a particularly exhausting search for the elusive instrument of choice, I was reflecting on the day and worrying about the fact

What Is Kid Watching?

- It is a continuous, systematic look at the process of how students learn.
- It is learning to see what's there and turning that knowledge into effective instructional invitations.
- It is reporting to students and parents about authentic learning experiences and growth (concepts and strategies) documented over time.
- It is valuing contributions each child makes within the learning community that is our classroom.
- It is helping the children realize who is an expert and who they can turn to when they need assistance.
- It is giving voice to students who might otherwise be silent.
- It is getting to know each child in as many different contexts as possible; to know each child as a person unique in all the world.
- It is the fuel for our desire to know more about the learning process as well as the continuous refinement of our craft as teachers.

Kid watching is not something apart from the curriculum but rather it is what holds it together and pushes it forward into new and often unexplored territory.

— O'Keefe, 1994

From "Kid Watching" in *Creating Classrooms for Authors and Inquirers* by Harste and Short, Portsmouth, NH: Heinemann.

Figure 2–5. *Features of Kid Watching.*

that many of the teachers were becoming overwhelmed by the freedom to make every decision from scratch. Tim captured the spirit of the day by exclaiming, "Be careful what you wish for!" I suddenly saw quite clearly how easy it would be if we simply made space to intentionally and systematically share how children were growing as readers, writers, mathematicians, scientists, social scientists, and members of the learning community. It was so simple. Throughout our curricular conversations we had focused on how we wanted our children to learn to think and work as readers, writers, mathematicians, scientists, historians, and so on. We simply needed a device that would provide the structured support necessary to share our observations of such growth with parents and give children and parents a chance to reflect upon their growth and change using three pluses and a wish (Mills 1990).

Heidi gave birth to the Center for Inquiry progress report (see Figure 2–6, p. 20), yet it is the teachers who have nurtured its growth by demonstrating how to gather, interpret, and share process and product information in compelling

Child's Growth as a Scientist/Social Scientist:
(Biologist, Geologist, Astronomer, Historian, Geographer, Anthropologist.)

2

Child's Contributions to the Classroom Learning Community:

Child's Growth as a Learner in General:

Center
for
Inquiry

1

PROGRESS REPORT 19___–19____
Richland County School District Two &
University of South Carolina
Small School Partnership

Student: _____

Teacher: _____

Grade: _____

Assigned to grade_____ for 19____ – 19_____

GRADING PERIOD: 1ST   2ND   3RD   4TH

	1	2	3	4	Total
Days Present					
Days Absent					
Days Tardy					

Child's Growth as a Reader:

Child's Growth as a Writer:

Student Self-evaluation
Student, please write three positive comments and a goal for yourself.

3

My growth during this nine week period:

+

+

+

Goals:

Parental Evaluation
Parent, please write three positive comments and a goal for your child.

My/our child's growth during this nine week period:

+

+

+

Goals:

TEACHER: _____ Date: _____

CHILD: _____ Date: _____

...atician:

The progress report includes:
- Child's growth as a reader
- Child's growth as a writer
- Child's growth as a mathematician
- Child's growth as a scientist/social scientist
- Child's contributions to the classroom learning community
- Child's growth as a learner in general
- Student self-evaluation
- Parental evaluation

Figure 2–6. *Center for Inquiry Progress Report.*

ways. Kid watching and reporting growth to parents continue to be focuses of our study group meetings four years into the project. In fact, Louise Jennings, our ethnographer, who joined our venture—or adventure—once we opened the Center, shares specific incidents that have influenced the evolution of our assessment strategies in Chapter 4. In closing, the central belief we all hold about assessment is this: the more we know, the more we see; the more we see, the more we grow and change as teachers. Hence, our evaluation procedures promote inquiry among the tall and small at the Center.

And So It Was

We welcomed students and their families to the Center with our curricular framework, progress report, and initial mission statement in hand. We invited all families, school board members, district administrators, and university partners to a school picnic intended to do the following:

foster a sense of community within classrooms and throughout the school

orchestrate transportation and after-school care procedures

publicly recognize the support we had received from the school board, district office, and university administrators

address personally any questions or concerns parents had, as it was a real risk for many of them to have their children leave their neighborhood schools to attend a place without a proven record of success in the community.

Only later would they find that we held our promise, a promise to:

know and care for all of the children intimately through looping in a small school setting

provide consistently rigorous opportunities for children to think and work as readers, writers, mathematicians, scientists, historians, artists, musicians, and dancers

hear and respect all voices

uphold democratic principles within the school and throughout the community

promote habits of the heart and mind, which include inquiry, imagination, perseverance, appreciation, confidence, joy, reflection, responsibility, and collaboration.

Only later would they find that all members of this small school partnership would truly strive to live the model they articulated in the final draft of the mission statement:

CENTER FOR INQUIRY MISSION STATEMENT

The students, parents, and staff of the Center for Inquiry, a genuine collaboration between the University of South Carolina and Richland District Two, are responsible for developing ourselves as more thoughtful, caring, and intelligent people who delight in learning and are committed to creating a more compassionate, equitable, knowledgeable, and democratic world.

References

Calkins, L., and S. Harwayne. 1991. *Living Between the Lines.* Portsmouth, NH: Heinemann.

Gilbert, D. 1996. *Creating Possibilities: The Evolution of a Teacher and a School.* Master of Arts Thesis, Columbia, SC: University of South Carolina.

Goodman, Y. 1978. "Kid Watching: An Alternative to Testing." *Journal of National Elementary School Principals* 574: 22–27.

Griffin, P., L. Burrill, and P. Smith. 1995. *The American Literacy Profile Scales: A Framework for Authentic Assessment.* Portsmouth, NH: Heinemann.

Harwayne, S. 1992. *Lasting Impressions: Weaving Literature into Writing Workshop.* Portsmouth, NH: Heinemann.

Jablon, J., D. Marsden, S. Meisels, and M. Dichtelmiller. 1994. *Omnibus Guidelines: The Work Sampling System.* Ann Arbor, MI: Rebus Planning Associates, Inc.

Kirby, D., and C. Kuykendall. 1991. *Mind Matters: Teaching for Thinking.* Porstmouth, NH: Boynton/Cook.

Meier, D. 1995. *The Power of Their Ideas: Lessons for America from a Small School in Harlem.* Boston: Beacon.

Mills, H. 1990. "Teachers and Children: Partners in Learning." In *Portraits of Whole Language Classrooms,* edited by H. Mills and J. A. Clyde. Portsmouth, NH: Heinemann.

OKeefe, T. 1996. "Teachers as Kid-Watchers." In *Creating Classrooms for Authors and Inquirers,* edited by K. Short, J. Harste, and C. Burke. Portsmouth, NH: Heinemann.

Power, B. M., and R. S. Hubbard, eds. 1996. *Oops: What We Learn When Our Teaching Fails.* York, ME: Stenhouse.

Rhodes, L. K., and N. L. Shanklin. 1993. *Windows into Literacy: Assessing Learners, K–8.* Portsmouth, NH: Heinemann.

Short, K., J. Harste, and C. Burke. 1996. *Creating Classrooms for Authors and Inquirers.* Portsmouth, NH: Heinemann.

Stephens, D., ed. 1990. *What Matters? A Primer for Teaching Reading.* Portsmouth, NH: Heinemann.

3

It's Our School

THE FIFTH-GRADE CLASS OF 2000
AUTHORS: HEIDI MILLS, CARA HARTLEY,
CAITLIN WATTS, KALA BELCHER, DENEAL COTTON,
DEANNA SPOONEMORE, AMANDA HASSEN,
SARAH EARLE, AND JULIE RILEY WAUGH

It is only fitting that a chapter be written by a group of fifth graders in Julie Riley Waugh's class. Most of the children in this class began living and learning together at the Center when they were in second grade. As they embarked upon a study of their school culture for their first inquiry project of this year, they truly actualized the vision of inquiry that we had all dreamed of when starting this school three years ago. Their piece reveals the power and potential of a shared philosophy across an intimate school setting. The children have such a solid, unwavering, and sophisticated sense of what matters, they simply take our breath away.

Like most of the amazing invitations in Julie's class, it all started with a simple conversation. Julie and I were talking about the new roles, responsibilities, and rituals that her fifth graders would inherit. We had established several rites of passage—renamed as "privileges" by the class—for the fifth graders, such as flag, car pool duty, and conducting visitor tours on Thursday mornings. We reminisced about past visitors who enjoyed the tours tremendously and valued the fact that the children were given such a prominent role in the school. However, deep inside, we knew that the tours could be more than delightful. We knew that the children had developed a sophisticated understanding of teaching and learning; we knew that they were accustomed to reflecting on their own growth and change; we knew they could tell the story of our school in honest and compelling ways; we knew that it was their perspective that mattered most. And so it was. Some of the children chose to tell the story by creating information packets and guided tours for guests, others created a virtual tour of the school in the computer lab for visitors who missed the live version, still others created a map of the Center from

24

an aerial view so that visitors could navigate their way from classroom to classroom, and finally, eight of the fifth graders invested in writing part of this chapter.

In Julie's words, "I felt it was important to start this crucial year with a strong sense of knowing our own place, the Center for Inquiry, and the lifetime learning habits of the heart and mind that it instills in all of its community members." "A sense of place" became the first concept to reunite learners and make interdisciplinary connections when school began. The students adopted a social scientist stance and began investigating the culture of their school. They made personal observations, posed questions, and then formed inquiry groups to better understand and communicate unique features of the Center. One group made extensive observations across classrooms. After returning, they interpreted their observations and identified themes or patterns they noticed across the school. Another group worked with Brent Petersen, the USC intern, to create interview questions for a diverse range of stakeholders including parents, teachers, children, and the district superintendent. A third group collected and analyzed artifacts that represented critical incidents in our history as a learning community. The fourth group accessed Web pages from other unique sites such as the Manhattan New School to discern how they might improve our own version.

While each group had its own mission, they were all united by and invested in genuine inquiry. Julie had masterfully initiated and sustained the project by focusing on the skillfulness of inquiry. She helped them learn to use primary sources such as interviews and artifacts as well as secondary sources such as Web pages and print materials written about the school. Throughout it all, she illustrated the importance of learning from the process and products. The classroom exemplified an apprenticeship model. Julie was their mentor. And because she was, the fifth graders will now become yours. Welcome to the fifth grade at the Center for Inquiry.

Kids Are a Part of The Curriculum

CARA HARTLEY

At the Center for Inquiry the kids are a part of the curriculum. For example in our Class we are doing inquiry projects about the Center. These have included, interviews, observations, collecting artifacts, and exploring the Internet to help gather information to write this chapter. After we have gathered all of our information, we separated into different groups such as the tour guidelines,

PowerPoint, tour and the chapter group. In our chapter group each member has a certain topic to write about such as, we love to read, we are good author's etc.

The first graders are learning to work as scientists by exploring the wonders of dirt and soil. The first graders have been collecting dirt from different area's such as colored from our freshly painted portables, neighborhoods, houses, and other areas at the center.

As you can see, the kids are a part of the curriculum too. To quote Mrs. Barnes, the first grade teacher, "The Center gives kids the freedom to explore their interests in building our curriculum."

Trust at CFI

CAITLIN WATTS

At the Center for Inquiry the teachers trust us enough to give us privileges that other schools don't have. Except we have to understand that there are responsibility's that go along with those privileges and if you forget those responsibility's than you have to pay the consequences.

An example of their trust is that they trust us enough to let us choose what we want to write for each month. Each month we have two stories we need to write the first one is a mandatory piece the class has to vote what they want to write about like for example if it was a family story you would write about something that happened in your family. And the other story you needed to write as your choice you could write about anything that you thought was appropriate.

Our school is a place were teachers allow us to talk about the news that is happening around the world but they trust us enough to remember not to bring in to many gruesome details into the classroom because it is not appropriate for school.

Another example of their trust is that after a math message or spelling test or a piece of writing that we have done a math message or spelling test or a piece of writing they allow us to check and rework or piece on our own.

At the center the teachers aren't the only ones who trust each other the kids trust their teachers and their classmates. As fifth graders at CFI we not only trust our teachers and our classmates but we trust the younger schoolmates.

Basically our school is held together by trust and love!!!!

Connections at CFI

KALA BELCHER

Part of CFI is connections. That may be connections to our lives, other people, books the past or anything else. Connections are good because they may break down anything we don't understand or it may even help teachers determine whether you understand or not. A lot of times someone will make a connection to something and everyone will go, "Oh, yeah." That leads to fun, experiments, and just plain warmth, like a fuzzy blanket hovering over all of us.

For example, the 5th grade class was having a Friendship Circle sharing news on the subject flooding. Philip asked the question, "When a flood already happens why doesn't it go down?" Zac, responded to Philip saying, "Cohesion or the flooding waters stick together." Thomas thought about the connection and said, "The flooding keeps spilling until the rain stops." Kevin, interested in that this was happening said, "The flooding is happening so fast!" Some others wondered if the sewer was spitting out the water. Tyler wondered if the flooding waters would go back up stream. It was such a wonderful conversation!

Not just one class contributes and learns from connections, all the classes do! For example, the kindergarten class was reading a book called *Red Leaf, Yellow Leaf*. After reading the book they connected other colors to it. They wanted to explore more so they went outside to find more colors. That's what I call fun!

Connections is really part of life at CFI and I think that's really a unique part of all of us!

Reading

DeNEAL COTTON

At the Center for Inquiry every grade, Kindergarten through 5th, loves to read. Kids read at break, under tables, and lunch and recess. This school is a reading machine.

We have lots of chapter books by famous authors like: J. K. Rowling, Sharon Creech, Karen Hesse and Roland Smith. Without reading we would be an unhappy school. Sometimes we go to the arena and someone reads to us. It's real fun.

Every other Friday we go to the Sandhills Library where we look for books. We also have D.E.A.R. time. D.E.A.R. time is when you stop what you are doing and read. D.E.A.R. means drop everything and read.

We mostly read chapter books at this school. Sometimes the staff might come and take us to the U.S.C. room or computer room and read with us. We read news articles and magazines. We love to read non-fiction and fiction books. Also we have literature circle groups. That's when 3, 4, or 5 people meet and read and share passages with each other. You often get to choose which chapter books you want to read. This is a great school.

Writers Workshop

DEANNA SPOONEMORE

At the Center everyone is committed a writer.

Every Tuesday and Thursday we have 15 minutes of silent writing, which is when you write without talking. Then, we have an hour to have an adult edit our work, write a story, write down your thoughts, do the steps in the authoring cycle, in order etc. An authoring cycle tells you the steps of writing a wonderful story. The steps that are in the authoring cycle are:

1st Ideas/Prewrite

2nd First Draft

3rd Author's Circle

4th Self Edit/Rework

5th Adult Edit

6th Final Draft

7th Publishing

Ideas/Prewrite is when you put your Ideas down on your paper. It's kind of like a whole story or an outline.

First Draft is when you have your story down on your paper, But later you add stuff to your story and it's sloppy. That's a Rough Draft.

An authoring circle is when you're done with your First Draft and you ask people if they would like to join you and some other people in a circle so you can share your First Draft of the story your working on, with them. After you're done sharing your with them, the listeners give the story teller ideas, make comments, and ask questions. Then, after the listeners give the story-teller ideas, make comments, and ask questions, the storyteller got ideas of what they can put in their story to increase it.

For example, the storyteller gets done with his/her story and it's only five paragraphs. Then, one of the listeners raise their hand and the storyteller calls on them and the listener says "I wish you made it longer because, it was so good." Then, the storyteller would put that down on his/her paper and then later the storyteller would look over all his/her questions, comments and make his/her choice.

The self edit/rework is when you correct your story, then you rewrite your story, but with your corrections in it. For example, if you have a sentence in your story that does not make sense, like this sentence—Where cat go?— You would correct the sentence, by yourself.

An adult edit is when an adult edits your work but the only difference is that at the Center you sit by an adult. Then, you read your story to them, and while your reading your story they put a notation or a mark over a sentence or word you guys need to talk about. Then, after your done reading it to them you talk about the sentence or word, so you can understand the sentence or word. I think this works because, if an adult corrects it for you, you won't learn how to spell the word and you will keep on wording the sentence like it was before the adult corrected it.

Final Draft is when you're all done gathering your thoughts, First draft, Authors circle, done with self editing, and have an adult, edit your story, poem, paragraph etc. It's also called a Final Draft when it's not sloppy and when it's in your best handwriting.

Last but not least Publishing. Publishing is when everyone in the class comes down to the carpet and then two people, who got pulled from the random cup, read their marvelous stories with everyone. While you're reading you hold a microphone and speak into it, so everyone can hear your story. Then, after their done sharing your story a few people gives the storyteller three pluses and a wish, but some people make connections, or tell stories, and after you tell stories about a person some people write stories about that person. For example, in the Fifth Grade Kala wrote a very powerful story about her Grandma dying. She received two pluses and one story for her story. Her first plus was from Katie. Katie stated that, "Kala's Grandma reminded her of Kala because, Kala was so strong." Her second plus was from Ms. Riley the Fifth Grade teacher. Ms. Riley stated that "Kala had showed that real stories from your own life can be powerful." Her first story was from Tyler. Tyler told a story about "His Grandpa." Then, later Tyler went on to write a story about his Grandpa.

Overall everyone at the Center is committed a writer and I think this is really unique because It's part of our daily lives.

Valuing Versatility

AMANDA HASSEN

At the Center for Inquiry we value each other and our work. This is what makes our school so special. Having the privilege to come to the Center is a privilege you don't want to lose.

When I think of valuing work, I think of the piece that the illustrator constructed and how they know people value their work. After Ms. Riley, our 5th grade teacher, reads a read-aloud to the class, we do something called a visual response. After everyone is done with his/her visual response we come up to the carpet.

We pull a name out of the random cup (a cup with everyone's name in it) to see who will share their visual first. In our class we share our visuals differently than other schools. Our class does something that we call "Save the Last Word for me."

"Save the last word for me" is when the illustrator of the visual comes up and picks three people that would like to say what they *like*, what they *see*, and *wonder*, about their piece. After the three kids are done saying what they want to say, the illustrator comes up and talks about his/her visual. That is why we call it "save the last word for me" because the illustrator gets the last word. I like "save the last word for me" because it tells the illustrator how much we value their time and work.

Valuing people's work is a big part about the Center.

Learning from Our Mistakes

SARAH EARLE

At the Center for Inquiry we learn from our mistakes. In second grade, Mackenzie was publishing one of her stories and she found a miscue. Mrs. Pender looked at the paper and said "Yes, you did make a mistake." and then Mackenzie said "Well at least I know how to spell that word." Mrs. Pender said "Yes at least now you know."

Also fifth grade does math challenges, which is when they figure out problems based on the day of school, Pretend it is the thirty first day of school They'd write,

Is 31 . . .

Odd or even?

Prime or composite?

Abundant, deficient or perfect?

What is it squared?

What is it cubed?

What's its Roman numeral?

Are there any proper factors?

Is there any thing special about this number?

The fifth grade would then answer all these questions and then two people would go up to the front of the room and share what they have. If they get a part of it wrong, someone would say "How did you get that answer?" and they would explain again and usually they find the miscue but if they don't they do it over and then they'd find them. These are some of the few examples of Learning from our Mistakes. There are a lot more. If you'd like to see, come on down and visit!

We Are All Teachers: Tall and Small

JULIE RILEY WAUGH

At the Center for Inquiry, we are all teachers. Yes, it's true, I am the official teacher; being a teacher is my job, my career, what I get paid to do. But when it comes to the little and big things that we learn each and every day, each and every person in this community teaches others.

I most definitely felt this as I listened to the students while they wrote this chapter. They chose words so carefully and eloquently. They said things in ways that I never could, in voices that are the most important, yet are often quiet in teaching and learning. They used words and ideas that we as adults use to explain the Center for Inquiry (I knew they had heard, but wasn't always so sure they understood) in meaningful contexts to explain them to others.

I was nervous when I sat down with these children and their first drafts. We had brainstormed a list of fundamental things that we thought were important ideas about the Center. As a whole class, we gathered information about the Center by interviewing, visiting classrooms, and studying artifacts. But what a task I was asking them to do! I was asking eight students to use all of the information we had gathered to write a chapter for a book . . . together!

The moment that Kala read her first lines about connections, all of my fears melted away. In what became a very long author's circle, I listened, offered ideas, complimented, and swooned. I almost lost my breath not once, but many times. I peeled off the residue of teacherly composure, joining the conversation with my eyes, ears, and heart. It was a dream. I was working as an author, with a group of passionate, committed authors. It was that simple.

We started our year with everyone teaching something to the class. It was an idea I borrowed from Tim O'Keefe and his class, actually. Many students taught us wonderful paper-folding projects; Kevin taught us about the states of matter; Tyler taught us about chess; Rachael taught us how to make dream catchers; and Richard taught us about the planets. After each person's lesson, I would ask everyone, "What have we learned from Kevin, or Tyler, etc., about being a good teacher?" The list we generated as a class is powerful and included: be patient; don't get upset too quickly; have confidence; be willing to try something again; it's OK to make mistakes; be an inquirer; reflect; make it fun; ask before you tell; let people try; connect new ideas to experiences we have had before; be willing to repeat things; say please; involve students; give students time; offer help with something at another time; and welcome people. I can say, most surely, that no inservice program in the world could remind me as much about what makes teaching and learning powerful.

I am thrilled that Heidi Mills approached me with the idea that our students would write a chapter for this book about the Center for Inquiry. It is all too appropriate, not only because the Center is a place where we are all teachers, but also because children are at the heart of all that we do at the Center. More than at any other school I have visited or taught in, teachers at the Center trust children to do hard things, to join conversations alongside us, to ask hard questions, and to speak confidently and eloquently about what is important to them in their own learning. Asking students to write this chapter was appropriate, in short, because no one else could have said it better.

4

Inquiry for Professional Development and Continual School Renewal

LOUISE B. JENNINGS

What is inquiry and what role does it play at the Center? For whom and for what purposes? As a school ethnographer, I entered the Center with these questions in 1996. I have been collaborating with Heidi Mills, Amy Donnelly, and others to document as much as possible about everyday life and work at the Center in order to address such questions. Our videotaped data and field notes are growing as we continue to work with the teachers and students to capture life and learning through inquiry. My prior work has focused upon processes of teaching and learning across the curriculum within classrooms (e.g., Jennings and Pattenaude 1998; Tuyay, Jennings, and Dixon 1995). I also was a member of a research team that investigated school restructuring practices across the United States (Snyder, Morrison, and Smith 1996). These interests combine naturally at the Center because, after a few observations, it became evident that not only is inquiry at the center of classroom pedagogy, but it also propels growth in many directions throughout the school community.

During my observations in classrooms, at schoolwide events, and at various meetings, I was struck early on by the ways in which all members of the Center community become inquirers, including students, teachers, parents, and teacher interns. As members of the community take up inquiry for different purposes and in multiple ways, they construct together a culture of inquiry. Within this school culture, inquiry has become a means of continual renewal and transformation. These observations led to the question: In what ways does inquiry influence change and transformation—both transformation for the inquirer and transformation of the learning environment,

33

whether that learning environment is a classroom, the school itself, or a professional development meeting?

Because inquiry is so pervasive at the Center, there are many directions to take in addressing these questions. Other chapters in this book focus upon inquiry within classrooms. In this chapter, I explore various practices of inquiry for professional development and continual school renewal. All Center teachers and teacher interns inquire into processes of learning in their classrooms, both individually and in collaboration with university researchers. As understandings have been transformed, teachers have enacted changes in classroom and school practices. Thus, this chapter describes inquiry practices that are at the heart of professional development and school renewal, focusing upon the transformative nature of these practices over the course of one school year, 1997–1998.

Why a "Culture" of Inquiry?

Many ethnographers examine cultural groups in order to understand how members construct together systems of shared meaning and how this shared meaning, in turn, influences members. As an educational ethnographer, I view schools and classrooms as small, particular cultures (Collins and Green 1992; Dixon, Frank, and Green 1999; Jennings 1998; Santa Barbara Classroom Discourse Group 1992). This perspective suggests that students and teachers, as members of a cultural group, construct both implicit and explicit sets of practices over time (Gumperz 1981; Goodenough 1963). By documenting events over long stretches of time, we can explore how members create practices of inquiry, illustrate how these practices change, and examine how these changes influence other practices.

Much of the work on inquiry in education considers inquiry as a basis for the curriculum. Short, Harste, and Burke (1996) have provided a way of framing inquiry-based curricula. They describe a cycle that is "anchored in underlying processes of inquiry" (54). The seven key processes interact in multiple directions and cycle and recycle. They include:

- building from the known
- taking time to find questions for inquiry
- gaining new perspectives (through dialogue, transmediation, knowledge systems/academic disciplines)
- attending to difference/anomalies/new knowledge

- sharing what was learned
- planning new inquiries
- taking thoughtful new action through reflection and reflexivity

The authors suggest that the nature of inquiry not only influences academic meaning making, but inherently leads to transformation:

> As a result of inquiry, learners literally reposition themselves both mentally and physically in the world for purposes of taking thoughtful new action. What we have learned has to cause us to interact differently in the world. From a social perspective we have to position ourselves differently. Our identity as well as the identity of others has been affected. We simply are not the same people. The ground has shifted in terms of how we stand in relationship to friends and knowledge systems. (59–60)

While Short, Harste, and Burke discuss transformation that accompanies inquiry as curriculum, many of these processes can be applied to other aspects of schooling. Imagine a school culture driven by the inquiry processes described in this cycle. Until I became involved with the Center, I had not considered how inquiry could support professional development, school renewal, and the nature of relationships within this community of learners. In this chapter, I address the question: How does inquiry for professional development influence changes with respect to relationships among students, teachers, and parents?

In another article, Short and Burke (1996) argue that, too often, our educational practices are not aligned with our beliefs about education, schooling, teaching, and learning. Inquiry can help educators interrogate their educational practices and beliefs so that they are more consistent with each other. In fact, beliefs and practices are ideally in dynamic interaction: our practices change to reflect altered beliefs and our beliefs change as we engage reflectively in practice. Thus, another research question I want to explore is: What is the relationship between beliefs and education practices and what is the role of inquiry in this relationship?

Inquiry and Professional Development

Inquiry became a natural avenue for professional development in addition to other avenues, such as peer coaching and inservices. The faculty and university partners meet weekly, to inquire into our educational beliefs and practices and to develop strategies for improving upon them. Thus, these inquiry meetings have been the root of much professional development and school renewal and are the focus of this chapter. The evolution of these weekly meetings was natural as well. At the end of the first year, the faculty members agreed that they wanted to meet during the summer to look more closely at teaching and learning philosophies and practices. The richness of those four half-day meetings led to the decision to continue these literature studies, or curriculum inquiry meetings, throughout the school year. In the fall of 1997, school and university faculty met each Monday after school; half of those meetings focused upon business such as announcements and school decisions; alternate weeks were dedicated to inquiring into our teaching and learning practices and philosophies. The structure shifted in January 1998, when the biweekly inquiry meetings took place on Thursdays from 11:00 A.M. to 12:30 P.M. At that time, the MAT interns facilitated a blanket reading fest with books and bagged lunches for each class. We now meet weekly. Regardless of meeting times, these gatherings provided an important opportunity for sharing professional insights and literature, observing and discussing one another's classroom practices via videotapes, and examining our philosophies and practices in inquiry-based education.

I have taken field notes and videotaped the majority of the meetings. Through these data, I examine the nature of inquiry for professional development. I also bring in data from other sources to show how these meetings transform practices in the classrooms, across the school, and throughout the larger school community with parents, thus contributing to continual school renewal.

Weaving Together Community, Assessment, and Inquiry

During the first year at the Center, the faculty asked many questions. Three prominent questions were: (1) What are the features of a supportive, effective learning community? (2) How do we construct one? and (3) How can we improve upon our methods of assessing and celebrating students' achievements? These topics were discussed formally and informally in 1996–97 as faculty developed the school philosophy and mission, constructed a narrative student progress report, and shared ideas on developing communities of inquirers in classrooms and as a school. We agreed to explore these questions, in addition to other topics and matters, during four summer meetings. In the following sections, I will describe events that took place from July 1997 through June 1998 to show the development and influence of faculty inquiry into assessment and building community.

Building Community Through Academic Practices

Heidi proposed that we incorporate time during the summer meetings to view videotapes that she had taken in each of the six classrooms in order to discuss processes of community building. We found this approach to be an effective means of "visiting" classrooms and discussing our practices. Peer coaching during the school year provided another vehicle for observing one another's classrooms in order to teach and learn from other teachers. However, by viewing videotapes, we were able to closely examine and discuss the moment-to-moment interactions and processes that constituted community building in classrooms. Heidi selected excerpts from each classroom that she felt illustrated various features of community building, but the discussions of the tapes naturally led to many more insights than Heidi had originally seen herself.

At the first meeting, we discussed an article titled "On Community," by Nel Noddings (1996). We discussed the difference between identifying characteristics of community and putting community at the center of classrooms; the difference between cooperation and collaboration; and the tension created by focusing on both community and the individuals that comprise that community. We then viewed tapes from three of the classrooms.

Rick DuVall's Fourth-Grade Class

The first tape brought us into Rick DuVall's fourth-grade classroom as he and students sat in a circle on the floor, sharing their written responses to a song about the Western movement that had been provided by another teacher, Tim O'Keefe. In this excerpt, one student, Dennis, introduced a perspective about Andrew Jackson that was challenged by other students, leading Dennis to further explain his point. Rick also made a connection between the topic and an incident in their own class community about sharing recess with an older grade. After watching this excerpt, Amy and Heidi opened the discussion:

Amy: One of my favorite things was when one of the kids said something and Dennis said "No, it wasn't that," so we see that whole notion of challenging to stimulate the conversation and to clarify the conversation and extend ideas.

Heidi: And we didn't see enough of this to really understand it, but Dennis' point was not the popular idea of the class. Most people were really down on Andrew Jackson and saying all these pretty radical things and he said, "No." I think that he thought that Andrew Jackson was doing the right thing at the time. And so for him to even put that idea forth to begin with was a real risk on his part and then when they challenged that idea he continued, which is what you saw.

Amy: Mm-hmm, and one other thing I really liked is also about building community—how you helped kids make those personal connections, like when you brought up, "That's like the time on the playground with the fifth graders and the ball." If they don't make those connections, we need to help them try to make them.

Michele (K–1 teacher): And to offer those personal connections when you're one voice in a crowd of voices. It wasn't like the teacher saying the obvious predetermined thing that you were looking for; it evolved naturally in the discussion.

Through this conversation we were able to celebrate Rick's teaching and also share our insights into the kind of community that he was constructing with his students. We were thus able to make visible some of the otherwise invisible processes of building a community of inquirers:

- encouraging learners to extend their thinking through our questions
- creating an environment where learners can challenge ideas and respond to and work through those challenges
- helping learners make connections between academic content and personal and community events

Later, during this same conversation about Rick's class, additional features of community building were recognized and supported:

Amy: A couple of times you did it, and a couple of times kids did it—that whole idea of asking the question, like "Do you think" or "Is that what you meant?"

Heidi: And I think the way that you posed questions—I think that the nature of the questions that you ask people were the ones that the kids were asking each other, like, "I wonder why humans were so caught up in this?" and encouraging people to take different perspectives; you didn't say, "Their way of thinking was wrong."

Amy: And it goes back to the article, the content of the conversation was a balance between facts and how people really felt about things.

Heidi: And yet it was a substantive conversation.

Amy: Really.

Heidi: I think it's a hard balance to strike. You could have talked about the playground for the next five minutes, but instead you made a connection to life at school and life at that time but then went back to the original topic.

Louise: One thing I've noticed at the Center that I don't see a lot in other class-rooms was how you write responses along with the students and share them with students. That makes you a learner along with the other learners, and students become teachers, so that there is more of a blend-ing of roles.

Heidi: Yeah, which is why I think that kids begin to adopt not only the way of thinking but also the language. The research in literacy clearly demon-strated that if your model of instruction is phonics, then the kids drop other kinds of strategies and only use sounding-out kind of cues because that's what's valued and demonstrated as important. And I think what you see here in terms of community is the way you interact with kids, they begin to adopt your way of thinking about teaching and learning and the language of the profession, too. For example, somebody said, "I made a connection." In a lot of ways the kids were talking to each other in the same ways that you talk to the kids.

Through this conversation, we developed and emphasized the impor-tance of building authentically, through use, a language for inquiry, a common language that all members of a class can access (Lin 1993). These conversa-tions also provided an opportunity to integrate existing research and theory with our own teaching practices, as we see in Heidi's connection to research on literacy. Other key ideas about building communities of inquirers included:

- posing questions in ways that encourage learners to take multiple perspectives
- creating substantive academic conversations that incorporate compas-sion; such conversations encourage learners to integrate opinions and feelings in ways that strengthen the academic content without substi-tuting for it
- creating flexible roles for students and instructors that position them both as learners and as teachers

The conversations that grew from watching videotapes of each teacher's classroom sometimes had wide-ranging effects. For example, when discuss-ing another part of the videotape of Rick's class, one teacher asked about one student's request to "speak into the silence" rather than raise hands dur-ing the class discussion. In explaining this notion of speaking into the silence, Rick described an inquiry that he and his class embarked upon during Thanksgiving: Students found that during some class discussions, they talked on top of one another without truly listening to each other. They decided to observe how groups of people conversed during Thanksgiving break. When sharing their findings, one student offered that his family members would wait for a pause in the conversation and "speak into the silence." The class decided to adopt this means of group communication, rather than raising hands and waiting to be called upon.

This discussion about one class' inquiry into communication had an extensive effect. As I observed in several other classes, teachers and students used the idea of speaking into the silence. In at least one class, members actually used that term in reminding one another not to talk over each other or when making a decision for what conventions to use for turn taking during a group discussion (e.g., "Shall we raise hands or just speak into the silence?"). In other classrooms, the spirit of speaking into the silence became more and more visible, whether or not that terminology was used. The way in which the original fifth-grade class code spread across the school illustrates how each class culture develops its own personality, yet there are common threads across all the classrooms.

Diana Stout's Third-Grade Class

The excerpt from Diana's third-grade classroom captured Diana's meeting with one literature study group. The students needed to resolve the problem of staying in sync with one another while reading the chapters of *The Chocolate Touch*. Diana joined the four students on the floor and orchestrated the meeting without making any decisions for them. One member of the group explained why she was having difficulty keeping up with the reading and other students offered strategies. Following the tape, we discussed the temptation to make decisions for students in the interest of time. Tammi, who taught fourth- and fifth-grade classes, initiated the conversation:

Tammi: I think it would have been real easy to say, "Okay, this is what you'll do." Diana, you might have had in mind that that's what they were going to do and that may have been the best solution, but you didn't say that. You let them go around, and everybody had input and they talked it through. It was a real-life problem that they needed to solve, and you didn't just say, "You guys work that out," and you didn't just say, "Okay, you can't work it out, this is what I'm going to do." Everybody's voice was heard, everybody's opinion.

Rick: I loved how when they weren't really coming to consensus and when it seemed like maybe they weren't getting where they needed to be, that Diana stepped in and offered some parameters—

Others: Right.

Rick: And still offered limited choices, but the ultimate choice was put back on them and the responsibility was back on them, but she gave them some wisdom and some advice.

A little later, Amy pointed out how Diana helped the students focus by asking questions such as, "What is the decision you need to make?" and "Is there a compromise you can reach?" then providing a summary check with each member.

Heidi: And so they had that sense of ownership and you were leading from behind, you were really providing the direction they needed. I mean, you knew they needed some guidance or you wouldn't have even gone over there to meet with them.

Diana: [Laughing] I just knew that group!

Heidi: But it was a really clear illustration of how you were negotiating with them and providing the leadership they needed from you as a teacher but the ownership that they needed as kids or as learners.

Michele: Mm-hmm, I thought that was nice.

Tim: The routines are so nicely established. You can tell, those kids maybe needed a little more guidance. Just the fact that kids are all off on their own doing literature studies I think is amazing, so you can tell that they're used to it and are comfortable with it. They know what their roles are, even though this particular group was having some trouble with it.

Tammi: A lot of times people think, "Center for Inquiry, kids just kind of learn on their own." And this is definitely a demonstration of how, no, there are parameters, there is still guidance, and yes they are in their little group on their own and they are expected to read on their own and expected to come to discussion when ready on their own, but we're not just saying, "Go to it."

We see here how all faculty members participated in the discussion and built upon one another's ideas, which parallels the expectations that these teachers have of students in classroom discussions. This discussion highlighted the importance of taking time to help students develop responsibility for problem solving. We discussed how teachers can "lead from behind" (Harste 1996) by doing the following:

- offering parameters, yet allowing students to decide on those parameters
- using questions to help students determine the focus or problem at hand
- providing summary checks by asking each student to state his or her understanding of the problem or solution
- supporting student ownership of the problem and the solution
- recognizing when groups need teacher input and when they can manage the work of the group on their own

During these discussions, teachers often shared some of their own tensions, as Tammi did in one of the previous dialogues. The following video excerpt provided an opportunity for faculty to discuss the tensions of creating curriculum with students, given the confined times and spaces of the school day:

Michele: I always worry, "When do I let them go, and when do I step in without being a control freak?" That's the first thing that struck me; I thought, I didn't see any apparent "Okay, how much am I going to be involved?" It was just so natural and such a beautiful balance of the recommendations and leadership without being controlling. I mean I love that, it was nice.

Heidi: It's so hard, especially when you have a lot of things going on and different groups are in different places, to have the patience to slow your teaching down enough to take that three minutes that you need to give them that opportunity to work it through. We all know that we have to do that to really make it work, and yet at the same time, we all feel the pressure to keep things moving.

Tim: So it's a wise use of time.

Heidi: That's what I mean!

Diana: It doesn't have to happen very often.

Heidi: Right.

Diana: Because then students from that group later become part of another group and they pass on what they learn about working together.

Michele: That's nice.

This conversation allowed us to explore multiple tensions: the desire to keep class work moving at a constructive pace, the desire to allow students to accomplish their group work independent of too much teacher direction, and the recognition that sometimes we need to slow the works and provide guidance to students. Michele pointed out how Diana had provided leadership without being too controlling. Diana and others discussed how taking that time to help students reflect on their group work can be time-saving in the long run, for this process helps students engage in group work more effectively. In short, this discussion allowed us to explore actions that we can take as teachers to help students develop effective means of collaborating *within* an authentic context of academic activity, rather than as a separate lesson.

This first summer meeting ended with questions: How do we develop as a professional community, including the mentorship of MAT interns? How can we involve parents? Through our discussions, we formed a community of inquiry among faculty that mirrored many of the same processes that we discussed regarding classroom community building. These discussions also provided opportunities for each of us to reflect on how these practices related to our own instructional beliefs and practices, both as K–5 teachers and university teachers. We agreed that visiting each classroom through videotape was a productive practice worth continuing in the following school year.

Continuing the Inquiry

As described earlier, we continued inquiry study meetings throughout the school year, meeting every two weeks to inquire into our own educational practices. In coding and analyzing my field notes from these meetings, I found we focused on two main themes throughout the year: strengthening our relationship with parents and developing assessment practices that would be congruent with the Center's philosophy.

Bringing Parents into Our Community of Inquiry

While students and teachers lived and learned the meaning of inquiry-based instruction on a daily basis, parents were not part of that daily construction. Most parents valued the school's philosophy and values yet had to rely on their experiences in more traditional schools to help them understand their children's experiences at the Center. The school sought to build a partnership with parents through monthly Curriculum Nights. During the first year of the school, Curriculum Nights were designed to bring the whole school together to explore different areas of the curriculum. For example, one night focused on writer's workshop and another on mathematics. However, understandably, parents' questions to teachers often revolved around the school's departures from traditional school practices, such as the absence of grades at the school.

Our focus on developing the partnership with parents evolved naturally, through inquiry. During the inquiry study meeting on October 13, 1997, we explored inquiry-based learning by discussing and exploring them together. First we brainstormed characteristics of inquiry-based learning, then asked questions that evolved from this brainstorming. Faculty agreed that the most significant question to inquire into at this time was: How can we strengthen our partnership with parents? That discussion led to the transformation of Curriculum Nights. At our October 13 inquiry meeting, faculty agreed that the whole-school focus of Curriculum Nights worked well in the school's first year, but a new structure was needed so that teachers could address topics that were pertinent to their own classrooms. For example, one teacher might need to involve parents in her class' expert projects that month, while another may see a need to develop, with parents, strategies for helping their students with homework. Faculty also agreed that the next Curriculum Night needed to inform parents of the principles and philosophy behind the school's inquiry-based practices. Staff provided other ideas for strengthening the partnership with parents, including methods of communicating with parents. Dori's dialogue journals and weekly newsletters were discussed as vehicles for informing and transforming relationships with parents.

In the spirit of inquiry, the faculty sought out methods for parent education from other sources, including faculty from another Center for Inquiry, one established earlier in Indiana with Jerome Harste. A grant from the Spencer Foundation supported periodic teleconferences whereby faculty members from each center could share knowledge and support one another through our endeavors. At the October 25 teleconference, we asked Indiana how they strengthened their partnership with parents. Among other ideas, they described how classroom photographs served as a basis for discussion with parents regarding classroom practices and the philosophies of learning that supported them. Since Heidi had been using videotapes so effectively, we agreed that videotapes from classrooms could be used in the same manner.

This was one of the many ideas shared at the next faculty meeting on November 10, when the subsequent Curriculum Night was organized. The original plan was to have a panel of faculty and parents describe their views of inquiry. From there, ideas were generated one by one, eventually leading to a format that was more in keeping with the spirit of inquiry. First, we borrowed another idea from the Center for Inquiry in Indiana by having parents write on graffiti boards their notions of what they wanted their children to be like as adults. Children joined this activity, showing their parents the ropes behind graffiti board writing. The cafeteria buzzed with almost one hundred adults and children generating their ideas. They shared these ideas as Tim wrote them on an overhead projector and facilitated the discussion. Tim was asked to document the discussion because of his ability to take thorough in-process notes. Then Heidi shared videotapes that captured teaching and learning processes in two classrooms earlier that day. Faculty and parents described the features they viewed in these videotapes that supported the kind of learning they had earlier identified as important for helping children grow into mature, responsible, learned adults.

In this way, inquiry into what it means to be part of an inquiry community has helped us find ways to bring parents into our community more solidly. Inquiry informed practices, as everybody discussed concerns, shared ideas with one another, and sought out other ideas from other sources. Practices were transformed as faculty focused upon various ways of strengthening parent communication and modifying curriculum nights to meet our changing needs.

Assessment Practices

We also bring parents into our community of inquiry in other ways. Student assessment at the Center involves parents as well as the students. During the first year of operation, faculty collaborated frequently to develop and continually revise the narrative progress report, seeking to construct a format that reflected student achievement as scientists, social scientists, mathematicians, readers, and writers. Students and parents participate in this assessment process: students and parents add to the teacher's comments by each writing three pluses (three positive characteristics) and a wish (a challenge to improve in a particular area) (Mills and Clyde 1990). While this is a time-consuming process for all involved, parents, students, and teachers have come to value its benefits.

During the second year of operation, faculty continued to ask the question: How can our assessment practices better reflect student achievement and promote growth? At the first summer meeting, in July 1997, faculty members revisited the four quadrants of assessment (see Appendix A, Figure A–1, p. 227). They reflected on the ways in which they were attempting to capture, interpret, and report growth and change from process notes and student products. At a subsequent summer meeting in August, we discussed the limitation of written reports when Dori shared what she had learned by inquiring into how video could be used to support student-led conferences the previous year. Tim added that parents and students appreciated his taping of students' expert project presentations as well. Faculty members agreed that they wanted to use video as another means of recording and sharing student achievement with family members. Many faculty decided to have all students bring a blank videotape to school for recording events such as student-led conferences, expert project presentations, and other achievements.

Dori's inquiry and her opportunity to share it with all faculty led to significant changes within individual classrooms. For example, in November, Michele videotaped the first graders' presentations on their expert projects, the culminating activity of their focused study on ocean life. Michele taped not only their presentations but also the period following the presentations when other students asked questions, which the presenter addressed, and offered compliments. Each student brought his or her videotape home, and parents and other family members were invited to watch the videotape, then write three pluses and a wish for that student. In this way, parents were brought into the process of inquiry, and their assessment was added to the student's own three pluses and a wish and that of Michele. Lora, who presented on manatees, received several responses from her family, including one from her teenage brother:

> + She was prepared for every question possible and answered it with a good response.
>
> + She had many models and representations to back up her information.
>
> + [She] stated her sources and used Websites off of the Internet.
>
> Wish: That she would have drawn the manatee with the steps on the board.
>
> [referring to a model that Lora developed for drawing a manatee].

Jonathan's mother wrote:

> + Jonathan seemed so confident and showed no signs of fear as he stood before his classmates. He seemed so at ease. . . .
>
> + I liked the way he was able to share facts about his animal without having them written down and before him.
>
> + Jonathan showed so much enthusiasm as he prepared his project and it showed in his presentation. I think he did a *wonderful* job. What a way to build self-esteem and make learning fun and enjoyable. Having the video available to parents is a big plus.
>
> Wish: To be able to see some of the other students' expert projects.

These examples illustrate how family members have begun to take up the language of inquiry. As they play a role in assessing the expert projects, parents and siblings become more attuned to learning processes by carefully attending to the student's presentation as it appeared on video. Lora's brother, for example, pointed to the effective models she constructed and her thoroughness in locating resources for her study. Furthermore, these opportunities to view and respond to students' presentations offer a time for families to celebrate learning. Both Lora's brother and Jonathan's mother applauded the experts for knowing their topics so well that they were able to present them effectively and answer questions with confidence. Like Jonathan's mother, many parents have expressed enthusiasm for videotaping the expert projects and the opportunity to celebrate their children's performances with them through their written responses.

On August 22, the faculty began to inquire into ways of improving upon the narrative progress reports. They started with an inservice on strategies for anecdotal record keeping. Tim has received national recognition for his work on kid-watching strategies, and he led the session. He also invited all faculty members to share their strategies, rubrics, and ideas for narrative assessment at that time. Through this structure, teachers had the opportunity to improve upon their own assessment practices by viewing and discussing those of their colleagues. For example, Dori's systematic attention to each child's progress was reflected in her class newsletters. Following the inservice on kid-watching strategies, Dori's newsletters increasingly focused upon individual students when class activities were described, as seen in these excerpts:

> Thank you **Vincent** for producing a graph on, "What did you have for dinner?" for the class to participate in. He took the lead from a Venn diagram that was on "What did you have for breakfast?" the day prior! I love to see children advance an idea further that we can all learn from. Way to go **Vincent!**

> While discussing "saxophone," **Betsy** wondered how long it takes to make one. After discussion on possible sources that would lead us to our answer, we decided on calling a local music shop. **Betsy** took the lead and so professionally called the shop herself. Please see what **Betsy** has found on the back of this newsletter!

> Thank you to **Nicholas** for bringing in a bird's nest which led us on a quest for information! The class wanted to find out what kind of bird eggs they were. **Devin** suggested we consult his dad who is quite a nature expert. Since he was not quite certain, **Aaron** brought in a book on bluebirds. After looking through the book, we predicted that they were Eastern Bluebird eggs! This is another wonderful example of collaboration with other experts, valuing the learners' interests, generative investigation, and learning skills through authentic use!

These excerpts indicate Dori's attention to both the collective learning experience and individual learners' contributions and growth through those experiences. By exploring and sharing methods for improving assessment, like Dori, faculty members have been finding effective ways to record and celebrate each students' growth as a learner.

As the first quarter came to a close, faculty discussed forms for filling out the content of the narrative progress reports. On October 13, they agreed to write three pluses and a wish for each section of the progress report. They debated about ways of summarizing progress and terminology that would be constructive and informative. Heidi agreed to gather excerpts from their progress reports from the previous year so that they could view one another's forms of expression. She compiled a three-page list of expressions, including her suggestions for further developing teacher comments on the progress reports (see Figure 4–1, p. 48). At the following meeting, the faculty members expressed their appreciation for Heidi's compilation, noting how useful it

Center for Inquiry: Progress Report

Sample entries that reflect our model from the 1996–97 school year.

Child's Growth as a Reader:

- has incredibly sophisticated verbal responses to literature that acknowledge a range of interpretations
- employs effective strategies when attempting unfamiliar words
- is beginning to examine a variety of genres
- chooses to read age-appropriate literature
- makes connections across texts
- chooses to read to herself and others quite often
- reads to find out information (research)
- reads with more confidence
- writes thoughtful responses to literature
- asks questions about new words
- enjoys reading and makes good use of her time during reading workshop
- selects challenging books that many of her peers would find difficult

WISH/GOAL: Most everyone simply said "to read more" in this section. While we would all agree with this and might say it, I would recommend an additional comment that reflects how the child might grow (process information or strategy use) or what the child might work on (giving more thorough responses to literature, making contributions to literature study group conversations, using context clues to construct meaning . . .). A couple of teachers made comments beyond "read more." For example:

- read longer and more challenging texts
- read across genres
- spend more time on task (involved) during reading time in class
- discuss more about the literature we share in class
- utilize more daily practice to become a more independent and fluent reader

Child's Growth as a Writer:

- expresses his ideas well through writing
- enjoys publishing and gives good feedback to those who read their work out loud
- self-selects challenging writing topics
- is really developing his ability to write about what he has read
- can write and draw connections between stories and personal experiences
- expresses feelings in writer's notebook
- is a risk taker in writing and makes an effort to write words, phrases, and sentences to convey meaning
- uses conventions of print including punctuation marks
- develops creative, innovative ideas for writing projects
- is improving neatness and mechanics

WISH/GOAL: I noticed that all teachers were more specific in writing than in reading. However, in both areas it seems that the word *skills* was overused or misused. For instance: Wish . . . would improve her spelling skills. "Strategies" would probably convey the message more accurately and it would even be more helpful to describe the nature of the spelling strategies used (For example, relying on visual memory, spelling the way it sounds, examining print around the room, etc.). I made the same observation in reading. For example, reading *skills* used rather than *strategies*—especially in relationship to scores on tests such as vocabulary or comprehension. My personal opinion about quantitative data is that examples like "index of control in spelling" informs parents about the ratio of invented to conventional spelling in their child's writing. Therefore it is specific without rating kids. Think about sharing scores carefully. It may not be helpful and may violate the nature of this instrument if we, or parents, misinterpret the value of the information.

Child's Growth as a Mathematician:

- uses mathematics as a tool to solve problems and answer questions
- is beginning to internalize basic addition facts
- demonstrates a grasp of place value
- is beginning to tell time on a standard clock
- demonstrating an understanding of place value
- uses math as a tool to examine our world
- explains his strategies and thinks about math concepts thoughtfully
- increased confidence and risk taking in math
- is becoming much more comfortable solving word problems

WISH/GOAL:

- work on basic division facts
- ask questions if there is something he doesn't understand
- memorize math facts to make problem solving easier
- work on logical applications of problem solving
- use mathematics in real situations
- practice all four basic math operations
- to practice subtracting with concrete objects—to internalize basic subtraction facts

Child's Growth as a Scientist/Social Scientist:

- locates relevant information from reference materials independently
- demonstrated incredibly mature and sensitive views during our study of the Civil War
- prepared and presented a wonderful expert project
- chooses academic tasks during center time
- collaborates with small groups to research topics of interest
- eloquently verbalizes questions and discusses topics of interest
- selected excellent topics for expert projects, always interesting and well thought through
- is able to bring artistic talent to science/social studies work
- seeks information by active participation and investigation
- during choice time he can be found in the science area observing the fish, turtle, gerbils, and spiders

WISH/GOAL:

- focus on understanding of topics we explore rather than trying to memorize facts
- read more in this area for recreational reading
- continue to integrate process skills (strategies?) in science (generate questions, interpret, conclude, test hypotheses)
- have her projects done on time with less help from home
- be serious and thoughtful when asking questions
- pursue her own personal inquiries
- become better informed of current events

As usual, the closer I look at who you are and what you do for children specifically and the profession at large, I am in awe. I hope you find my selections helpful as you embark upon another year of observing, interpreting, and sharing your children's growth.

Heidi

Figure 4–1. *Heidi's Notes on Progress Reports.*

was for them as they searched for ways to describe their students' progress and challenges.

By approaching assessment as a collaborative faculty inquiry project, the teachers and university partners made terrific strides in developing assessment practices within a single year. Additionally, these practices have influenced relationships among students, teachers, and parents in several ways. For example, by involving family members in assessing students' expert projects through video, Michele and other teachers have helped family members take up the language of inquiry and better understand and appreciate the less traditional forms of instruction that occur at the Center. Similarly, newsletters that focus on individual students' processes of learning and accomplishments as well as whole-class activities help parents see the otherwise invisible processes and benefits of an inquiry-based approach to learning. Many parents' concerns about assessment without the use of a grading system have fallen by the wayside.

Discussion and Implications

By looking closely at the work accomplished during and as a result of inquiry study meetings, we can see how inquiry has played a significant role in professional development and continual school renewal. Through these meetings, many of the principles of inquiry introduced by Short, Harste, and Burke (1996) were addressed. We brainstormed our beliefs about teaching and learning to build from what we knew. We took time to develop questions and gained new perspectives through videotapes of each classroom and dialogue. Faculty members constantly shared what they learned from their own classroom inquiries. We took time during our meetings to plan new inquiries. Finally, I have sought to illustrate how thoughtful new actions grew from these inquiries.

I asked at the beginning of the chapter how inquiry might influence the relationship between beliefs and practices. By closely examining teachers' practices through videotape, faculty members were able to make explicit their beliefs and study how practices may or may not have been aligned with those beliefs. Faculty were also able to articulate beliefs that were more implicitly held, such as the importance of taking time to help groups of students collaborate more effectively. By examining beliefs through actual instructional practices, faculty members were able to clarify the philosophies that underpinned their practices both individually and as a school. Gloria Ladson-Billings (1995) has also found videotape to be an effective medium that allows faculty members to view and discuss one another's practices and beliefs.

In 1997–1998, the faculty specifically focused upon beliefs and practices regarding building communities of learners, strengthening partnerships with parents, and developing effective means of assessment. The inquiry on community helped faculty uncover various processes of community building as seen through practice in each classroom. These meetings underscored the importance of creating environments where our questions can help learners extend their thinking and consider ideas from multiple perspectives, where learners can challenge and work through one another's ideas, and where substantive conversations integrate personal connections with strong academic content. We also discussed our beliefs about the flexible and dynamic roles of teachers and students in these learning communities (Putney and Floriani, in press). Students in all classes at the Center, even kindergarten, have the responsibility to contribute to the learning process. These are communities where students can be teachers and teachers are viewed as learners. However, teachers have the responsibility to help students learn to work together effectively, and in such cases, they practiced a lead from behind strategy and authentically integrated lessons on collaboration within academic activities. Students and teachers in these learning communities were creating a common language (Lin 1993) of inquiry, one that parents and other family members were able to acquire through their interactions with the school. This common language was shared among faculty members as well when Heidi compiled the list of terms that they used in narrative progress reports.

Parents were brought into the language and culture of inquiry through strategic efforts and also through assessment practices. Another question that I posed at the beginning of this chapter was: How does inquiry influence changes in relationships among students, parents, and teachers? By systematically and intentionally examining beliefs and practices of assessment and the partnership with parents, teachers found new ways of bringing the family into a closer relationship with each student's learning process. Such transformations occurred schoolwide, through systematically and carefully restructured Curriculum Nights as well as through specific teachers' efforts, such as involving families in assessing videotaped expert projects. Furthermore, many parents have commented through interviews that they have begun to look at and talk to their children in new ways that reflect the principles of practice at the Center.

One area of inquiry emphasized by Short, Harste, and Burke (1996) that continues to challenge us is attending to difference. These inquiry meetings provide an important time for celebrating our own learning as professionals and learning from the excellent practices that each faculty member offers. As some of the transcripts indicate, these meetings allowed faculty members to discuss some of the inevitable tensions that they face and how those tensions can be resolved. We are each sufficiently critical of our own teaching practices. However, we are challenged to find ways to bring in points of view that may be at odds with our colleagues' perspectives. As Short, Harste, and Burke (1996) point out, tremendous opportunities for learning grow out of exploring differences and complicating an issue by seeking to understand it in all its complexity. However, as much as we value such opportunities, it can be uncomfortable to discuss opposing points of view. Many of us are accustomed to school environments where decision making and professional development is not viewed as a collaborative endeavor. In such situations, we worked in isolation and were given few opportunities to discuss one another's practices. In a democratic school environment where faculty have a strong voice in school policy decisions, we, like our students, are learning how to communicate in constructively critical ways. How can we continue to be sensitive to one another while learning to ask the hard questions of each other?

Even when we are faced with such challenges, inquiry is clearly at the center of professional development and continual school renewal. It has been important to create a structured time and space for faculty members to inquire into their beliefs and practices. It has been difficult to carve out the time needed for inquiry study meetings. On occasion, these meetings have been taken up by important and real school business that requires immediate attention. In addition to finding the time for these meetings, we have come to see the importance of creating a *predictable structure* that includes strategies that promote professional reflexivity—studying ourselves to outgrow ourselves. In one of our discussions, Heidi suggested that such a structure include:

- making space for stories
- recognizing the power and potential of curricular conversations
- developing and sharing burning questions
- discussing theory, beliefs, and practices that grow out of viewing videotapes, sharing transcripts of classroom events, and/or looking at student artifacts
- honoring teachers' ways of knowing
- allowing the focus of meetings to emerge from the teachers' concerns, interests, and questions

Although the university partners organize and facilitate the meetings, we are attempting to lead from behind with the teachers just as they do with their students. Hence, the format of the meetings has evolved over time, but the emphasis of learning from colleagues remains constant. It has also been important that we all bring inquiring minds, questions, and beliefs to these meetings. Without time, a predictable and productive structure, and a spirit of inquiry, these meetings would likely motivate little real change and growth in classrooms, in the school community, or among the educators themselves. I conclude with questions worthy of further pursuit:

- How can schools create structures that foster inquiry for professional development and continual school renewal?
- How can those structures be maintained once the initial motivation for their creation has been threatened by many other competing demands?
- How can we remain flexible to altering those structures without risking losing them completely?
- How can we foster constructive critique and support honest communication in ongoing professional development and curriculum inquiry endeavors?

While we are asking these questions, we struggle in this new school year to find the time to return to inquiry study meetings, as a series of events and commitments are clamoring for our attention. However, we have seen the influence of inquiry in helping us grow and learn. Personally, I have grown tremendously in my own teaching practices by learning from and with my teacher-researcher colleagues at the Center. Each of us has come to see the power of inquiry for professional development and continual school renewal, and we will always find a way to make room for it in our school culture.

References

Collins, E., and J. L. Green. 1992. "Learning in Classrooms: Making or Breaking a Culture." In *Redefining Student Learning: Roots of Educational Change*, edited by H. H. Marshall, 59–86. Norwood, NJ: Ablex.

Dixon, C. N., C. R. Frank, and J. L. Green. 1999. "Classrooms as Cultures: Understanding the Constructed Nature of Life in Classrooms." *Primary Voices* 7 (3): 4–8.

Goodenough, W. H. 1963. *Cooperation in Change.* New York: Russell Sage Foundation.

Gumperz, J. J. 1981. "Conversational Inference and Classroom Learning." In *Ethnography and Language in Educational Settings*, edited by J. L. Green and C. Wallat, 3–23. Norwood, NJ: Ablex.

Harste, J. 1996. *The Semiotics of School Reform.* Paper presented at the International Reading Association Preconference Institute, Atlanta, GA.

Jennings, L. B. 1998. *How Democratic Classroom Practices Support the Academic Study of Tolerance and Justice.* Paper presented at the National Conference of Teachers of English annual meeting, Nashville, TN, November.

Jennings, L. B., and I. Pattenaude. 1998. "Making Meaning and Beyond: Literate Strategies for Exploring and Enacting Tolerance." *New Advocate* 11 (4): 325–343.

Ladson-Billings, G. 1995. "Toward a Theory of Culturally Relevant Pedagogy." *American Educational Research Journal* 32 (3): 465–491.

Lin, L. 1993. "Language of and in the Classroom: Constructing the Patterns of Social Life." *Linguistics and Education* 5 (3 and 4): 367–409.

Mills, H., and J. A. Clyde. 1990. *Portraits of Whole Language Classrooms.* Portsmouth, NH: Heinemann.

Mills, H., T. O'Keefe, and D. Whitin. 1996. *Mathematics in the Making.* Portsmouth, NH: Heinemann.

Noddings, N. 1996. "On Community." *Educational Theory* 46 (3): 245–267.

Putney, L., and A. Floriani. In press. "Examining Transformative Classroom Processes and Practices: A Cross-Case Analysis of Life in Two Bilingual Classrooms." *Journal of Classroom Interaction.*

Santa Barbara Classroom Discourse Group. 1992. "Constructing Literacy in Classrooms: Literate Actions as Social Accomplishment." In *Redefining Student Learning: Roots of Educational Change,* edited by H. Marshall, 119–150. Norwood, NJ: Ablex.

Short, K., and C. Burke. 1996. "Examining Our Beliefs and Practices Through Inquiry." *Language Arts* 73: 97–104.

Short, K., J. Harste, and C. Burke. 1996. *Creating Classrooms for Authors and Inquirers.* Portsmouth, NH: Heinemann.

Snyder, J., G. Morrison, and R. C. Smith. 1996. *Dare to Dream: Educational Guidance for Excellence.* Indianapolis, IN: Lilly Foundation.

Spradley, J. P. 1980. *Participant Observation.* New York: Holt, Rinehart, and Winston.

Tuyay, S., L. Jennings, and C. Dixon. 1995. "Classroom Discourse and Opportunities to Learn: An Ethnographic Study of Knowledge Construction in a Bilingual Third Grade Classroom." *Discourse Processes* 19 (1): 75–110.

5

Creating Curriculum with and for Children

MICHELE SHAMLIN

"Inquiry is the building of curriculum with students . . . and using their ideas and interests to inform the curricular path" was my hesitant response to the interviewers' request for my definition of inquiry. During the interview for a teaching position at the newly approved Center for Inquiry, I readily admitted that my knowledge and experience in the rhetoric of inquiry was limited. After more questions that delved into my educational philosophies and beliefs, the interview ended. I left the interview feeling certain that I would not be hired because the new magnet school would offer inquiry-based instruction, and my experience with inquiry was limited. I'm thankful I was wrong. The interview team saw potential in my responses, as my implicit beliefs reflected fundamental features of an inquiry-based model. Within a few days, I was hired as the kindergarten teacher at the new elementary school of choice.

That interview was three and a half years ago, and it has been three years since we opened our school. In that time I've spent many hours reflecting on my past years of teaching and the circumstances that brought me to this latest juncture in my journey as an educator. Embedded in these reflections were memories of key events and experiences that marked the evolution of my growth as a teacher of inquiry.

My Journey as a Teacher

The Early Years

I began my career in education as a first-grade teacher. I followed the district's curricular guidelines and used all of the designated textbooks and programs.

My students would eventually attempt most of the things I asked of them, but they were neither enthusiastic nor particularly motivated. Each student achieved at least a modicum of success, but I knew in my heart that something was missing.

As the years passed, I used every technique, gimmick, and strategy I could find to rouse my students from their apathetic slumps. I noticed that eyes began to sparkle and backbones straightened when the lesson or activity involved a topic that interested the children. Finding a way to study topics of interest while meeting the district's guidelines was often more than I could handle. I did not give up. Gradually I learned more ways to involve the children. They offered their ideas, opinions, and questions about topics, activities, field studies, and tests. Also, we began to create alternate forms of assessments together, such as rubrics and checklists. The students and I worked together to make our classroom a place that interested and challenged all of us.

After ten increasingly successful years at the elementary level, a middle school principal asked me to come to his school and teach seventh-grade science. He was concerned about his middle school students' apathy and lack of success in the classroom. He had heard about me, my passion for children, and my unconventional ways. Undaunted by the fact that all of my experience was at the elementary level, he begged me to give middle school a try. Being something of a daredevil, I agreed.

To say that teaching middle school was challenging would be quite an understatement. I found myself reading, planning, researching, and experimenting to discover ways to interest, stimulate, and involve the reluctant adolescents in the classroom. I enrolled in graduate courses in an effort to learn more. By closely watching and reflecting on my own actions, I eventually worked my way back to the foundations of what I believe about learning and about education. It took some time examining my own actions and beliefs before I could differentiate between what I knew in my heart to be true and what I had blindly accepted from others. Once my beliefs were firmly in place, I set about the task of making my actions reflect those beliefs. As I grew as a teacher and learner, I had eight wonderful years with some fabulous middle school students. Many of my colleagues complained about students' apathy and lack of motivation; that was not the case when the students and I worked together to pursue our interests.

Then I accepted the kindergarten position at the new school of choice. Once again I found myself nervously facing a new challenge. After all, I had never taught kindergarten and the change in grade levels was huge. I immediately began to read about teaching young children and talk with teachers of young students. I spent hours pouring over Bobbi Fisher's *Joyful Learning* (1991) and Carole Avery's *And with a Light Touch* (1993). This search proved to be very encouraging. The information and advice I received led me into kindergarten with the confidence that, once again, building curriculum with students was best practice, regardless of age and experience. I started the year as a learner with my young students.

The things I found to be important in an early childhood program were the very same things I held close to my heart as the catalysts of my successful experiences in middle school. Certainly the content was different, some strategies and skills were different, and the degrees of student participation and motivation varied, but the foundations of my classroom, those beliefs and subsequent actions on which I based every aspect of my teaching, held true regardless of age, level, or grade. Therefore, the potentially difficult transition I feared never occurred. Instead it was relatively smooth, as I learned that inquiry was inquiry wherever one went and whatever one pursued.

Living and Learning Through Inquiry

Given that inquiry is a philosophical stance and not a set of methods or activities, there was no scheduled time for inquiry. Inquiry pervaded each day in our kindergarten classroom. We inquired about everything—reading, writing, math, rain forests, animals, friendship, and much more. Our inquiries continued into and throughout first grade. The topics were diverse and at times complex, yet we pushed through, determined to satisfy our curiosities. My students and I learned and grew a lot.

One of the most amazing things I experienced was the magnitude of the power that existed in building curriculum with students and allowing the interests and ideas of the children to drive the direction of our studies. Early in the spring semester of kindergarten, I decided to focus on the concept of growth and change over time. I based this decision on a comment made by a student as we observed how our school had been evolving from isolated, unattractive portables to an appealing learning village. My students and I had been watching the painting, the landscaping, the addition of awnings, and the construction of an outdoor arena. One day, Lora commented, "We've been talking about how we grow up. Our school is growing up, too." Right then I decided to broaden our focus on personal growth and change to the conceptual framework of growth and change over time. In the course of our study we discussed many things—seasons, people, schools, holidays, traditions, folktales, and much more. My MAT intern planned a trip to the zoo as a part of our look at growth and change in animals.

The children loved the zoo animals and were quick to record their observations and questions in journals. I noticed that our focus on growth and change was evident in their questions: "How big is a giraffe when it is born?"

"Where do mother sea lions keep their milk to feed the babies?" "Why do baby horses walk as soon as they're born, but it takes us a year?" As we talked about our observations and questions during lunch, I was struck by the depth of the conversation and the thoughtfulness that went into the children's hypotheses.

At school the next day, we had a rich conversation about our zoo trip, as individuals shared excerpts from observation journals with the class. In the midst of our talk, Elise said, "I have a suggestion. Why don't we do expert projects on animals?" Students in the upper grades had been doing expert projects for several months, and my kindergartners wanted to do them, too. "If they can do it, we can do it," I heard over and over. Believing strongly in the need to follow the children, I agreed.

In an exciting conversation about animals and how much we were all fascinated by them, each child chose an animal to study. We spent an afternoon brainstorming ideas for our proposed expert projects. The children and I negotiated a list of required criteria and another list of suggestions. For instance, each project would share five facts about the animal, focusing on growth and change. There would be a minimum of two illustrations. The children would do all of the writing and drawing. Each project would have a title. Each child would write his or her name and the date on the project. One of the suggestions was that children would try to find poems or songs to support projects. Finally, we brainstormed ways that parents could help. The list of requirements, suggestions, and parent guidelines were typed up and sent home. We decided that projects would be due in two weeks, and each child would prepare a presentation for the class during which he or she would share the learned information.

The projects were nothing less than phenomenal! Each child chose to focus on growth and change in her or his own way. Hutton shared the changes in hunting practices as cheetahs grow. Melissa explained how the eating habits of wolves change as they grow. Lora showed the stages of development for young kangaroos. The list goes on and on. I realized that focusing on a concept such as growth and change while encouraging the children to pursue their own interests pushed my young inquirers beyond attaining surface level information. We invited the first graders to a project fair during which the kindergartners set up their projects around the classroom and shared them with their older, yet still young, colleagues.

I paused often during this entire experience to step back and reflect on the propelling nature of inquiry. To me, the expert projects seemed like an appropriate place to stop with one cycle of inquiry and pursue another. We did pursue another area of interest, but it was not necessary to stop and look for our next topic. During the projects, several students mentioned that their animals of interest were found in rain forests.

On the day after our project fair, we sat in Friendship Circle to discuss and savor the experience. At that time, Hutton looked around the group, took a deep breath, and said, "Miss Shamlin, we want to study rain forests." I looked around the circle at the nodding heads and realized that they had already discussed this and were only waiting for my approval to proceed. Needless to say, I agreed.

Secretly, I predicted that this study would be brief because rain forests are fairly removed from *our* world. I was quite wrong. Within days, our room was filled with books, videos, posters, and pictures, and one wall was in the process of being converted to a rain forest. Children made toucans, parrots, monkeys, sloths, plants, vines, trees, and many other animals and insects. We also learned songs about the rain forest.

Our first social action project stemmed from our study of the rain forest. Elise was very concerned that rain forests were being cut down. She proposed that our kindergarten find a way to help. Her enthusiasm was contagious. In no time, Elise and some allies had organized a campaign to collect aluminum cans, "sell" them to recycling centers, and send the money to a rain forest federation. Parents got involved, as did other students at our school. An area of our classroom turned into a recycling center. In the midst of this excitement, I was learning a lot about living through inquiry. I witnessed firsthand the generative nature and the incredible power of an inquiry-based classroom.

Current Questions

Offering an inquiry-based education was not the only responsibility involved with living and learning at our school. Our school served as a national demonstration site for educators from across the nation. We have hosted numerous visitors who were interested in seeing an inquiry-based school in action. They read related literature, visited classrooms, asked questions, talked with teachers and parents, and filled out observation sheets. We were encouraged to read the observations and reflect on the information and questions that the visitors shared.

During the past two years, visitors have asked many questions about various aspects of our classroom. I have readily shared the things I have learned—my thoughts, my beliefs, and my own questions. However, I became increasingly dissatisfied with my ability to answer some of the recurring questions that bombarded me week after week. In particular, I was dissatisfied with my explanations about building curriculum with and for students. I found myself able to offer only vague descriptions and advice about "listening to the students and following what they say." That was true, but I knew it was so much more than just listening. It was this dissatisfaction that propelled me to search for a deeper understanding of what it really means to build curriculum with and for children. I wanted to intentionally and systematically examine how I created curriculum with my students. In so doing, I would become a more planful, thoughtful teacher, and I could make greater contributions to the profession by making the implicit features of inquiry-based curriculum development explicit.

I decided to embrace my doctoral research and dissertation as an opportunity to pursue these issues. When the next loop began, I entered our classroom full of new kindergartners, determined to investigate our time together. Specifically, I wanted to examine how we created curriculum together and how the curricular framework supported us. The following is a composite of two days in October.

A Composite Day in Kindergarten

(October 29–October 30, 1998)

Book Browse (7:40 A.M.–8:05 A.M.)

I greeted nine of my students with a quick welcome and a hug as they entered the classroom. Students could be dropped off at school up to thirty minutes prior to the official beginning of the school day, which is 8:05 A.M. The students who arrived early had time at the beginning of each school day to engage themselves in sustained literacy activities, while other students arrived with only enough time to unpack their book bags prior the official beginning of the day.

As the students unpacked their book bags and talked with one another, they began to explore different books that had been placed in the reading area. Two students chose to read a nonfiction big book. Six students began looking through books about animals, all nonfiction choices. The animal books were kept on a bookshelf designated for focused study. Matthew got his focused study journal and looked through it.

Joey, one of the six children with animal books, asked me to read to the group. I immediately joined the students on the red carpet. Stephanie explained their plan. She said, "We don't want to hear a whole book. We're looking at the pictures, and we need help with the captions." I agreed to provide the help they were seeking. As the rest of the students arrived at school, I greeted them from the floor while reading whichever captions the children indicated. More students joined us on the red carpet. Soon there were small groups looking at pictures and slowly working to read the captions. They consulted me when a word proved too difficult to conquer. My usual response involved questioning the students about the strategies they typically used and then guiding them through the process.

"What do we do when we come to an unfamiliar word?" I asked.

"Get our mouths ready by looking at the first letter?" Stephanie queried.

"That is certainly a strategy. What else?" I added.

"We try a word that makes sense and matches the letters," Joey explained. He then proceeded to decode the word. As Joey demonstrated, the children knew some strategies; they just needed a little support and encouragement.

Morning Friendship Circle (8:05 A.M.–8:30 A.M.)

As the schoolwide morning announcements began over the intercom, the students began to quietly put away the books and gather on the red carpet—the common meeting area of the room—in a circle. After pledging allegiance to the American flag, observing a moment of silence, and listening to the announcements, the students took turns telling the news events that they wanted to share.

Caroline began Friendship Circle by telling the class about the need to have a warming rock for a pet snake. "We went to the pet store yesterday," she shared, "and got Nuby [her pet snake] a warming rock. The pet store man said that snakes had to stay warm. I told him that must be because they are cold-blooded. He stared at me. He asked me how old I was. I told him five. And he told my daddy that he couldn't believe I knew about snakes being cold-blooded. My daddy told me to tell the man what it meant, so I did. He couldn't believe it."

As she paused, I asked, "So, what did you tell the man?"

She looked surprised at my question and replied, "I told him that the snake's inside temperature changes with the outside temperature." She received several compliments from members of our community.

Jordan then shared that her cousin didn't know what cold-blooded and warm-blooded meant. "And he's in the third grade!" she exclaimed. The other children gasped and expressed amazement that such a big boy would not know such a simple thing.

Joey asked, "Is he okay? I mean is something wrong with him?" Jordan thought about his question for a moment and said, "No, but maybe something is wrong with his school."

Paxie continued by asking, "Are we going to do expert projects?" Several students wanted an explanation about expert projects. I asked Paxie if she would like to explain. "See, an expert project is when you pick one thing and study it really, really hard. Then when you know a lot of stuff, you make a project and bring it to class," she offered. "When it's your turn, you do a presentation. That means you teach everybody in the class what you know—even the teacher!" All eyes turned to me for confirmation.

I agreed with Paxie, "That is an excellent description of an expert project. Paxie remembers when her sister, Dani, did expert projects when she was in my class. In answer to your question, Paxie, I hope we will decide to do expert projects. What do the rest of you think?" I predicted they would respond enthusiastically, as expert projects had been given a place of honor in rituals that pervaded our school. The response was unanimous; we decided to do expert projects on an animal of choice.

Marcus had asked to share next. Rather than telling his original news, Marcus chose to say that he wanted to study either wolves or ducks. "I like mammals the best," he offered, "but I really want to learn about ducks." I assured him that either animal would be fine with us.

Alex told about an upcoming trip his dad was going to take. "He's going all the way to Taiwan. He'll be gone for a long time. I'll miss him," he sadly shared. Everyone nodded sympathetically and murmured words of comfort.

Jessica told the class about her cousins coming for an unexpected visit. She was not pleased with the surprise. "They slept in my bed!" she exclaimed. "I had to sleep on the floor. I hope they leave soon."

McKay concluded our news sharing by telling about a girl she knew who had some fish, a turtle, a parakeet, and some tadpoles for pets. "All she needs is a mammal and she'll have all of the groups we studied!" McKay exclaimed.

Joey immediately commented, "But she's a mammal herself!"

McKay looked surprised. "Oh!" she said. "Ding!" I smiled knowing that McKay had simply used an expression I used often in conversation with my colleauges. *Ding* held a shared meaning among the faculty. We used it to confirm or validate the obvious. Basically, it was a softer version of "duh!" Obviously, the teacher talk had also become part of the children's repertoire.

Our Friendship Circle concluded after we quickly reviewed the daily forecast that was printed on the board. We ended by joining hands and singing "Make New Friends," a traditional camp song.

Whole-Group Time (8:30 A.M.–9:00 A.M.)

The students moved from the circle and gathered on the floor in front of the chair where I sat to lead our whole-group times. After discussing the date and the day of school, we began a shared reading session. By the middle of October, we had settled into the routine of reading two big books during each shared reading experience: an old favorite and a less familiar big book.

Our old favorite of the day was *The Little Yellow Chicken* (Cowley 1996). As I pointed at the words, we read each page. When we finished, Stephanie said, "I've been thinking about the chicken's grandmother [the little red hen]. I was thinking before that she was just mean because she told the little yellow chicken not to share with the frog and the bee and the beetle."

Amber supplied, "She was grouchy because everybody wasn't nice to her in her story."

Stephanie continued, "Well, I've got another idea. Maybe she wasn't really mean. Maybe she just didn't trust the frog and the bee and the beetle. She was a bird, so maybe she didn't know about amphibians and animals without backbones like the bee and the beetle."

Before I could say a word, Joey chimed in, "Yeah, I bet you're right. It's just like the birds in *Feathers and Fools* [Fox 1989]. Remember? They had a big war because they didn't understand each other. Can we read that again?" I agreed that it was time to revisit that book. Also, I complimented Stephanie on her insight and Joey on his connection.

Our new big book for the day was titled *Duck and Hen* (Cowley 1992). Before opening the book, I asked our usual questions while pointing to the appropriate parts of the book, and the students answered in unison: "What is this called?" (the front cover); "What is this?" (the back cover); "What is this?" (the spine); "What is this?" (the title); "What is this?" (the author's and illustrator's names); and as I opened the front cover, "What is this page called?" (the title page). Then we proceeded to read the book together.

I used a pointer to direct the students' eyes along the appropriate path. When we finished reading the book, we discussed the strategies they had used to read the unfamiliar text. At the conclusion of our discussion, McKay made a comment. She said, "I think the author didn't know much about birds."

I thought about her statement for a second and asked, "Why do you say that?"

She readily answered, "Well, there isn't anything really much about birds, real birds. Real birds can't talk, so that's just make-believe. She could have put in some stuff like how they breathe through lungs and they lay eggs and they're warm-blooded. You know, to make it better. More real."

Alex disagreed: "I think the author does know about birds. She had to know about ducks and hens or the story wouldn't have made sense."

Joey shared a connection. "It's like *Feathers and Fools* [Fox 1989] again. Except that book was about peacocks and swans instead of ducks and hens. I'm glad the duck and hen decided to notice their differences but stay friends."

McKay maintained, "I still think it would have been a better story if the author had used more real stuff about birds. Maybe I'll write a story like that." I told her that I certainly hoped she did.

Brief Read-Aloud (9:00 A.M.–9:10 A.M.)

We ended our whole-group time with a brief read-aloud. Although I had planned to read a different book, I decided to read *Feathers and Fools* since it had been mentioned twice that morning. The students were completely quiet as I read about the strife between a group of peacocks and a group of swans that resulted from focusing on their differences. When the focus on differences led to fear, the birds gathered weapons with which to protect themselves. After a horrible battle during which all of the birds were killed, two eggs hatched, one revealing a baby swan and the other, a peacock. The baby birds noticed their similarities and decided to be friends.

The children were quiet as I finished the book and closed the cover. As always, I asked, "What are you thinking about?" Paxie said that she was feeling sad because so many birds died.

Alex agreed and added, "They weren't very smart. They should have talked about what scared them."

Caroline remarked, "Yeah, they needed to have a Friendship Circle to solve their problems. That's what we do." Since there were no further comments, we moved on to Explorations.

Explorations (9:10 A.M.–10:10 A.M.)

Explorations involved free choice within and around eight major learning centers that were positioned around the room. During Explorations, students were able to choose between the book center, art center, blocks, housekeeping, computers, the sand table, the manipulatives area, and the writing center. There were no teacher-imposed restrictions for Explorations during the first months of school, other than a limit of four people per area. We had, however, begun to discuss some requirements that the children would have to complete during Explorations. We planned to begin those "teacher choices" after Thanksgiving.

While many of the children chose to participate in the usual activities that were available during Explorations, there were some students who chose activities that related to our investigation into the world of animals. Marcus, Sean, Shane, and Chelxenn chose the blocks area. After a brief discussion, they decided to construct a zoo. As I listened to their conversation, I realized that this was not merely a superficial reference to our animal study. "We need to put the groups together. You know, the mammals and reptiles and birds and all of them. That way people can go see the group they like the best without having to walk all over the place," Sean offered.

Shane agreed, "Yeah, and we need to put the reptiles and amphibians close together, too." Marcus wanted to know why that mattered. Shane explained, "Because they're all cold-blooded, and we'll have to make sure they stay warm in the winter and cool in the summer. That will be easier if they're close together." The other boys agreed, and they worked quietly for a few minutes.

Then Sean said, "You know, everybody needs water to drink and take baths and stuff but the amphibians need another water place, too." I asked why. Sean explained, "They'll need water to lay their eggs and so the babies can grow up in it." I was amazed at the depth of their thinking and planning.

Allie, Caroline, and Jordan were in the art area, working on some drawings of animals. As each finished her drawing, she taped it to the wall in the animal gallery. The animal gallery appeared early in our focused study on animals. There was a section of one wall that McKay and Sean had asked to use for animal art. Since that day, all of the children had made artistic contributions to the animal gallery.

Alex and Jonathan spent over half of Explorations time by the aquarium, observing the fish. They had their faces pressed against the glass as they watched our six fish. I joined them at the aquarium. "What are you guys doing?" I asked.

Alex replied, "We're wondering about these fish."

I asked what they were wondering.

Jonathan explained, "Well, we're trying to count how many times they open their mouths. Alex says that's when they are breathing. We want to know if they all breathe the same number of times." I debated over whether or not to guide the boys in their investigation and decided to wait until they had exhausted their own ideas.

"Let me know what you find out," I commented.

Alex looked up. "When we're through," he said, "we're going to count our breaths and see who breathes more, us or fish." I complimented the boys on their investigation and told them that I hoped they would report their investigation to the class. They agreed and went back to work.

Joey, McKay, and Matthew were hard at work in the writing center. I sat down with them and asked if they would tell me what they were doing. Joey answered immediately, "We're not writing yet. We're just talking about what to write. You know, we're planning." I told him that I always spent some time thinking before writing.

"What are your plans so far?" I asked. McKay seemed frustrated as she shared that Joey did not like her plan.

"He said my story won't make sense," she explained.

Joey defended himself: "I did not say that. I said that it would be better if you wrote about two different kinds of animals instead of writing about two animals in the same group."

McKay argued, "But *Feathers and Fools* is about two birds!"

Joey responded, "But so is *Duck and Hen* and you didn't like it!"

Matthew remained very quiet, so I asked his opinion.

"I'm just going to write my own story," he shared. "I don't care if anybody doesn't like it. My mom will." I agreed and suggested that Joey and McKay work on their stories separately for awhile.

"Maybe you could get back together and share them after you've got your thoughts on paper. Sometimes that makes it easier to discuss than trying to decide everything before you even start writing." They both began writing.

Later, I asked McKay what she had decided to do. "I decided to write about three animals. That way I can use two mammals like I wanted to and a different animal like Joey said. It's a reptile!" she added. I complimented her on her ingenuity and told her that I would like to read her story when she finished. She agreed.

Jessica wandered around from center to center for a while. Finally, I invited her to join me on the red carpet for a game. She agreed only after some very strong persuasion on my part.

Morning Recess (10:10 A.M.–10:30 A.M.)

The students lined up at the door and went out for recess. Ten of the children went straight to the playground equipment. Three played on the tire swing. Four went down the slides, while others simply climbed the ladders. After about ten minutes, Kenan suggested that they play a game. Joey, Christopher, Kylie, Elizabeth, Sean, and Caroline decided to play Cheetah with Kenan. The game was a variation on tag. The person who was "it" was instead "the cheetah" and ran around chasing the others. When a child was tagged, she or he became the cheetah and chased the others. At the end of recess, Jaretta, my kindergarten assistant, waved her hand, and the children lined up behind her. As the children entered the classroom, I squirted some soap into their hands, and they washed their hands in preparation for lunch. After washing their hands, they went to the red carpet and sat down for Sharing Time.

Sharing Time (10:30 A.M.–10:50 A.M.)

Kenan was the first to share. "I want to tell you about the study me and my dad are going to do," he said. "We were talking about bears hibernating and all. I thought that bears hibernated in the winter because of the cold.

Then I started thinking that didn't make sense because bears are warm-blooded. And what about polar bears? The cold weather doesn't bother them. Anyway, my dad and me are going to find out why bears hibernate and if it's because of the cold and if it is, how come. That's all," he concluded. A few students raised hands to ask questions and give compliments. Kenan called on Christopher.

Christopher said, "That's a cool study, Kenan. I like it!"

Next, Amber asked, "Is that what you're going to do your expert project on?" Kenan tilted his head to one side as he thought about it. "I don't know yet," he answered.

Finally, Jaretta commented, "I think it's very special that you are studying things on your own, Kenan. Be sure to report back to us about your findings."

Chelxenn shared a book he had made about fish. "I have an aquarium at home," he said. "That's what gave me the idea." He showed the cover of his book and turned each page so the others could see. The title was *Fish*. He had written his name as author and illustrator. Each page showed a different fish. There were no words other than the word *fish* on each page. As he closed the book, Chelxenn announced, "That's all." Three children raised their hands for questions and compliments.

McKay asked, "Why didn't you use any more words?"

Chelxenn grinned sheepishly and said, "I didn't know how to spell them. Anyway, pictures can tell a story, can't they?" McKay agreed, and Chelxenn called on Sean.

"I like your book," said Sean. "Did you make it at home or in Explorations?" Chelxenn said that he had made it at home.

Margaret commented, "That's a great idea, Chelxenn. We should write stories about our pets and put them in a book." The other students noisily agreed. I asked Jaretta to make a note that we would start some pet stories during writer's workshop.

Amber shared a new doll her grandparents had sent. Several children asked to hold the doll. Amber agreed that they could play with it during afternoon Explorations.

Allie shared some photographs of her new pet rabbit. "I got it for my birthday," she said. "Can I bring her to school one day?" I told her that she could certainly bring the rabbit if her mother could bring it and take it back home after a short while. Allie grinned and said that she had already asked her mother.

McKay raised her hand and asked, "Aren't you going to tell us about your bunny?" Allie then shared that her rabbit breathed through lungs, would have babies some day, had "hair called fur," and was "hot-blooded."

When she finished, Joey said, "Of course, your rabbit is a mammal." Allie nodded at his comment.

Then Shane asked, "Is hot-blooded the same thing as warm-blooded?"

Allie quickly corrected herself: "I meant warm-blooded." Amber confided that she had always wanted a bunny while Allie sat down on the red carpet.

Paxie shared a nonfiction book about dogs. "This is my dog book," she said. "This one is like Little Anne [her pet] and this one is like Sam [another pet]. I'm going to use this book when I do my expert project on dogs. You can get color copies at Kinko's. That's all," she concluded. Christopher complimented her on sharing the book and asked if he could look at it later. Paxie said he could. Everyone applauded as she took a seat on the red carpet.

Lunch, Read-Aloud, Interlude, and Snacks (10:50 A.M.–1:00 P.M.)

The students quickly took seats in the cafeteria and began eating and socializing. After about twenty-five minutes in the cafeteria, we stood up and cleaned around our table. The students then discarded their trash, emptied their trays, and lined up at the door. We returned to the classroom, where Jaretta read a book.

When she finished reading, Jaretta announced that it was time for Interlude. The children got their towels and spread out for rest time. At 12:45 P.M., the students got up, folded their towels, got their snacks, and sat on the red carpet for snacks and conversation. Afterward, we gathered on the red carpet for our afternoon whole-group time.

Whole-Group Time (1:00 P.M. –1:30 P.M.)

Our afternoon whole-group time consisted of a focused study session. We gathered on the red carpet to talk about organizing our information by using a Venn diagram. This is how the conversation evolved:

MS: I was thinking yesterday about how we have been talking about three kinds of animals. What three kinds of animals have we talked about?

Students: Mammals, reptiles, and birds!

MS: Mammals, reptiles, and birds. I want to show you how we can use a Venn diagram to compare the three. Now, we used two circles when we compared mammals and reptiles, but we haven't done it with birds, too. This will be a good opportunity to practice with three circles.

Christopher: Uh oh!

MS: Okay, there are our two circles like when we had mammals and reptiles. This circle was about mammals, and this circle was about reptiles. What was this in the middle?

Students: Both!

MS: Now that we are adding birds, we need a third circle. Let's say this one is mammals [sounding out and writing]. I usually label my circles so that anybody who comes in will know what it is. If it was just an *M* up there, they might think it was monkeys instead of mammals. Now, what do we want this circle to be?

Students: Reptiles.

MS: Okay, *rrrrrrr* [sounding out and writing].

Marcus: I have an *r* in my name.

MS: You sure do. Let's think about our questions. Maybe we can use our questions to start out guiding our Venn diagram. That way we can use the information we have learned about these animals. We can put it right there on it. Okay, let's think about mammals first. What covers the body?

Students: Hair!

MS: Hair. Is that true with reptiles?

Students: No.

MS: Is that true with birds?

Students: No.

MS: So, where do I write that?

Students: In the mammals circle.

MS: Just in the mammals circle. Right?

Christopher: Like a hairy bunny!

MS: What about reptiles?

Students: Skin.

MS: Dry, scaly skin. Do birds have dry, scaly skin?

Students: No!

Christopher: No, they have feathers!

MS: Okay. Dry, scaly skin for reptiles and feathers for birds. None of that goes in the middle. Now let's think about how babies are born.

Students: They give birth.

MS: Most mammals have live birth. Do either of the other two? Remember, we are talking about most of them. There are exceptions.

Students: No.

MS: So we'll put live birth in the mammals circle. What do most reptiles do?

Students: Lay eggs.

MS: What do birds do?

Students: Lay eggs.

MS: So where are we going to put that? Birds and reptiles share that characteristic. Steph, where are we going to put it? Come and show me. [She does.]

Students: In the middle.

MS: There you go. It's between reptiles and birds—in the intersection of just those two because it's not true for mammals. Okay, let's move on. Are they warm-blooded or cold-blooded? Mammals are. . . .

Students: Warm-blooded!

MS: Reptiles are. . . .

Students: Cold-blooded!

MS: Birds are. . . .

Students: Warm-blooded!

MS: Okay, so what's the only one that's cold-blooded?

Students: Reptiles. [Teacher writes it on the diagram.]

MS: Now, let's think for a minute. Christopher, go and sit at the table right behind you. That might help you leave others alone and you can still see. Okay, now let's think about where we are going to put warm-blooded. Where do we need to put it for birds and for mammals? Jordan, why don't you give it a shot? See if you can point to the place we should write warm-blooded. You can do it; you're looking at the right place. Exactly right! Good for you! We didn't put it in the very middle because that would include reptiles. Is everybody with us? Cool. Okay, where is the skeleton? Mammals?

Students: Inside.

MS: Reptiles?

Students: Inside.

MS: Birds?

Students: Inside.

MS: Chelxenn, why don't you come up and show us where to write inside skeletons. Think big; we'll help you if you have a little trouble. It needs to show that all three of the groups have inside skeletons. Where can we put it? Ding! Perfect! Okay, so what am I writing right here? Inside skeleton. You know what? You guys might have been noisy when we started, but you are doing some serious stuff here. This is big-time hard stuff. Okay, how do they breathe? Mammals?

Students: Lungs.

MS: Reptiles?

Students: Lungs.

MS: Birds?

Students: Lungs.

MS: Chelxenn showed us where to write characteristics for all three groups. Okay, now the last question, how do babies get food? Mammals?

Students: Mommas make milk!

MS: Mothers produce milk. Do any others do that?

Students: No!

MS: So, I need to go ahead and write that in the mammals circle. What about reptiles?

Students: Get it by themselves.

MS: Is that true for birds?

Joey: Birds get worms.

MS: Ah ha! How do the baby birds get food?

Joey: The parents eat worms, and then they throw up in the babies' mouths.

MS: Okay, why don't we just say that a parent brings them food. Okay, do you know what I think is really cool? We've got something in almost every place. The only place that is still empty is for what two animals?

McKay: Reptile and mammals.

MS: We don't have anything that they share but birds don't.

Joey: How about they have teeth?

MS: Hmmm, they have teeth. Actually, I'm trying to decide about birds. Do birds have teeth?

Students: No!

MS: Joey, where are we going to put teeth up here? Thanks. Isn't that cool? Marcus?

Marcus: Those circle things, it's kind of like we count them like this—first, second, third. It's like *Star Wars* first, second, and third.

MS: You're right. That's a great idea for Explorations. There are characters that are in all three, aren't there? Like, isn't Jabba the Hut only in one of them?

Christopher: Jabba the Hut is in two of them, the first one and the last one.

MS: Oh. Isn't that cool? Marcus, great idea and great connection!

Jonathan: You could add one circle and do four.

MS: It's really hard to do four and be able to show all of the relationships. I'm glad you mentioned that. When we add the next group of animals, we will have to find a different way to show similarities and differences. We won't be able to use Venn diagrams anymore.

Joey: We'll probably have to use lines.

MS: Be thinking about that because the lines idea will work. Jordan?

Jordan: Maybe we could make our own thing [Venn diagram]. Like that one but about something else. Maybe during Explorations time.

MS: Great idea. You could construct one about lots of things. Caroline?

Caroline: When I was at home yesterday, I did an uppercase *R* and a lowercase *r*.

MS: Good. Stephanie?

Stephanie: I was thinking when we add the fourth group, we could just use another circle.

MS: Why don't you investigate that during Explorations? Then report back to us. Elizabeth?

Elizabeth: I'm going to make one about me and my sisters.

MS: That would be fine. Now, the point in doing this is . . . just a second. Joey, can you hold your thought? We have all our information written about birds on a chart. We have all our information about reptiles on a chart. We have all our information about mammals on a chart. The good thing about a Venn diagram is that we can see how they are alike and how they are different right here on one diagram. With the three separate charts, we have to go around and look at each of them. With the Venn diagram, we know everything immediately. So, this shows how they are alike and how they're different. Okay?

Students: Okay!

MS: Now, we are going to make journals a little bit different for you. Instead of having a specific time to write in your journals, you can write whenever you choose to. It's an invitation for Explorations now. If you would like to write in your journal, Jaretta and I will hang around down at this end of the room and, if you need help, we will be here to help you. We will be more than happy to help you. The journals are right over there. If you choose to write, how many pages will you use?

Students: One.

MS: One, and you'll put the date on it. You can write on the back of the page, too. It can be a Venn diagram if you want or it can be something that you've thought about animals, a question you have, or something you want to study. Matthew?

Matthew: Penguins can swim.

MS: Some birds do swim. You could write that in your journal. Now, listen. If you choose not to write in your journal today, that is fine. Journals are serious business, not just to scribble in. [We talked regularly about encouraging the use of marks to represent letters and words. In this excerpt, I was discouraging aimless scribbling.]

McKay: What if I want to write a lot?

MS: Then you can use more than one page! Is everybody clear?

Students: Yeah!

Following the conversation, I dismissed students to go to Explorations.

Explorations (1:30 P.M.–2:00 P.M.)

Our afternoon Explorations time was similar to the morning Explorations time. Kenan moved to the blocks area when Marcus decided to go to the computers. While Kenan was in blocks, the boys decided to make a pet store instead of a zoo. When I asked why, Sean told me that it was too hard to make a zoo with blocks. "We need some other stuff," he said. I told him to let me know if I could help. He agreed and went back to work. The boys did not talk as they worked during the afternoon. Instead, they seemed intent on following their own ideas.

There were more artists adding to the animal gallery. Also, Amber and Paxie had joined the writers in the writing center. They were busy making a list of the dogs they liked out of Paxie's dog book. When I asked what they were going to do with the list, they both shrugged and went back to work.

Once again, Jessica had difficulty choosing an area. I guided her to the art area and waited until she became engaged in creating a picture. Then I joined two students at the easel to read some big books.

Clean Up and Pack (2:00 P.M.–2:10 P.M.)

When Explorations time ended, we cleaned up the room, and each student packed his or her possessions to take home. When the packing was complete, students deposited their book bags in a circle on the red carpet. They then lined up for a brief afternoon recess.

Afternoon Recess (2:10 p.m.–2:30 p.m.)

All of the children played Cheetah during the afternoon recess. Jaretta and I had to caution the children to play safely. They were rather rough as they tagged one another. Finally, I ended the game by suggesting that they go to the playground equipment. They all went. At 2:30 p.m. Jaretta lined up the children, and we returned to the classroom.

Afternoon Friendship Circle and Dismissal (2:30 p.m.–2:50 p.m.)

The students entered the room and came to sit in front of their book bags for our afternoon Friendship Circle. We joined hands and sang "What a Wonderful World" (Weiss and Thiele 1967), which had recently become a part of our afternoon ritual. We then shared our highlights of the day and our compliments to one another.

Four students named Book Browse as their highlight. Amber elaborated, "I liked reading the captions. There's more information there." Six students said that the morning Friendship Circle was their highlight. Five children named our focused study session as their highlight. Two chose Sharing Time, while the remaining five selected Explorations. I found it interesting that the five students who chose Explorations were the boys who had worked on the zoo and pet store.

Kenan thanked the other boys for letting him join them in the blocks area during the afternoon Explorations time. McKay thanked Joey for his suggestions about her story during the morning Explorations time. She added, "I appreciate it, Joey, even though it made me real mad." Elizabeth expressed her excitement about seeing Allie's pet rabbit and reminded Allie to ask her mom to come soon.

We ended our Friendship Circle by once again joining hands and then squeezing them to show personal friendship for everyone in the class. Each person squeezed the hand she or he was holding and so on until the squeezing returned to the originator. At that point, everyone lifted their connected hands and smiled. We then moved to the classroom door and exchanged hugs as we filed out of the room for the day.

Reflecting on What I Value Most

As I chronicled the composite of two days, I realized that our journey into the world of animals had precipitated changes across the curriculum. From Book Browse to our closing Friendship Circle, the children's words and actions were influenced by our focused study on animals. Actually, the effect was more than just an influence; our focused study into the world of animals permeated the day. As our venture progressed, we went from discussing animals only during focused study time to talking, writing, reading, drawing, thinking, creating, playing, and sharing thoughts, ideas, questions, and insights about animals. As a result of our close look at animals, we began to notice animals all around us, at school and at home.

As I planned our focused study sessions with various ways to reinforce and extend our thinking, the children were offered a multitude of opportunities to examine animals from various perspectives. Without being prompted, the students read about animals during Book Browse, shared about animals during Friendship Circles, offered information that they had learned outside of our classroom, made choices and decisions during Explorations that alluded to and included animals, and brought artifacts that reflected insights and observations about animals for Sharing Time.

There were occasions when students demonstrated that they had internalized content about animals. For example, when Caroline related her experience at the pet store, she showed that she understood the meaning of warm-blooded and cold-blooded. Kenan's question about the reason bears hibernate showed that he, too, was considering bears in light of the content he had internalized.

Kenan's question about bears also demonstrated that he was pursuing personal inquiries on his own. He knew that learning extended beyond the classroom as he included his father in his quest.

There were indications that the students realized the value of extending their thinking and the thinking of others. When Chelxenn shared the book he had made, he was questioned about his reason for using pictures instead of words.

Reading, writing, and mathematics were used as tools for learning about animals. Earlier in the school year, the children were interested in learning to read and write because they had been taught to expect that in school. As our focused study progressed, the children desperately worked on reading so they could learn more about animals. They displayed an intense interest in writing because they wanted and needed to record their ideas and questions about animals. When mathematics was shared as a way to organize information, the students embraced the notion of charts and graphs and worked to find ways to support their interests.

The children became more independent as they sought to read and write by themselves. They listened to me and their peers, practiced the strategies they heard and saw, and then worked to make the ideas and techniques manageable without too much adult assistance. Stephanie reminded me during Book Browse that they did not want me to read to them; they just wanted help with the words they could not figure out alone.

Stephanie extended everyone's thinking by asking our views on the little red hen. She offered a new perspective for us to consider when she suggested that the little red hen was nervous because she did not understand amphibians and invertebrates.

The students demonstrated growth in working together appropriately. There were less interruptions, and they talked to and with one another rather than directing all comments to me. Instances of inappropriately working together were less common. McKay and Joey displayed a certain sophistication as they discussed the story McKay planned to write. The children began to use words to solve disagreements and problems rather than inappropriate actions.

Our focused study on animals provided a new lens through which the students viewed the world. They discussed animals at home, brought the discussions to school to share with their classmates, made choices and decisions all day based on their interest in animals, and posed questions and made observations based on their understandings.

I became less of a monitor and more of a participant in our study. The children assumed responsibility for bringing in new information, questioning current understandings, posing new questions, and searching for answers. They even took responsibility for initiating expert projects.

As I entered the Center for Inquiry, I had strong beliefs about teaching and learning, yet I was not able to name them. These beliefs had developed throughout my teaching career. As I highlighted earlier in this chapter, I stumbled on to many sound practices that reflected my beliefs, not realizing that these beliefs and practices were indicative of an inquiry stance. However, I solidified my beliefs, and practices that supported those beliefs, by explicitly teaching my kindergarten students to be intentional about their inquiries. This propelled my realization that I, too, needed to be intentional about my own inquiries. Initially, this realization manifested itself in my inquiries into teaching and learning. However, as inquiry began pervading my thought patterns, my habits, and my interactions with my students and colleagues, I began to realize that my approach to inquiry as a philosophical stance also formed the basis of who I had always been as a person. Thus, my journey into approaching inquiry with intention influenced not only who I was as a teacher but also who I was as a person. With this in mind, I realize that I have become a stronger learner, a more effective teacher, and a better person.

References

Avery, C. 1993. *And with a Light Touch: Learning About Reading, Writing, and Teaching with First Graders.* Portsmouth, NH: Heinemann.

Cowley, J. 1992. *Duck and Hen.* Bothell, WA: Wright Group.

———. 1996. *The Little Yellow Chicken*. Bothell, WA: Wright Group.

Fisher, B. 1991. *Joyful Learning: A Whole Language Kindergarten*. Portsmouth, NH: Heinemann.

Fox, M. 1989. *Feathers and Fools*. San Diego, CA: Harcourt Brace.

Weiss, G. D., and B. Thiele. 1967. *What a Wonderful World*. New York: Atheneum Books for Young Readers.

6

Giving Children Voice

Daily Rituals That Support
Learning Through Conversations

TIMOTHY O'KEEFE

(Excerpts from a classroom audiotape dated 5/17/99: whole-group literature discussion in response to "Letter from a Concentration Camp" [Vchida 1990].)

Elise: I think it's sad because the people wouldn't give them so much food and the people were still starving.

Dani: What I wanted to ask was, is POW a homophone?

TO: Dani wants to know what POW means. [Reading from the story] *"My father was taken as a P.O.W."* Does anyone know what that means?

Jack: Prisoner of war.

TO: You know what that's called Dani? When each letter stands for another word? That's an acronym.

Jack: I noticed that in this story and *The Bracelet* that both of their dads got sent to a prisoner of war camp because they worked for Japanese companies. I think that Yoshika (the author) got sent to one during the world war or his mom or dad did.

Courtney: I remember when he said when people are in war they get crazy. I want to know what that means.

TO: What do you think it means?

Courtney: They get all crazy and they almost kill their own persons on their own teams.

Elaina: I think it means like in *Number the Stars* some man went against who he was. They do things that they *know* are stupid.

Hutton: On page 60, near the upper middle, I agree that war makes people crazy like Courtney just said a few minutes ago. I agree that war makes people crazy.

TO: Can you point to any examples of things that make you agree?

Hutton: Like the war in Yugoslavia, a lot of innocent people are getting killed by NATO and NATO is trying to help. It's really just . . . you know.

Sarah: I think that war makes people crazy, too. Like Napoleon was so crazy about war that he started a war by trying to take over the world. He thought he was so great because he had won so many fights and things.

Lora: They treated good people bad like the family. The people, the soldiers, they didn't even think about it. They were being bad to other people. They should say something to the soldiers like, "Think about you being us. Would you want to live this way?"

TO: So they should put themselves in the other's place.

Lora: Like *The Moccasin Game*.

Faith: Was Herman one of his friends from Germany? I was sort of wondering if he was. Because from reading the story it sort of sounded like he was.

TO: It did say that he had a very German name. I think that raises an important question. The Japanese were put in internment camps because we were at war with the Japanese. But we were also at war with the Italians; we were at war with the Germans. The Italians and the Germans did not have to go to the internment camps. In the story, Jimbo asks the question, "Why?"

Joe: Were there lots of German people and Italian people in America?

TO: Sure there were lots of Germans and Italians in America, just like there were lots of Japanese Americans.

Joe: Then how come they didn't go?

TO: That's the question that Jimbo asks. What do you think about that?

Hutton: Because Japan started the war by sinking almost all of our navy so maybe they were more angry at the Japanese Americans. I remember something from somewhere, maybe *The Bracelet* or something like that, maybe they thought the Japanese Americans were being spies for Japan. Maybe they were extra angry because they sunk almost all our navy.

Jonathan: One of the bestest parts in the story was when he says that "just because I look like I come from Japan it doesn't matter." It just doesn't matter. It's sort of sad.

TO: It's sort of sad. He was just as American as everyone else born in America, wasn't he? Good point.

The longer I teach, the more I realize the power of children's voices. In this exchange about the short story "Letter from a Concentration Camp" the second-grade students in my class demonstrated for me the learning and teaching potential of conversations.

When I played this tape for some other teachers this summer while participating in a staff development program, one person said, "I just cannot believe the level of conversation. You were talking about social injustice while we were talking about *Frog and Toad*." I quickly responded that my class loves Arnold Lobel and that *Frog and Toad* stories are wonderful literature. "Still," she responded, "it's hard to believe that these were second graders."

Her assumption that young children are not capable or ready to handle complex, important issues is one that is common, even among thoughtful educators. I continue to be amazed at the understanding demonstrated by young ones over issues of equality, slavery, war, injustice, freedom, and so on. Realizing how articulate and sincere my students can be has forced me to examine my role as their teacher.

Examining the Role of the Teacher

The teacher's role in an inquiry-based classroom is just as important as that of a traditional classroom teacher but, perhaps, a little more delicate. It includes rejoicing in discoveries, prompting and supplying opportunities for genuine conversations, bringing areas of authentic inquiry to the forefront, sharing wonderful literature, encouraging questions, and helping children seek answers to these questions. It is a balance of what is important to children—what *should* be discovered/uncovered—with the given curriculum of the district, which we hope is based on national standards—what *must* be taught. As cited in the Preface, at the Center for Inquiry, we believe that inquiry is a stance we take toward learning, learners, knowledge, and schooling rather than a particular teaching method. I know it is my right and my responsibility to collaborate with my children when making instructional decisions.

I have also come to realize that so much of the teacher's power or influence in the classroom does not come from what we do but rather what we don't do. By *not* stepping in and deciding what's appropriate to talk about, by *not* capitalizing all of the instructional time with our agendas or the agendas of textbook writers, by *not* talking so much, teachers open the door to true inquiry. In an environment of trust and equality children freely and naturally teach and learn from one another, and in so doing, they do far more *uncovering* of curriculum and truth than we could ever hope to *cover* by trying to control all of the learning that takes place during a given year.

Judith Lindfors' look at power and control in inquiry dialogue clarifies some of the issues surrounding the question of who is in charge. Teachers must consider these questions: "Who has the right to influence the shape of the dialogue? Who has the right to pull for another's verbal participation?" (1999, 154). Beyond these guides for how conversations are run, teachers would benefit from asking, "Who selects the stories we will read and discuss? Who defines the routines we will use to encourage conversations? Who decides what must be covered within a given year, and where will the real emphasis will be placed? Who decides which resources will be used?"

Some of these decisions are made for us. The textbooks in the classroom, for instance, are selected by a committee of teachers and administrators with representation from all of the schools in the district from a list of books approved by the South Carolina State Department of Education. So, if we choose to use a textbook on plants, it will pretty much be the same textbook that all of the second graders use throughout the district. *How* the books are used, and indeed, *if* they are used at all is up to us.

Some critical decisions are simply made by me. I have decided, for example, that our daily business meetings will occur in the mornings. The plan for the day is laid out: activities such as going over details about lunch, attendance, and outstanding assignments, sharing news and public journals, and so forth all seem well placed at the beginning of the day.

On the other hand, some important decisions are shared. Students often suggest ideas for shared reading, how to organize the class newspaper, and when the class needs a general peer tutoring session on something in which many children need assistance.

Some decisions are made by default. If we have had a few class discussions about a shared reading, it is simply logical to mix it up and share ideas through a different format in subsequent literature discussions. Lindfors describes this as "sharing the creating of territory" (1999, 170). This is true in the larger structure of discussions—what we discuss, the format of the discussions—as well as within conversations—considering when turn taking is appropriate, when we may overlap others' remarks, when one topic shifts to another. Put simply, a teacher in an inquiry classroom must accept that there is a balance of power among all participants.

Still, the teacher's role in an inquiry-based classroom remains a paradox. Teachers take responsibility for a leadership role in the classroom, creating curriculum and bringing our own experiences and expertise to the group. At the same time, many teachers try to work themselves into the background so as not to privilege their own voices and to ensure that children's voices are heard and valued above all else. It is not as simple as stepping into the background and letting things happen on their own. It is more about helping children learn to take hold of conversations, to initiate them, and to orchestrate them.

My ideas about conversation have evolved over the years that I have been teaching. Early in my career, I found myself leading most discussions. Discussions often followed the pattern of me asking a question, calling on a student whose hand was raised, listening to the response, offering a remark as to the quality of the response or making a qualifying remark or restating the student's response, and then asking another question and calling on another student.

These days I often find myself trying to speak less and listen more. In listening to tapes and reading classroom transcripts it has become clear that when I don't capitalize the talk, the students are more willing to contribute and their ideas and questions often spark ideas in others, which fosters real dialogue for long periods of time. When I open up the floor to the ideas of the group, the children have more of a vested interest in the proceedings. There is ownership and responsibility, respect, and a willingness to risk that simply do not occur in the same way when I call on each participant and react to or evaluate his or her contributions.

Dialogue, according to Peterson and Eeds (1990), "is . . . more than an exchange of information and sharing of ideas, dialogue requires personal investment. It cannot be pursued in a passive state. . . . Dialogue is demanding work, requiring that all involved have initiative and wide-awake imaginations. Tension and anxiety are not foreign to it" (14). This authentic dialogue is what I strive for in my classroom. It is the primary vehicle for meaning to be constructed and shared in my room. It also provides the richest data for me to assess growth and change in my children's thinking.

Real dialogue, like all authentic language, is generative (Harste, Woodward, and Burke 1984). Conversations spark new ideas and connections. Often in the classroom, conversations must come to an end because we run out of time. Often there is disagreement and, occasionally, frustration. There is also laughter and playfulness with language. Conversations beget conversations.

At times, authentic conversation in the classroom is not difficult to achieve. There are subjects that young children naturally find fascinating and easy to talk about. A provocative story, for example, is usually an easy tool for launching into a lengthy dialogue. A news story about a popular singing group or current, media-driven cultural icons, such as Pokémon or Beanie Babies, also serves as a connection for children to make in class, even children who don't usually become involved in discussions. But what about science, current events, geography, mathematics, or language? It's natural to think that achieving grand conversations about these topics would surely be more challenging and difficult to maintain. What about drawing parents into important classroom conversations? Are there ways to invite parents into our fascinations and investigations? Could these conversations be used to uncover and investigate curriculum content that we are expected to have covered by testing time in the spring? Is there a way for large concepts or ideas to take hold and be a framework for conversations for a long period of time?

Much of what follows considers this last question. As issues of peace and freedom dominated much of the national news, I sought to use these ideas to frame much of our curriculum during the spring of 1999. These concepts became the touchstone for many of the invitations and conversations in the classroom and at home.

In the following sections I will answer these questions and explore my role as the classroom teacher in fostering these conversations. In so doing, I wish to make clear that this is not a "how-to" look at classroom conversations. Rather, this chapter is intended to be a *retrospective* view. I would not presume that what occurred in our classroom this year could be duplicated in the same form in other learning environments or even in my own classroom in years to come. While there might be some ideas in this chapter that can be easily adapted for use in other settings, good ideas alone do not make the difference. It is the stance we take as teachers that propels our inquiry and that of our students into new and often unexplored territory.

Trusting the Process

I am the first to admit that everything isn't always smooth in my room. Leaving space for conversation is a little messy at times. There are long periods of silence that used to make me feel uneasy and make me want to rush in with something—anything—of my own to fill the void that I saw as wasted instructional time. There are still students whose voices I do not hear, either because they choose not become a part of our conversations or because I cannot seem to find the right way to invite them in. There are children who hold the floor for far more than their share of time, thus limiting the opportunities others have to speak. In fact, it has helped me to realize that one never becomes a perfect teacher. "There is no getting teaching right. As professionals we are always learning and growing" (Short, Harste, and Burke 1996, 48).

But there are moments of excellence and beauty in the classroom. These times, when the class conversations and routines continue effectively without any intervention or management on my part, are the times I treasure as an educator.

Without exception, each year I learn more and more that effective classroom practice comes from knowing children and listening to their voices, from knowing curriculum and realizing how and when to become an instructional leader and when to be simply a participant in the grand conversations that make up our school year. This balance of talking and listening, leading from the front and leading from behind, teaching and learning alongside the students, explicitly sharing content while promoting an inquiry stance, is the stuff that great teaching is made of.

Leaving Space for Real Talk

I went through Madeline Hunter's PET (Program for Effective Teaching) training—a staff development model used by the South Carolina Department of Education—in the 1980s along with most of my colleagues. Phrases such as "time on task" and "teach to the objective" (a.k.a. "T2O") made sense to those who embraced a transmission model of instruction. "Bird walking," or straying from the subject at hand, was to be avoided in the model lessons from which our evaluations arose.

All of this staff development came at a time when I was noticing remarkable things about my students. Some of the most effective teaching and learning happened when we bird walked.

The most interesting and memorable teaching moments did not emerge from formal lesson plans, but the occasions when the children listened to and asked how a guitar is tuned or when a student's mother came into class in the middle of the morning with the limp body of a red-tailed hawk she had just found killed on the road. Some of the most brilliant mathematical insights developed when students shared problem-solving strategies or when they created their own mathematical stories. Students' breakthroughs as writers often grew out of opportunities to learn from their young colleagues during strategy-sharing lessons or with their spontaneous insights as we ended, almost sadly, a great read-aloud book. My social studies lessons often paled in comparison to discussions we had about current events, politics, recent scientific breakthroughs, countries changing leadership, or even forms of government—all straight from the news of the day.

While I never really believed that the transmission model of instruction made sense in light of what I was seeing in my students' learning, something about "time on task" still made me a little nervous. We say to one another in professional meetings that we need to trust children as learners, but saying those words and living that life are sometimes difficult to reconcile. With pressure from high-stakes tests, curriculum guides, long-term planning maps, textbooks, units to cover, and district-mandated objectives, it is difficult for us to trust ourselves, our students, and the process.

Literature Conversations

Spaces for conversation may take the form of simply leaving time for talk after reading aloud a picture book, a chapter from a chapter book, or some other shared reading. The questions I often ask after closing the book for the day are: "What do you think?" or "Does anyone have anything to say?" The immediate pause is often followed by a trickle and then a flow of ideas as children follow up on one another's comments, make personal connections or connections to other stories, disagree, clarify or seek clarification, recall favorite passages, or note wonderful language used by the author.

As I mentioned, this year, the concepts that were the touchstones for our class during the second semester were peace and freedom. The idea for these came mainly from the news about the conflict in Yugoslavia. This is a country that we knew very little about, and yet it was the major international news focus for the spring of 1999. Because there is a large military base in our school district and many local soldiers and their families were affected, the fighting had particular significance and stories were shared almost daily during our news time.

Not everything in our curriculum was neatly woven into these big ideas. Certainly mathematics went its own direction and, occasionally, we'd stray from this by exploring areas of physical science. While we were busy studying other topics not dealing with peace and freedom there were still opportunities for us to reach back to this touchstone through news articles and current events, which we shared almost daily.

Many stories were introduced for shared reading that centered around the themes of peace and freedom, including "Letter from a Concentration Camp" and "The Tree House." Both of these short stories come from the edited book *The Big Book for Peace* (Durell and Sachs 1990). Some of the power of this conversation is known only to the participants. However, the reader may vicariously engage in the experience by knowing that Joseph had done his expert project only the week before on the Holocaust. This was a topic that he chose entirely on his own. His classmates chose a variety of other topics, from biographies of relatives, to animals, to ships, to countries. Joseph chose the Holocaust.

Other inside information is discussed as well. In our class Language Journal, for instance, there had been many references to typos during the second semester of second grade. This public journal, like our Science Journal and Math Journal, housed a collection of written questions and observations made by the children each morning. The children wrote in these journals and published their thoughts at subsequent class meetings. Every few days some-one in the class would record in the Language Journal a typo found in the newspaper, on package labels, or even in published books. Notice how the children transform the notion of typo in the next conversation.

Even without all of the contextual information, this conversation is a powerful one. It occurred at the end of the second-grade year and I had reached a place in our small-group conversations where I was consciously trying not to interject too many of my own opinions and ideas.

"The Tree House" by Lois Lowry, was a text I chose to share with the children. First we all read the story. Some read quietly, seated alone at the ta-bles. Others read in groups of two or three, supporting one another and dis-cussing the story independently. When everyone had finished reading the story and had recorded some notes to help in the formal discussion, we gath-ered in larger groups of four or five to share ideas.

The story is about two friends who have a conflict over possessions. One child's grandfather builds her a tree house. Her neighbor and friend becomes jealous and asks her father, who is out of work, to build her a tree house of her own. The two girls overcome their difficulties by literally deciding to build a bridge.

In the conversation that follows, I sat with Ali, Elaina, and Joseph and recorded what was said. At first we referred to notes that we had taken while reading, but we soon found ourselves simply having a conversation.

(Excerpts from a classroom tape dated 5/26/99: small-group discussion of "The Tree House.")

Ali: I highlighted *Finally she called across the fence. "Would you like to borrow some of mine?" she asked. And Leah said, "Yes."* Chrissy is finally trying to be nice, I think. At first she started being really mean, then she started to be nice. And just about where they made the bridge I wrote, "I like their idea." Then I highlighted, *"I don't really hate you Leah," Chrissy said. "I don't really hate you either," Leah replied. They sat together on the porch and looked around happily.* "I'm glad they're getting along," is what I wrote.

TO: You know how Ali highlighted the part about the bridge? In my notes I wrote that the bridge is a metaphor. It's almost like they were at war but the bridge—

Elaina: Connected them.

TO: That's a good way to put it. It's like a symbol for them becoming con-nected again.

Elaina: When they were mad, it's like the bridge was a friendship line.

Joseph: I was wondering about where it said, *You reached it by climbing a ladder, a ladder.*

TO: But read the whole sentence.

Joseph: You reached it by climbing a ladder, a ladder to the best tree house ever.

TO: Did anyone else notice that it was kind of odd that the author said *a ladder* twice? Joe said to me earlier that it was probably a typo.

Elaina: It's not a typo. It's just like . . . I'm just using this as an example. I went up a ladder, a ladder. It's just repeating the same word twice. There's nothing really wrong with it.

TO: It's just an effect that the author is trying for?

Joseph: . . . *a ladder, a ladder.* . . . It shouldn't have it twice.

Elaina: It's like you're stuttering on a word or something.

Joseph: . . . *a ladder, a ladder.* . .

TO: Here's another example: I had some money, some money for some ice cream. It's just an effect.

Ali: It's like, his name was Sam, Sam the seahorse.

Elaina: It's not a typo; it's not wrong. . . .

Joseph: . . . *a ladder, a ladder.* . .

Elaina: It's an effecto! Instead of a grammero or a typo, it's an effecto.

Joseph: I wrote that Chrissy is going to be best friends with Leah again. And I got it right.

TO: Good prediction.

Elaina: I noticed that there's an alliteration at the beginning because it says *marvelous, magnificent.* Afterwards I thought it was a very deep thought: *two shiny, brass hinges and a small brass bell that rang when you pulled the string.*

TO: That's a nice description of the tree house. Even if you didn't have a picture you could imagine it.

Elaina: And it said, *It's all mine isn't it?* on page 31 at the very top. I thought it was just kind of bratty, I'm going to say. Then it says *Just mine and nobody else's?* That's selfish!

TO: The way you read . . . that was just the way I heard it in my head.

Ali: I think why she wrote *Keep Out* and stuff, I think it's sort of . . . Her grandfather started this because he's the one who said . . . If he would have said that everybody else could play in it, too, she probably would have let everybody else in.

Joseph: Her grandpa said that it was just for her.

Elaina: It's like her grandpa influenced her to say that.

Joseph: It's like Saddam. No, like Hitler. He made the people think that the Jews were bad.

Elaina: He made them believe that the Jews were their trouble.

Joseph: And the guy made Chrissy think that Leah was bad.

TO: I see exactly what you're saying. The way I looked at it was . . . She asked him if he made it for her and he said, "Yeah, I made it for you." I don't think it was saying, "you can't have other people here."

Ali: She didn't understand, probably.

TO: I think she understood it the way she wanted to understand it.

Ali: She's probably thinking, "Well it's mine. I can do whatever I want with it."

Elaina: She didn't understand the way *he* was telling *her* . . . I underlined *I hate you, Chrissy. I hate you.* I wrote that they were kind of acting . . . In my way, I'd say "cuckoo."

TO: I thought they were getting a little carried away, too. Chrissy was mean to say, *"No you can't come in. This is my tree house."* Leah got immediately carried away. Instead of just getting her feelings hurt, she just started hurting Chrissy.

Elaina: [Quoting from the story] She stood silently for a moment. Then she said, "I hate you, Chrissy." Then Chrissy goes, "I hate you too."

Joseph: If she whispered it, how could Chrissy hear her? They were, like, in a yard.

Ali: I think that Leah got a little bit carried away. Maybe she shouldn't have said, "I hate you," She might have said, "That's mean. Maybe you shouldn't be so mean," or something like that.

Joseph: Chrissy said, "I hate you too."

Elaina: Joe, it's not really her fault. She started it.

TO: Joe, what you said about whispering, I think she said it in a soft voice but, apparently, she said it in a loud enough voice so the other kid could hear.

Joseph: She was up in the tree house. And she was on the ground. That doesn't count how high the tree was.

TO: Maybe it wasn't actually a whisper. Maybe *whisper* wasn't the right choice for a word there.

Elaina: I highlighted *He was making Leah a tree house. Chrissy laughed to herself. She knew they didn't have extra money now for things like paint and brass hinges.* And I also did *never in a million years.* I thought just because she has paint and brass hinges, it doesn't mean that it's better than somebody else's.

Joseph: Leah's was better than hers.

Elaina: It just means she's got more than the other. Wow.

Joseph: Leah had all those pictures on her wall and she had—

Elaina: curtains, fruit—

Joseph: —wastebasket.

Ali: Chrissy didn't really have that stuff. She said, "I don't really have curtains or a rug."

TO: They both lied a little bit, didn't they?

Ali: Just to brag. They wanted to be better than the other one.

Elaina: I wrote that doesn't mean anything. Then I highlighted *Do you have any books I can borrow?* Then she starts to be a little kinder.

TO: That was the turning point in the story.

Elaina: Yep! Then they turned around like they were going back to being friends the way they were before. Then I wrote that they started telling the truth to one another instead of keep lying and lying and lying. Lora was my partner. When it said that the board would go from one house to the other over the fence and they could visit one another by walking across the board, I went, "Hooo, very scary!"

Ali: I don't know how a fence could be that low, you know, to get to the porch.

Joseph: It would probably be the tree house porch. But they would have to be the same height.

TO: There were two things that I thought were great metaphors. One was the fence. It's something that divides people, right? Like this is your property, this is my property. And then the board, or the bridge, is what connects people.

Elaina: I thought it was kind of cute when Leah says, *"It's not very high,"* Leah pointed out. *"If we each came out half way and held hands we could help one another across."*

The discussion continued for quite a while. As a participant of this literature study group, I was able to get to know these children better both as readers and as the wonderful individuals they are. I got to understand how they react to what they read as well as their sense of what is right and wrong in how people interact, their sense of fairness and justice. What is essential in this kind of discussion is that everyone feels as though he or she has important contributions to make. In this lengthy dialogue, all of us taught and learned from one another. Everyone demonstrated how our previous experiences are essential to our current understandings of text. Everyone's voice was heard and respected. Our focus was on interpreting, not simply comprehending, the text.

Sometimes the most valuable tool we have as evaluators and curriculum writers is also a valuable gift we can give to children: time and silence to be filled with rich language and wonderful ideas. By creating this empty space, by ritualizing it and valuing it, we impart importance to it. Children soon rise to the occasion, realizing their responsibility to fill it with *something*, not necessarily something important or novel, but something that says who they are and how they understand.

For me, there is the added benefit of discussing literature with friends. It may be selfish, but I enjoy hearing others' points of view. I become a more careful reader. I realize that my point of view isn't necessarily the right one. I am able to contribute and at the same time learn. In this discussion I was able to point out symbolism and metaphor in the context of our conversation. But it was Elaina who brought up alliteration. Joseph, with his literal interpretation, made us look closely at word choice. Ali helped us understand what motivated the characters. Perhaps more important than the skills, strategies, and literary devices we uncovered, this discussion helped us to value good literature and hunger for more, to value other's opinions, and to see worth in one another's insights.

Responding to Literature
Through Written Conversations

Another way to encourage dialogue is through written conversations. This conversation on paper encourages participants to share ideas while developing fluency with writing. Written conversations demonstrate the real purpose of writing while encouraging children to teach and learn written language conventions from one another. They help children become flexible and thoughtful writers (Short, Harste, and Burke 1996).

In a written conversation, partners have a discussion on a single sheet of paper using a single pencil. This is a useful tool for getting children to know one another as well as an avenue for thought-provoking, generative analysis of shared experiences. It is one way to stimulate literature study. I invite children to respond to literature several times each year in my class in response to a shared reading experience. Written conversations may follow a read-aloud story or a story that children have read on their own or with friends.

The children are almost always anxious to participate, as a written conversation is a quiet yet intimate way to connect with an individual classmate. During the first few written conversations at the beginning of the year, I do not put any restrictions on what the children write, as long as they write about the story. As a result, many of the exact same questions are asked over and over, including "Did you like the story?," "What was your favorite part?," and

"Who was your favorite character?" Later, as we used the written conversations as a tool to begin whole-class discussions, it became obvious to us all that the convergent questions, the ones that only required a "yes" or "no" answer or an answer of only a few words, did not serve us well. Gradually, as the children's questions grew more sophisticated, their written responses became more personal and more important. I found that the children were putting more of themselves, more of their personalities into their questions and answers.

During our focus study on peace and freedom, the chapter book I read aloud was *Number the Stars* by Lois Lowry (1989). Most days, after closing the book from the day's installment, we simply talked about the story. The children were totally engrossed in the book. The bravery of the Danish resistance during World War II and the friendship of Anne Marie Johansen and Ellen Rosen helped clarify our focus study, fueled conversations about history, and initiated personal inquiry studies among the students.

In response to Chapter 15, "My Dogs Smell Meat!", I asked my students to pair up for written conversations about the story. We had just read a wonderful section in the book in which Anne Marie had outsmarted German soldiers while on her way to deliver a secret package to her uncle who was smuggling Jews out of Denmark to the freedom of Sweden.

In a written conversation between Jack and Sarah (see Figure 6–1, p. 92), the students were still using some of the questions we identified earlier in the year as not being too challenging or likely to reveal much about the other's interpretation ("What's your favorite part?" and "Who's your favorite character?"). The tag question, "Why?" was discovered early on as a way to ask some of the same questions but in a way that requires longer, more thoughtful responses. Both young writers clarified their answers because of the extra *"why?"* Jack when he commented on the author's cleverness and Sarah when she wrote about Anne Marie's strength as a character. The style of writing is naturally informal in both language and writing conventions (*I dunno* and *Duh,* for example); however, these two still made some critical points and challenged one another to do more than simply recall details from the story. Jack was a little evasive, but Sarah pursued him and restated her question with her own ideas as an example in an effort to get a quality response from him on her rather vague question about his feelings.

In ViLora Lee and Ali's written conversation, there were many opportunities for the children to answer very briefly, but each of them carefully explained her points to the other (see Figure 6–2, p. 93).

When ViLora asked if the book made Ali scared, and when Ali asked if ViLora thought there would be any more surprises in the story, each girl had the opportunity to answer with a simple "yes" or "no," yet both children

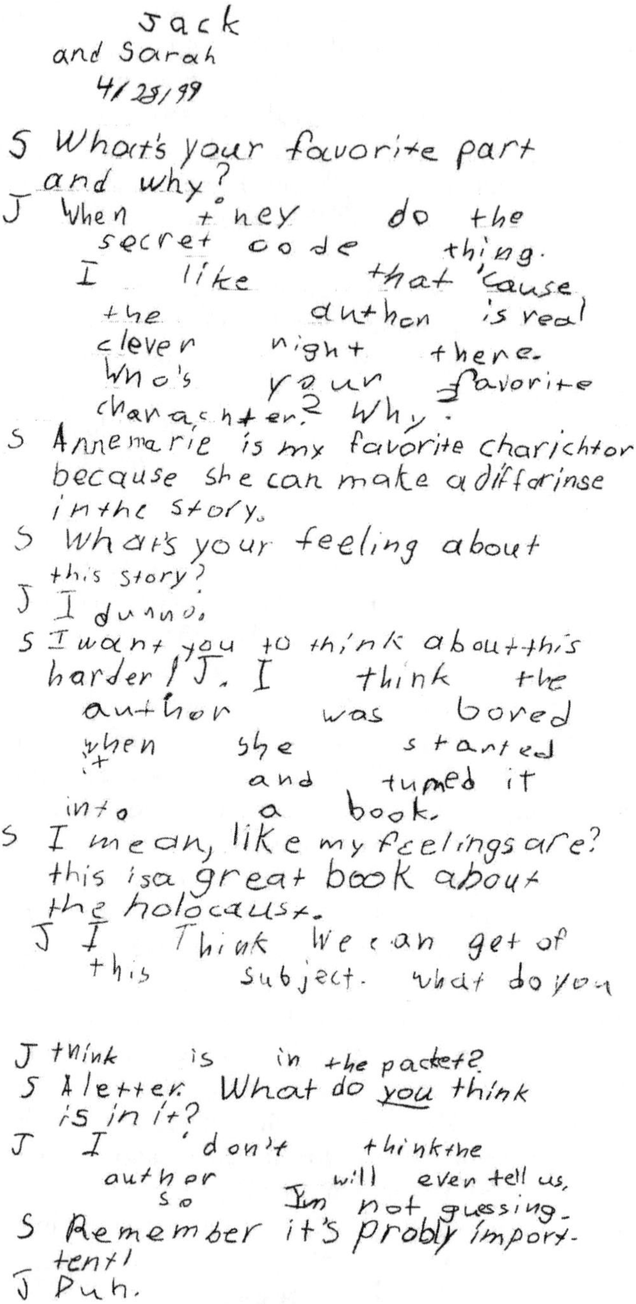

Jack
and Sarah
4/28/99

S What's your favorite part
and why?
J When they do the
secret code thing.
I like that 'cause
the author is real
clever right there.
Who's your favorite
charachter? Why.
S Annemarie is my favorite charichtor
because she can make a diffarinse
in the story.
S What's your feeling about
this story?
J I dunno.
S I want you to think about this
harder! J. I think the
author was bored
when she started
it and turned it
into a book.
S I mean, like my feelings are?
this is a great book about
the holocaust.
J I think we can get of
this subject. what do you

J think is in the packet?
S A letter. What do you think
is in it?
J I don't think the
author will even tell us,
so I'm not guessing.
S Remember it's probly import-
tent!
J Puh.

Figure 6–1. *Jack and Sarah's Written Conversation.*

ViLora Lee Ali   4/28/99

A.c. What do you think the hankerchif
Was for Maby it was like
v.L.L a caver that hase something
like a code in side. Dose
r this book make you scared?
A.C. yes, the Author made you
Scared and curiose
Wern't you suspis os when
they tricked you about
the cofon? v.L.L not relly we hade
an idea it was for the pepol
to excape. What do you think
is going to hapen next?
A.C. I think the boat will Sail
away and it will be the
end. Do you think the
will be any more surprises
in the story. v.L.L Of corse I think
that there will some thing
hapen to the bote but
An mary will save it.
Do you think that we
shud read more of thes
Aoters books? A.C. Of course
I do. Do you? v.L.L yes
Do you think this book
is as good as Dr. Dolitel?
A.C. I think its better and
more exiting.
                    Bye
                    Bye

Figure 6–2. *ViLora Lee and Ali's Written Conversation.*

Taylor Hutton 4-28

T.N. Do you think their's a lesson
to the story. Why or Why not?
H.CCThat c wation sumpt
me! Do you think ther
is Something ales about
that hakk rchif, if you
do what are you thenking?
TN. Maybe there is Something inprinted
on the back. Why do you think
Amerys mother acted So serius
about the hanterchif she
Whasit setyus. I dout
rheber her being sheds.

Figure 6–3. *Taylor and Hutton's Written Conversation.*

made thoughtful responses going well beyond mere completion of the written conversation task. Each was clearly interested in sharing thoughts and seeking ideas from the other. Their predictions and analysis of the story show me so much about them as readers who approach text with enthusiasm. It is exciting, yet not surprising to me, that both of these readers were interested in exploring more of Lowry's work.

Hutton and Taylor revealed a shared understanding and sophisticated interpretation of the text through their written conversation (see Figure 6–3). Taylor demonstrated that he was interested in morals or lessons to stories through his first question, and Hutton clearly yet thoughtfully questioned the assumption that underpinned his last question. Both young colleagues were pushing one another as learners through this focused talk on paper.

By reading over sets of written conversations, I get to know each child more clearly as a reader and as a writer. Not only do I get a good idea about their use of writing mechanics through their writing, but these artifacts also serve as windows into their understanding. Through these conversations on paper, children reveal so much about how they read and interpret texts.

Of course we do more than just respond to stories through written conversations. The children write literature responses, draw pictures to represent ideas, and read and discuss in pairs, small groups, and large groups. Written conversation is just one way to get children to express themselves openly and to learn from the interpretations of others.

Promoting Conversations Among Parents

One way that I foster conversations among parents is through our weekly newsletters (Mills and O'Keefe 1999). These generally have several sections that include what we are focusing on in the classroom curriculum, important whole-school information, dates and details for such things as field studies, and an open-ended project or activity for the children to do at home. This has become known as the Newsletter Project. These educational invitations are often connected to what we are studying. If measurement is a focus in mathematics, for example, the project might be for the children to measure ten things at home and to create a chart or graph to display their findings. When the students have just finished presenting expert projects in the following newsletter, I usually ask the parents and children to watch the videotapes of the presentations and fill out evaluation forms.

It is customary for me to include in each newsletter an invitation for parents to respond to the activity and to describe for me how they think their child did on it. I give the parents the option of writing three pluses (or positive observations) and a wish for something the child might need to work on or focus more on in the future (Mills 1990). Many parents use the three pluses and a wish format; others simply write their thoughts in a narrative or list form.

As with classroom invitations, there are some newsletters that invoke lots of energy and enthusiasm. There are also those that don't seem terribly engaging. I think that the time that parents spend working with their children is almost always well spent.

Many invitations for the projects come from suggestions made by the students. If something has gone particularly well in class, someone might suggest that we do the same with parents. Parents might also suggest projects to include in the newsletters. The story "Letter from a Concentration Camp" was such a powerful springboard for our class book talk that I thought it might do the same at home. Here, I include an entire newsletter as an example. The invitation I have referenced is in the second paragraph.

Dear Parents,

The expert projects are coming along very nicely. We have left a lot of time in school for the children to work on these and I am pleased with the children's accomplishments. Mahogany asked this morning about whether or not her parents could help her edit her paper. You remember that we said that these projects will reflect the children's work as much as possible. Mahogany's request, followed by the way with similar questions from other children, leads me to conclude that we should allow parents to edit their children's work, to the same degree as parents help during writing workshop. So, please feel free to edit for writing mechanics (spelling, capitalization, punctuation, etc.) but please let the words belong to the children. I think this will go a long way in giving the children the confidence to do more on their own in third grade. Thanks for your patience and understanding about this.

We read a really nice story this morning called "Letter from a Concentration Camp." The story is about a child and his Japanese American family who were relocated to an internment camp during WWII. The story is told through a letter written from a young child to his friend. Since we have been thinking about war and peace and history this piece fit in perfectly with what we have been considering. Since the expert projects are due on Friday, the only other homework this week will be for you to please read the story with your child and have a written conversation about it. You may take turns reading, read it in chorus together, read it silently, etc. Then please write some comments about your child as a reader. Please also have a written conversation about the story. These can be very far-reaching and so feel free to discuss other things that this story reminds you of. There will be no reading log, math handouts, or any other written homework so that you will have time to really read, listen, think, and write about this story. This will be our last newsletter project of the year so let's make it one of our best!

Tim

So many children used this as an opportunity to transcend the actual reading and writing task. They shared insights, feelings, and values. Lessons were taught about history and connections were made to other great pieces of literature as well as to family histories.

The actual written conversations are priceless documents of growth in the progress of these children as learners. The questions and answers are records of much more. These are snapshots of children and their parents as thinkers, believers, teachers, dreamers, seekers of understanding and justice. Their ways of communicating go beyond what can happen between the classroom teacher and the students. In short, these are conversations that *need* to occur at home. There are lessons here that go beyond the standards in reading and language arts.

Melissa and her mother *assumed* comprehension at the point when they put pencil to paper (see Figure 6–4, p. 97). Each assumed that the other had

Tuseday, may 17, 1999

Melissa

Letter from a concentration camp

I can't belive they have to sleep on army cots, and live in horse stalls. Isn't it bad?

I agree with you. The Japanese Americans were treated more like animals than people. Why do you think the government did that to Jimbo and his family?

Maybe becas they look like japanese. and their father work for japanese. do you think they new this was going to happen?

No, I think they were really surprised because they thought of themselves as regular Americans I think Jimbo was right — war makes people go crazy! Do you think Jimbo felt like an American or a Japanese boy?

American. he speaks american he eats amercan he lives with amican he is in a american country

he is amecan
what do you think

I think you have a good point! It is much more important to look at how a person acts and feels than how a person looks on the outside. That really doesn't tell us a lot about who a person really is!
            I now you are rite

Figure 6–4. *Melissa's Written Conversation with Her Mother.*

a perspective that was interesting and that they could demonstrate and learn one another's perspective through writing. Writing mechanics and reading comprehension were used for the purpose of learning about the ideas of another. In this case the person each was learning about was one of the most important people in her life.

Melissa expressed her outrage in her very first comment and didn't really even need the tag question "Isn't it bad?" Likewise, her third comment was followed by a question: "What do you think?" She may have been seeking reassurance for her feelings, but she was sincerely asking for a valued opinion. To prove how strongly she felt about Jimbo's status, Melissa used her own kind of italics for emphasis in her third response, *"He is an American."*

Amy wrote clearly and explicitly about her daughter's reading habits. This was important information to me as Melissa's teacher. It is the kind of information that adds tremendously to my knowledge of children as language users. Her first plus was equally important to me. It showed me that Melissa's mom was noticing one of the same things I noticed about Melissa as a reader—her passion (see Figure 6–5, p. 99).

There were many other responses to this activity that demonstrated the power and potential of parents' voices in the curriculum. Among them were the written conversation between Christine and her mother, Van. Christine's parents came to America from Southeast Asia. Van's response to me about this project speaks clearly of the feelings and information they shared about the story (see Figure 6–6, p. 99).

Christine obviously had a sense about the injustice of putting Japanese Americans into internment camps, but her mother took this opportunity to give some important context to the story. When she wrote to me that she had explained about the constitution and prejudice to Christine, it was another important reminder to me that parents are truly their children's greatest teachers. The significance of their written conversation speaks for itself (see Figure 6–7, p. 100).

Parents were teaching content as well as sharing their values and ideas. When Joe first asked his daughter Dani if Jimbo was born in America, she responded, "No. California." He wrote to me that she tickled him with that response, which he helped clear up. He also added, "Dani always makes me proud of her compassion for others."

Ali's mom wrote to me of Ali's "expression and great feelings about what she reads." She also wrote about the emotions they both felt about the story and concluded with, "How lucky we all are for the great lives we have . . ." If the newsletter project led these two— and others—to be grateful for the lives we have, then it served us well.

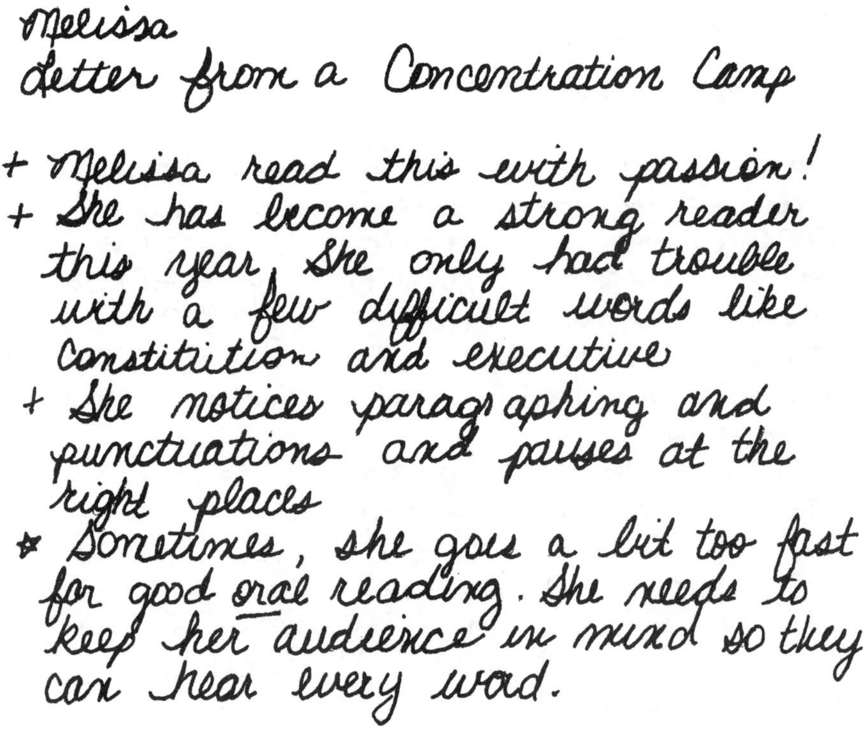

Melissa
Letter from a Concentration Camp

+ Melissa read this with passion!
+ She has become a strong reader
this year. She only had trouble
with a few difficult words like
Constitution and executive
+ She notices paragraphing and
punctuations and pauses at the
right places
* Sometimes, she goes a bit too fast
for good oral reading. She needs to
keep her audience in mind so they
can hear every word.

Figure 6–5. *Amy's Three Pluses and a Wish for Her Daughter Melissa.*

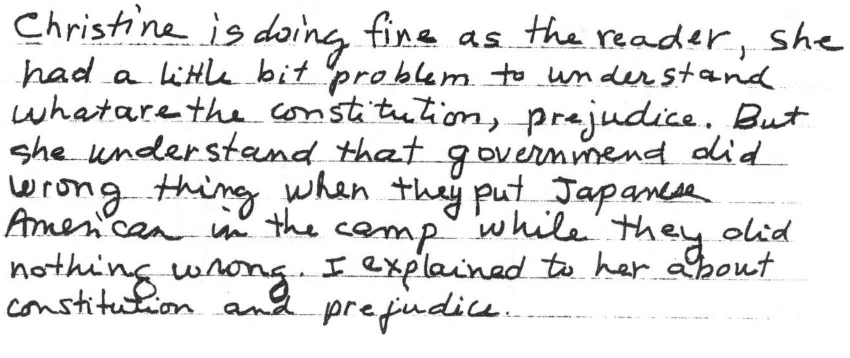

Christine is doing fine as the reader, she
had a little bit problem to understand
whatare the constitution, prejudice. But
she understand that governmend did
wrong thing when they put Japanese
American in the camp while they did
nothing wrong. I explained to her about
constitution and prejudice.

Figure 6–6. *Van's Comments About Her Daughter Christine.*

christine
Van Tran

_Do you know why these Japanese American were put into the concentration camps?
Because Japan were at war with americans
_Why did his father have to go to POW camp?
Because his father worked for a Japanese company.
_Is it right for the goverment to put the Japanese American into prison?
NO because they didn't do anything wrong.
_Why did the government go by their looks?
Because government is prejudice, because Japanese Americans have different look from them (the government) so that why Japanese Americans were sent to concentration camp and German Americans or Italian Americans were not sent to concentration camp because they are white.
_When the president Roosevelt put Japanese American into the concentration camp, did he do it against the constitution?
Yes because the constitution say they have to have a trial before they go to prison.

Figure 6–7. *Christine's Written Conversation with Her Mother.*

Promoting Academic Conversations

As I mentioned earlier, many of the most exciting conversations emerged simply because I made a concerted effort to slow my teaching down enough to make space for children to talk. I have already detailed structured literature study through small- and large-group discussion, written conversations with peers and parents, and invitations for parents to describe their children as learners. There are other daily rituals or curricular structures in our class that promote real talk.

Public Journals are large notebooks kept in the classroom in which children write comments, questions, observations, and insights on various subjects. After the children or I write in the Math, Science, or Language Journals, we tabbed the pages with sticky notes. At the next morning business meeting the contributors read their entries aloud to the class and elicit responses.

Among Science Journal entries were "I noticed that the frog's eyes are on the top of his head," . . . "I wonder why leaves on plants are different colors," . . . "Did you know that the China wall is so long you can see it from the moon?" . . . "Why does the gerbil play at night and sleep at day?" . . . "It seems like when the temperature around you is warm and then you get cold you get goose bump. . . ."

Here are some entries from the Math Journal: "I wonder if the numbers never stop," . . . "How fast does the earth go around the sun?" . . . "My theory EVEN + EVEN = EVEN, ODD + ODD = EVEN, EVEN + ODD = ODD," . . . "7 + 7 + 7 = 21 so ODD + ODD + ODD = EVEN," . . . "On the Titanic there were 2,227 people and there was only enough lifeboats for 1,100 people. So 2,227 − 1,100 = 1,127 people must have died."

In the Language Journal the children wrote: "Why are white things really white but white people aren't?". . . "aa is lava and it is in the beginning of the dictionary,". . . "The menu thing in the cafeteria said ,and. You're not supposed to write it like that,". . . "In the dictionary snazz is not a word but we still use it."

Through Public Journals children have a chance to teach and learn from one another. The conversations that often follow each published entry are wonderful.

Dialogue Journals are small notebooks in which the children and I simply record short, written conversations. These are ongoing through the school year. The children and I correspond about twice each week and the subjects range from vacation plans to family life to questions and comments about literature.

The News and Current Events are shared almost daily. The children and I share articles from the newspaper, children's magazines, nature magazines, or notes we have written about things we have heard on the radio or seen on TV. We use the globe and wall maps constantly to find the locations mentioned in the stories. Along with the news reports are often comments about the stories from the reporters as well as the rest of the class.

Sharing personal news is a more open sharing that is done during many morning meetings. This includes news about family birthdays, a best friend who has moved, a pet who has died, a father who got a new job, an aunt who had a baby, and so on. The children simply write their names on the board under "Other items of morning business."

True Conversations

In order for authentic conversations to take place, a set of understandings that allows members of the group to speak freely must be in place. Everyone should know that his or her ideas are worthy of consideration, even if someone disagrees with them. There must be trust not to take differences of opinion personally. Everyone should realize that, while he or she can opt out of conversations, it is an important responsibility to participate. There is an established expectation that we all share in the classroom talk so that we can teach and learn from one another. There is an understanding that everyone is capable of understanding complicated and serious issues. It is a given that questions are important and each child realizes that he or she helps make each day a learning experience with his or her queries and contributions.

Our classroom practices reflect our beliefs as teachers (Short and Burke 1996). As our beliefs change and we come to know more about how children learn, our practices parallel these changes. In years to come, my classroom will look different in many ways, just as it is very different now than it was when I first began teaching twenty years ago. So it must be. Listening to children closely requires changes in our practice. However, the classroom sounds—active children, singing, debates, discussions, laughs, sighs, questions, demands, squeals of delight, exclamations—the sounds of intrigue, surprise, and wonder should remain essentially the same. No two school years are ever alike, but the sounds of inquiry should remain constant. These are the sounds of true conversations.

References

Durrel, A., and M. Sachs, eds. 1990. *The Big Book for Peace*. New York: Dutton Children's Books.

Harste, J., V. Woodward, and C. Burke. 1984. *Language Stories and Literacy Lessons*. Portsmouth, NH: Heinemann.

Lindfors, J. 1999. *Children's Inquiry*. New York: Teachers College Press.

Lowry, L. 1990. "The Tree House." In *The Big Book for Peace,* edited by A. Durell and M. Sachs, 30–38. New York: Dutton Children's Books.

———. 1989. *Number the Stars*. New York: Dell.

Mills, H. 1990. "Teachers and Children: Partners in Learning." In *Portraits of Whole Language Classrooms,* edited by H. Mills and J. A. Clyde. Portsmouth, NH: Heinemann.

Mills, H., and T. O'Keefe. 1999. "What Really Matters in Literacy Instruction." *The New Advocate* 12:1, 39–54.

Peterson, R., and M. Eeds. 1990. *Grand Conversations: Literature Groups in Action*. New York: Scholastic.

Short, K., and C. Burke. 1996. "Examining Our Beliefs and Practices Through Inquiry." *Language Arts* 73: 97–104.

Short, K., J. Harste, and C. Burke. 1996. *Creating Classrooms for Authors and Inquirers*. Portsmouth, NH: Heinemann.

Vchida, Y. 1990. "Letter from a Concentration Camp." In *The Big Book for Peace,* edited by A. Durell and M. Sachs, 57–61. New York: Dutton Children's Books.

7

Becoming Reading Researchers

JULIE RILEY WAUGH

"What do you notice?" I asked everyone after we took a few moments to compare the data we had gathered.

"I notice that on challenging books, we went down," Caitlin Funk chimed in quickly, "and on moderately hard books we went up, and on easy books, we went down."

"Maybe the books were supposed to be hard for us," Caitlin Watts explained, "but we're just getting to be better readers. That's maybe why we have less challenging books."

"That's a neat thought," I added. "I like how you're immediately jumping to looking at your data and trying to interpret your data, or say, why did that happen? We've been trying so hard to read challenging books, why on earth did it happen that we went down?"

Inviting Fourth Graders to Become Researchers

We were reflecting on data that we had gathered about how many books we had read as independent readers, and this was only the beginning! I knew that asking students to reflect on their own learning and work helps them develop a heightened awareness of and sense of responsibility for their own learning. I hoped asking students to research their own reading would urge them and allow me to push them to challenging new places as readers. I had no idea, however, how becoming reading researchers would change students' individual and class reading practices. I was headed for a delightful surprise.

Research Needs Purpose

My invitation grew, literally, from a large pile of reading logs. Reading logs are what students use to record their nightly independent reading and share something about what they read. I ask students to complete one every week, and I collect them each Monday.

As I was pulling together resources from files to create narrative progress reports, I looked at the pile of reading logs and gave a sigh; I realized how much valuable information about my students as readers sat in that pile. I also realized that there was no way I would have the time to look through all of them carefully, together, to learn more about my students' growth as readers or about our whole class as a group of readers. I am grateful that I turned to my students for help. Inviting my students into the process allowed me to know them as readers through the concrete evidence provided through their reading logs.

Inviting my students into the process also allowed them to carefully reflect on themselves as readers. I've learned through teaching at the Center that reflection is an important part of the way we serve as mentors for our students. Along with demonstration, engagement, and celebration, reflection is a crucial tool for inquiry. Learning is propelled through reflexivity. When learners intentionally and systematically study themselves, they outgrow themselves as learners (Short, Harste, and Burke 1996).

The math that students would use to do their research would be no less significant. I was not asking students to solve certain kinds of problems, I was asking them to "reason and communicate mathematically," which The National Council of Teachers of Math (NCTM) recognizes as some of its major student goals (NCTM 1989). By inviting these students to become researchers, I gave them the opportunity to use math as a important tool, instead of learning math as an end goal unto itself. As Whitin, Mills, and O'Keefe express in their book *Living and Learning Mathematics,* "True mathematical literacy must originate not from a methodology but from a theory of learning—one that views learning not as a series of enjoyable activities or problem solving techniques but as a way of knowing and learning about the world" (1990, 166). Math helped us know more about ourselves as readers.

The natural, meaningful integration of our engagements, merging our worlds as mathematicians, readers, and researchers is yet another compelling purpose for this investigation. Teachers often leave math behind when they integrate curriculum, maintaining a traditional stance in which "math is assumed to be a fixed body of knowledge and learners absorb what is covered" (Schoenfeld 1993) long after they abandon such stances about other disciplines. If teachers share naturally integrated mathematical experiences, more teachers will search for such integrated ties. In turn, the shared potential may help math find its rightful place in the integrated curriculum. We try to make interdisciplinary ties like this explicit at the Center, not only to one another as teachers but to parents and students as well.

The Process of Becoming Researchers

Students use their reading logs to record what they read, the number of pages they read, and one thing they want to share about their reading each day. On December 9, 1998, I handed ten weeks' worth of reading logs back to the students and asked them to put them in chronological order. I also gave them Reflecting on Your Reading, a structured form with spaces to include numbers. I asked students to categorize the books they read as either easy, moderately hard, or challenging and to record the number of each. Then I asked them to categorize the books they read by genre—picture books, historical fiction, mysteries, fiction chapter books, nonfiction, poetry, biography, or series fiction. I included places to add genres, because I suspected some of their reading would not fall into any of the others. The Reflecting on Your Reading form also asked reflective questions after students calculated their numbers, like "What was your favorite book?"; "What was your most challenging book?"; "Which books would you recommend to your classmates?"; and "What did you learn about yourself as a reader from looking at all of your reading logs?"

The next step we took was to figure out how many books we read as a class. I created a form titled Reflecting on Our Class Reading to give them a place to do this. I asked students to collect the numbers from each category (level or genre) for their table. Then, we collected numbers from each table as a whole group and asked one person to add together each category for the entire class. After they did this, every student recorded our total numbers on his or her sheet.

Reflecting on Our Class Reading asked students "How many books did we read as an entire class?"; "What fraction of these books were easy?"; and "What fraction of these books were challenging?" For homework, I asked students to show the genre "information in a way other than with numbers. Be creative. Bring your representation to class tomorrow to share your findings."

We repeated the entire process on March 2, 1999, about ten reading logs later than our first research session. The process was virtually the same, with an important difference: now, we each had two Reflecting on Our Readings and two Reflecting on Our Class Readings forms to compare. In addition to our initial procedure, we looked at the numbers of books and genres side by side as a class, and I asked students to compare both of their Reflecting on Your Readings forms with the help of a Comparing Your Reading Reflections form.

Sharing Data in New Ways

In our first round in December, I shared overheads of some of the students' representations of our class data to help the class think about what we learned from this process. It was this discussion that caused students to articulate the math skills and strategies they used, and it was math that allowed us to look at our reading in new ways.

Rachael used a key and symbols to represent the class data (see Figure 7–1, p. 108). When talking about her graph, Rachael added, "I used my table's information in my graph, too, because I didn't want to waste it." Little did Rachael know that, along with illustrating her personal investment to our research process, she had added our first comment about using mathematical information as researchers and making decisions about what information is important. The door she opened would not be closed, and students intertwined observations as mathematicians and researchers throughout our reflections together.

Richard and Kevin chose to represent our class data using bar graphs (see Figure 7–2A, p. 109, and 7–2B, p. 110). Each plotted the different genres on the x-axis of his graph, and the numbers of each genre on the y-axis. Both showed our data in similar ways, but the size of each graph and scale of the numbers were different, causing the graphs to look different.

It was Zac's representation using base ten blocks (see Figure 7–3, p. 111) that caused us to look even closer at Kevin's bar graph. That Zac had chosen such an interesting and familiar way to represent our data was fun. We had used base ten blocks as a class just weeks before to explore division, and that, along with their visual appeal, may have been the reason that the students started to really notice the values in Zac's representation.

"I notice that Kevin had five for poetry, and Zac had six," one student offered. As we went back to Kevin's bar graph, we looked more closely at the divisions he used for his y-axis, and spoke about how to read the values in his bar graph. Sure enough, we realized, Kevin's graph showed six as well. His bar was just above the first line, and each line represented five books. Students were beginning to see that "how a set of data is graphed both conceals and reveals information" (Whitin and Whitin 1998). Having multiple representations of our class data encouraged us to compare our data in new ways.

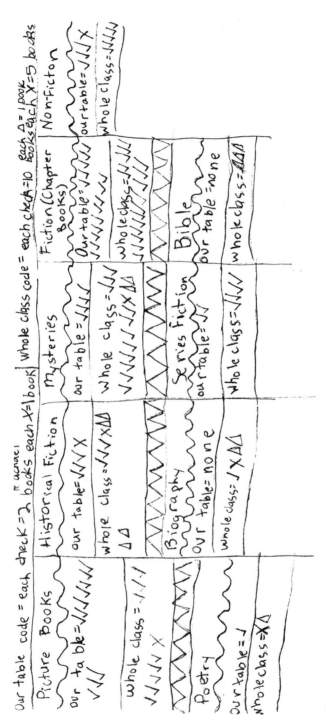

Figure 7–1. Rachael's Bar Graph Representation of Class Reading.

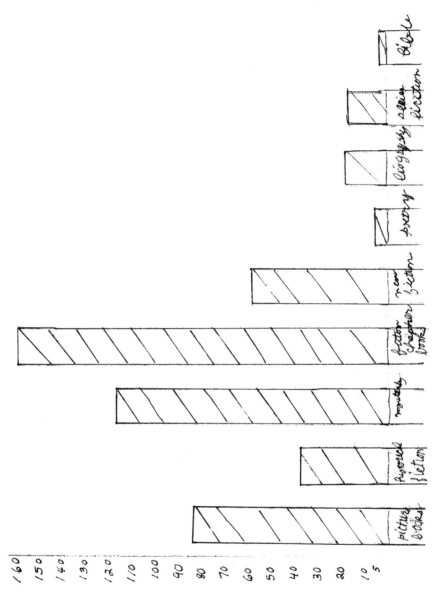

Figure 7–2A. *Kevin's Bar Graph.*

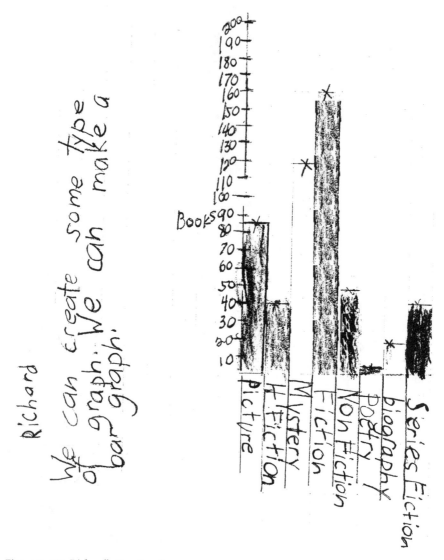

Figure 7–2B. *Richard's Bar Graph.*

Zac's base ten blocks also took us down another road when Kevin said, "I notice that in Zac's, that the top part [referring to the easy, moderately hard, and challenging categories] and the genre part are not the same." By Zac representing the difficulty categories as well as the genres, and by Kevin noticing the number difference and knowing that both groups were representing the same books and should be the same, they helped us realize just how messy data gathering can be and how important looking carefully at numbers in data

Figure 7–3. *Zac's Base Ten Graph.*

is. Zac and Kevin had catapulted us to one of the most important places of all—the "why" associated with the numbers we found.

Gathering the number of books each student read was no small task. Many students quickly started their research by categorizing each line, or entry, instead of each book as easy, moderately hard, or challenging. Some of these students would not realize their mistake until long after we had collected all of our class numbers and tried the Reflecting on Our Reading forms a second time, over ten weeks later. In our conversation about comparing our two rounds of class numbers, I offered, "I might even argue that the first numbers are higher than the actual number of books we read, because during the first round, more people were counting entries instead of books."

"Next time we'll probably do it even better, because we will have already done it two times," Caitlin Watts added positively.

Rachael said that in our first round she had put one of the Dear America series books she was reading in two genres, historical fiction and fiction. Others nodded their heads, and we realized that there was a reason that we had a larger total in our class genres than we did in our difficulty categories because we had often double-dipped into genres. We had accounted for many books more than once.

"I know I messed up," Caitlin Watts added. "I put Dear America books in fiction and historical fiction. I know that's one reason that we got a little bit of a higher number. I saw Megan using little signs on the reading logs," Caitlin continued. "She knew she wasn't counting that book twice, or something like that."

"In connection to writing your books down in two places," Katie continued, "Ms. Riley gave me the idea of writing all of my books down on a sheet of paper, and after I got done writing it, I would check it off, so that I wouldn't count it twice. I think Caitlin Funk did something like that this time." Our first attempt at gathering our reading data had shown us to be careful about collecting not only the numbers of books that we read but also about not counting the books more than once. Looking at graphical representations of our class data had helped us hone our research and data-gathering skills. We would not forget them as we went into our second round of Reflecting on Our Reading.

The Need for New Mathematical Skills

Before Kevin told us about his first bar graph, he said, "I wanted to do a pie graph, but it was too hard—all of those angles and stuff." This need to know, combined with the fact that, as a class, we explored fractions, decimals, percents, and geometry between our first and second Reflecting on Our Reading projects was a powerful incentive for me to do a mini-lesson on circle graphs. My teacher-researcher instinct had kicked in. The decision I made to do a mini-lesson came from listening to Kevin and acting on my instincts about what he needed, not from the next page in the math textbook.

It was intentionally right before I asked the students to represent the data from our second round of Reflecting on Our Class Reading. I put two pictures on the board (see Figure 7–4, p. 113).

"What do you notice about these circle graphs?" I asked.

Thomas started our conversation off. "We know 25 percent would be one-fourth. Remember when we studied fractions? You cut one-fourth, and

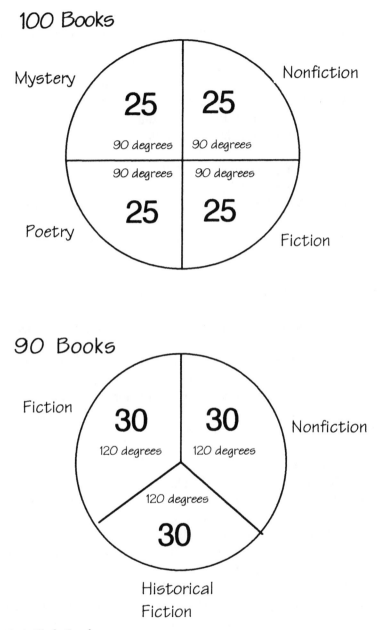

Figure 7–4. *Circle Graphs.*

four 25s equal 100 because every time we did 25 percent there has to be one-fourth. It's like cutting a circle in half, and turning it in another direction and cutting it in half again. That's why there is a group of 100 books, because four 25s equal 100. Because you add three other 25s."

"You could also think of it as money," Will offered. He also wanted to talk about the 90 books circle graph. "You know a Mercedes? You could think of . . . This is a little different than the one-hundred books graph."

"What makes this one different than the one-hundred books graph?" I asked.

"Well, it doesn't have four sides," Will answered, "even though 30 [percent] is more than 25 percent."

We briefly talked about the difference between the numbers that made up the graphs.

"About the one where you split it into fourths, what we just did with the information, most likely your answer wouldn't be 100. And so sometimes it might be harder to split into different parts," Megan pushed.

"It's an added challenge, if you choose to make a pie graph," I said with a smile.

"What do you notice about the angles in this graph?" I asked the class.

"On that one, it's right angles," Caitlin Watts said, pointing to the graph on the left. "On that one, it's bigger, obtuse angles." Caitlin led us to discuss the difference between the two kinds of angles, and how she thought I had chosen the degree values for each. I was interested in asking students to look closely at the degree values in the angles.

"How many degrees are in the inside angles of a circle?" I asked.

"360," Robert said proudly.

"How did you know that?" I asked him.

"Because a 360-degree roll [in an airplane] is all the way around," he answered, with a smile.

I pointed out to them that four right angles make a circle, that $90 \times 4 = 360$. "That's how I used the relationship," I closed with. "It's all relationships. I challenge you to do a circle graph."

I had hoped my mini-lesson would help students connect concepts they already knew to a circle graph, so that they would feel like they knew enough to try using one to represent our class reading data. It was important to me that I not show them step by step how to construct one, because the construction was their challenge. Unfortunately, no one tried one. Perhaps I gave a little bit too much information, so that students felt shy about just jumping in to try. What was important was the authentic opportunity to introduce circle graphs when there was a need to know how to make them.

A Second Round of Data

Will and DeNeal's data representations went on the overhead projector together. "Since they're both bar graphs, they're kind of the same," Katie noticed. "I like the key that Will used."

"Will used a key instead of color. A solid equals ten books, and an empty square equals one. You can't just look at the bars, which I think is kind of neat," I added.

Will explained his process. "When I did this, I was gonna make the empty ones five because some had to go really low, so when I looked at the other ones, some are, like, six. The one on the right, it has six, so I would have to make it one."

"So when you tried to use five, you couldn't represent all of them?" I questioned.

"So nothing goes below one, so I put one," he answered.

Rachael provided us with a new way of looking at our second round of class data, through her chart of percentages. It engendered rich conversation about data.

Bruce started us off. "I notice that what you did was percentages for each one. When I first just glanced at it, I notice you included 100 percent. That was the total number. I also like how you did percentages and you must have had to do some division for that because you had to decide, like, how many, like, the tenths and stuff."

Caitlin Funk continued. "I noticed that you put the number in front of the percentage of what, of how many books that there was because people may have gotten confused about 'How many books was this?' and 'How many books was that?'"

Rachael's chart also pushed us to think as researchers.

Katie shared, "I have something that maybe we can do if we do this again, . . . we could take all of the things that we did after they were done, like their graphs or whatever they did, we could put it to their old ones and we could make connections or comments about how different [they are] or what's similar about them."

"Neat," I said, smiling, and attempted to clarify, "So looking at Rachael's old way that she represented it, and her new way, we probably would learn a lot about what she learned about math."

"One thing I wish we would have done," Bruce continued with an idea, "is the first time I wish somebody would have done one like this and we would have been able to compare them in percentages. So we could really look at some of the other ones. That would have been neat." Katie and Bruce had internalized the strength in comparing data over time by mulling it over on their own. I realized the value of allowing them the time, investment, and trust to do this.

The Power of Comparison

Students started their comparisons on a personal level. After they completed the second round of Reflecting on Your Reading forms, I asked the students to look at them side by side with Comparing Your Reading Reflections.

The conversation that happened when I put copies of our Reflecting on Our Class Reading next to one another engendered amazing connections between math and interpreting ourselves as readers.

Caitlin Funk and Caitlin Watts, who began our conversation, were not the only ones eager to talk about what they noticed when they compared our data side by side. Amanda had observed something, too.

"On mysteries, the second time we went down, but the first time we were up because a lot of kids were reading the Woodland Mysteries. This time, we haven't been reading much of them. Last time we had 117. This time we have only ten." (See Figure 7–5, p. 117.)

"We've read all of the Woodland Mysteries," Sarah explained.

Caitlin Watts had another theory. "I think the last time was a longer period," she said. Her thoughtful skepticism pushed our conversation to the next level.

"You know that's neat," I replied. "I am so glad you brought that up because it's so important when we're comparing. It's like in fractions, you're not going to compare quarters and halves, right? But indeed Caitlin, I think we are pretty close on time. I think both of these were about ten weeks in time. But you're right. There may have been a little more time on the first round. Thanks for bringing that up."

"On the first one I calculated that we read more books," Philip continued. "I think that the reason why is because we are reading a lot more chapter books and chapter books are usually a lot longer than picture books."

"Again Philip," I added, "I like how you immediately jumped to the 'why.' It's good to think about, because when you are just looking at the numbers, do they necessarily mean that we're reading less or we're not reading as hard? It doesn't necessarily mean that."

"In connection to what Philip said," Katie offered, "how he was talking about since we're reading more chapter books, well, most of the books I was reading was chapter books for whole weeks. That's maybe a reason why numbers went up and down."

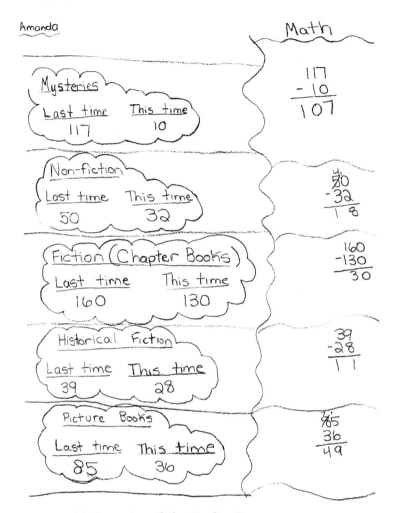

Figure 7–5. *Amanda's Comparison of Class Reading Data.*

"I also agree that it could be because we are reading more harder, challenging books. That's the reason we're not reading as many books as last time," Shelby commented.

"That's something I want us to think about as we look at these numbers," I said. "We don't want to get discouraged because I think there's something to that."

In one short, concentrated class discussion, our reflective analysis with comparing number data had allowed Caitlin, Amanda, Philip, and Shelby to deal with variables and reciprocity in highly contextualized, meaningful ways.

The students jumped very quickly past the numbers they saw in front of them. Because they had gathered the data, they were able to successfully analyze data in a way not possible had they not been integrally involved in the process of gathering it.

I noticed that there was a "continuity" between what I was doing as a teacher-researcher and what these students did in "approaching" research "for the first time" (Bruner 1960). They *became* researchers, and we were exploring, without a doubt, within a culture of inquiry.

Setting Goals

We culminated each research round with each student making at least three personal reading goals and all of us together making class reading goals. We posted all of these goals for everyone to see. These goals were important because they represented the "So what?" part of our research. The goals we set helped us put what we learned from using math in our research to good use.

On December 9, we came up with the following class goals:

- Read more nonfiction, biography, and poetry
- Read more challenging books
- When you go to the library, try to get one reading book that you truly read
- Read more each day

Many of the student's personal goals were similar to our class goals. These goals were monumentally important in our student-led conferences, for they drove students' presentation of reading growth with numerical data to support their claims and helped them articulate what they wanted to accomplish as readers. They were equally important for me as I completed narrative report cards. I had numerical data to show students' growth as readers, and the data also allowed me to have goals for students, so often similar to their own goals for themselves as readers.

These goals informed curricular decisions for me. Sarah noticed it and mentioned in one of our conversations, "I noticed that we have been reading more poetry books, and I think that maybe it's because of our goal. Ms. Ducworth [our MAT intern] has been introducing us to writing poetry, like haikus, and cinquains, and Ms. Riley has introduced us to some new poetry books."

When reflecting on how we thought we did with our first round of goals, Amanda said, "I think we've done better than the first one. I think we worked really hard on [reading] biography and poetry."

I added, "Especially that goal of different genres. I know that Ms. Duc-worth and I have made some different choices about the different books we share with you because of those goals, so that's been really good for us, too."

Our experience as reading researchers informed my choices of books to make visible on the book rack, which are always inviting and enticing to students. Our research results and goals were in the forefront of my mind when I ordered books in the spring for our next year together as a group. Keeping track of the books students read over the summer became part of the mandatory summer work, which will allow us to reflect on ourselves as readers at the very beginning of next year.

When we completed our second round, we reassessed our goals. We kept:

- Read more challenging books
- When you go to the library, try to get one reading book that you truly read
- Read for more time each day

Zac had proposed that we challenge ourselves to more than just non-fiction, poetry, and biographies, and change "Read more nonfiction, biography, and poetry" to:

- Read more widely across genres

Bruce had the process idea that we should "keep lists of books that we read individually and as a group. And that would also help when we do the Reflecting on Our Readings because then we'll know how many. We could put our initials by the book when we write them down. That would help in two ways."

So we added:

- Keep track of the books we read as a class

Sarah had earlier introduced us to the idea of a class book journal, in which people could recommend good books they read. She offered, "If you see someone poking their nose in a book, you could ask them to try it, or try to find it at the library." So we made our final goal:

- Use our book journal more

Shortly after we made this goal, one student noticed that she would get to the library and forget the books that her peers had recommended in our book journal. She suggested that we take our book journal with us on trips to the library, and she was eager and willing to take responsibility for that job. Our goals had expanded!

Some Final Reflections

Through conversation and examination of student products, students used numerous mathematical skills, strategies, and concepts in reflecting on themselves as readers.

- Students sorted and categorized data, representing it so that it was numerically accurate.
- Students created graphic representations of group data, choosing appropriate and varied ways to create informational text from the data.
- Students recognized numerical miscues in their data and adapted their data-gathering strategies to avoid further miscues.
- Students added and subtracted numbers in context to find totals and differences.
- Students found fractional values for different difficulty levels and genres within the entire group.
- Students created bar graphs to represent data and interpreted bar graphs, including successfully reading axes.
- Students used different symbolic ways to represent numerical values.
- Students connected percentage values to unit numbers.
- Students used manipulatives, such as base ten blocks, in new contexts to represent numerical data.
- Students found a need to know more about making circle graphs, and took part in a mini-lesson about circle graphs.
- Students compared and analyzed numerical data, incorporating and considering sophisticated variables and the concept of reciprocity.
- Reflective analysis allowed the classroom community to look carefully at the processes and practices of using numbers as researchers.

In using all of these mathematical skills, the classroom community grew as a community of readers.

- Students used numerical data and its various representations to set individual and group reading goals that were grounded in prior practice.
- Individual and group reading goals encouraged students to read more challenging texts.

- Students used numerical data to articulate their reading growth with concrete evidence to back up their statements.
- Numerical data became integral in assessment, as a part of student-led conferences and teacher narrative progress reports.
- Individual and group reading goals helped the teachers make curricular decisions about classroom texts.
- Individual and group reading goals reminded students to read more widely across genres.
- Students became more aware of one another's reading as well as their own. They shared books in a book journal and found books for others, often keeping personal goals in mind.

Going Further

The skills students had to use as they became researchers for our Reflecting on Our Reading engagement assures me that it was worth our while. I had no idea how far this engagement would push my students as mathematicians and researchers. The analytical reasoning students used to compare our reading habits over time has convinced me that Reflecting on Our Reading should be a periodic touchstone for our lives as readers and researchers.

Knowing that this engagement will continue brings forth questions for me:

- How do I encourage students to try making circle graphs to represent data without forcing them to make them and showing them how, step by step?
- In what other areas can our newly honed research skills help us grow?
- How can more rounds of Reflecting on Your Reading help students show their reading growth for the entire year?
- Are there organizational structures that I can use to facilitate Reflecting on Our Reading every nine weeks next year?

I suspect that my students will be important in helping me find the answers to these questions.

References

Bruner, J. 1960. *The Process of Education.* Cambridge, MA: Harvard University Press.

National Council of Teachers of Mathematics (NCTM). 1989. *Curriculum and Evaluation Standards for School Mathematics.* Reston, VA: NCTM.

Schoenfeld, A. 1993. "When Good Teaching Leads to Bad Results: The Disasters of 'Well-Taught' Mathematics Courses." *Educational Psychologist* 23 (2): 145–166.

Short, K., J. Harste, and C. Burke. 1996. *Creating Classrooms for Authors and Inquirers.* Portsmouth, NH: Heinemann.

Whitin, D., H. Mills, and T. O'Keefe. 1990. *Living and Learning Mathematics.* Portsmouth, NH: Heinemann.

Whitin, D., and P. Whitin. 1998. "Learning Is Born Doubting: Cultivating a Skeptical Stance." *Language Arts* 76 (2): 123–129.

8

Refining and Expanding
Our Notions of Inquiry, Talk,
and Classroom Community

RICK DUVALL

As we were preparing to open the Center for Inquiry in the summer of 1996, I spent considerable time studying state and district curricular guides, trying to connect the curricular mandates to my own personal interests and areas of expertise. I also spent countless hours wondering what my future students' interests and areas of expertise might be. Given the fact that inquiry is a philosophical stance and not a teaching method or a set of activities, it was paramount that my students and I "wander and wonder" (Merriam 1991; Short 1993) into the curricular mandates. We would need to approach the mandated curriculum through first recognizing, and ultimately capitalizing upon, our interests, observations, insights, and questions. While I viewed the curricular mandates as important, my philosophical stance was that their importance was truly magnified when our interests actively guided us into addressing the mandates, rather than allowing the mandates to passively guide our questions.

As the teacher of the incoming fourth graders, I also felt a special obligation to the Center, in that my students and I would be the first group to complete a two-year looping cycle at the Center before the students would move on to middle school. Consequently, while I wasn't entirely certain of what our first focused unit of study would be, I knew that I wanted to ground our study conceptually in the notion of community through independence and interdependence. The fourth-grade students would be leaving behind their former classmates and their nine different schools to come to the Center. While they would all have prior educational histories, most of them would not have had common prior experiences with school and with one another. Subsequently, they would lack a sense of community.

After studying the curricular mandates, I thought we might begin our first focused study with a social studies slant, investigating the early explorations of North America. After all, I had spent quite a bit of time earlier in the summer on an extensive backpacking trip, and perhaps I would be able to make some personal connections between the early explorers and my recent experiences as the students and I were getting to know one another. I also thought we might start with a more scientific slant and study rocks and minerals, another mandated unit of study. I had attended a weeklong rock climbing institute at Yosemite National Park during the summer and had collected numerous rock specimens that I found fascinating. Either of these topics could easily be a vehicle for building upon the conceptual framework of independence and interdependence. However, I wasn't sure that my enthusiasm for these topics would transfer over to the students, whom I had yet to meet.

As I met the students and tried to elicit from them the topics that they were interested in exploring, most of them initially lacked enthusiasm for any topic. They seemed apprehensive about even posing possible topics to study. It was as if they didn't trust that I would actually value what they said, or they felt that I had an answer that I wanted them to say and I was merely trying to prompt them to say the "right" topic. Dennis, one of my students, even commented, "Mr. DuVall, if you don't know what you're supposed to teach us, just look in one of those teachers books. It'll tell you." I realized that before we could really inquire into any topic, I would need to attempt to cultivate their curiosity and get them wondering about their world again.

Cultivating Curiosity

We spent a little time discussing how to observe something closely. I demonstrated how I could use sensory data to record my observations by looking carefully and listening attentively, and perhaps even touching lightly, smelling deeply, and tasting slowly. We went on observation walks to as many different types of environments as I could find near our school—wooded areas, empty fields, the edge of a large pond, paved parking lots, and a construction site. Each time we went to one of these places, we took careful observational field notes of what we observed.

After several of these walks, I guided the children to look over all the notes they had taken and then to mark those observations that they found particularly intriguing. I then explained that they might turn some of those observations into wonderings. I asked for a volunteer to share an observation that was intriguing. Lauren stated, "I noticed that one bush, well, half of it was beautiful and real green but the other half looked dead. It was weird! I don't know how it could be like that." I agreed that it sounded very intriguing and suggested that she might explicitly state her wondering as something like, "How can half of a plant appear to be very healthy while the other half appears dead?" The students and I then tried to turn our observations into "why" and "how" questions. I distributed tagboard sentence strips on which the students could write their wonderings. We then turned our bulletin board into our Wonder Why Wall so that students could publicly display their wonderings.

The students began to pose more wonderings over the next several days, and we spent time each day trying to locate texts and other information about one another's wonderings. We discussed in small groups and as a whole class what we were finding. The students seemed to be noticing things around them more intently. They also seemed to be becoming more comfortable with ambiguity when they couldn't quickly locate answers to their wonderings.

A Community Emerges

I was pleased with the sense of community that was becoming evident in our class. The students were becoming more independent in that they were beginning to assume more responsibility for their learning and were relying upon me a little less to tell them exactly what to do and when to do it. Simultaneously, they were becoming a little more interdependent, as they were taking great pride in finding information that would help answer some of their classmates' wonderings and not just their own. However, no common topic for study was emerging. I still had the curricular mandates in the back of my mind. I was wondering how I was going to teach what was expected if I kept waiting for a common thread to be spun from the children's wonderings. I also began to doubt my own kid-watching ability because I was sure that, amidst all of the wonderful things that were happening in our room, a common theme had to be emerging. I believed that I just wasn't able to see it.

I decided to confront this issue explicitly with the children. At our Friendship Circle (our class meeting) the next morning, I shared with the students the science and social studies units that were mandated by the school district. I asked them if they saw a unifying theme between the questions we were asking and the topics we were expected to explore. The children were as baffled as I was. Patrick said, "It seems like it would make sense to just go ahead and study the things we really care about first." I agreed with him that maybe we could all independently inquire into a topic that was personally meaningful. The students excitedly agreed. I realized that I could seize this opportunity for the students to acquire some of the inquiring habits of the heart and mind that would serve them well in later studies.

For the next few weeks, the students explored topics that they had chosen. They posed their own wonderings from multiple knowledge domains and utilized various resources in attempting to find answers to their wonderings. This culminated in each of us presenting an expert project to the class.

I next made the decision to focus everyone on the early exploration of North America. After spending about a week and a half immersed in books, music, and art prints dealing with the era and addressing each of the mandated curricular objectives, each student again chose a topic that had personally intrigued her or him from all that we had discovered during our time of immersion. The students then posed wonderings and began trying to answer their questions about their focused early exploration topics.

While the students remained unbelievably focused and seemed to be extremely engaged in the process, I still felt that it was a bit contrived and unnatural. I desperately wanted the students to use their new habits of the mind and heart, namely their heightened curiosity and their honed observational skills, to venture off into inquiring about something that was truly heartfelt, something that genuinely mattered. I wanted the students to explore something that would propel us both as learners and as people, something that would strengthen our unity and our sense of community. I still couldn't fathom, however, what that something might be.

The Students Find Their Voices

I had been making issues of social justice and equity explicit to the students in almost everything that we had read during the first couple of months of school. Regarding books and articles that we read during our focused studies, I was constantly asking questions such as "Whose voice is represented there? Whose voice isn't represented? What might be the perspective of the missing voice? Why do you think that voice isn't there?" I asked the students similar questions about works of fiction that we studied in our literature study groups. However, our discussion almost always centered around others—people outside of our immediate classroom community. Occasionally, I would try to make connections between these discussions and members of our own class during tense moments of disagreement. I never included myself as the object of these discussions, though.

In establishing routines and procedures at the beginning of the school year in our classroom community, I had agreed with Glover (1997) that "an important part of establishing routines and developing a strong sense of community at the beginning of the year involves learning to know the people around us. When we do this, we come to appreciate what they can teach us about ourselves and the world" (32). Consequently, I had attempted to provide my students numerous opportunities each day to engage in dialogue with one another and with me. I knew that children use language to make sense of new experiences by finding ways to relate them to prior knowledge and, subsequently, they put these experiences into words in order to see new patterns emerge in them. I also knew that having the opportunity to talk with peers and teachers influenced the quality of the students' thinking because from a Vygotskian perspective, thinking is an internal dialogue, an internalization of the dialogues we have had with others (Vygotsky 1978). I consciously had reflected a great deal upon the reciprocal relationship between talk and the creation of a learning community—that a learning community is created through talk, and, subsequently, the type of talk that emerges in a learning community greatly affects the rigor of that community.

However, I had never really contemplated how much I controlled the discourse in the classroom, nor how much my control contributed to an enormous sense of inequity in the class. Furthermore, I had viewed talk as a tool of inquiry. I had never given much thought to inquiring into talk itself or into how we better can utilize talk as learners.

On a late October morning, after about two months of being together, Stephanie announced at Friendship Circle, "This weekend I visited some of my relatives and I noticed that we all talked at the table but nobody raised their hands. It made me think of us in our room. I think we need to figure out ways to talk without having to raise our hands."

I asked the students to respond to Stephanie's ideas. Allison said, "Well, I agree. Nobody in my family raises their hands when they want to speak to all of us."

Patrick then zeroed in on the root of the problem, "Yeah, Mr. D., you probably control the talk in here a little too much. You say you want us to control ourselves and you don't want to control us. But you decide who can talk when we have discussions."

Most of the other children meekly looked at the floor. They probably felt as uncomfortable as I did. A few others nodded their heads in agreement with Patrick. I realized that, while I wanted the children to use talk as a tool for learning, I was able to be honest and admit that I essentially controlled the talk when we discussed issues as a whole group. I discovered that most of the children in our class didn't view our whole-class discussions as learning, but rather as performances of what they had already learned.

I explained that I guessed I was afraid that if I didn't exert some type of control over the discussions, they might quickly get out of hand. While all the rest of the students now looked down at the floor, Patrick looked me straight in the eyes and, with a genuine expression of anguish, asked, "Don't you trust us?"

Feeling quite vulnerable, I hesitantly swallowed my pride and answered that, indeed, I did trust them. Before anyone could then remind me that actions reflect beliefs—we had spent considerable time discussing how you can tell someone's true character and beliefs by observing his or her actions far more than by listening to his or her words, I hoped to rectify the situation by quickly asking, "So, what do you think I should do?"

Shannon reminded us of what we had discovered true inquirers do— they immerse themselves in the topic being studied before they rush to ask lots of questions and certainly before they attempt to present answers, which was exactly what I was asking the students to do in my moment of panic. She said, "Well, you don't need to do anything. I mean, we need to get more information about the problem first. Maybe we could watch our families and try to notice what they do, like, how they talk and stuff."

Excited that at least one of the students realized, in spite of me, that we could apply our inquiring habits to trying to solve this dilemma, I suggested to the students that we gather data on our families during the next week. We decided that we would discuss our findings the following Monday. Ashley asked, "Does it have to be our family? I mean, like, could I watch people talking at the mall and places like that?"

Megan added, "And at church?"

I said that I thought those were great suggestions. I invited the students to gather as much data as they could find from any setting where people were naturally conversing. All week the students informally shared the data they were collecting with one another and with me.

The following Monday, the students said they needed a couple more days to gather more information before trying to reach any conclusions. Finally, on Wednesday, we shared the data we had collected. Matthew said, "You know, sometimes it's hard to listen and sometimes it's easy."

Brandon nodded and added, "And sometimes it's hard to talk and sometimes it's easy."

The other students agreed. Most of them had gathered some data dealing with differences in speaking and listening patterns in different contexts. I asked the students to look through their data to see if they could identify patterns that emerged. After a few minutes, most of the students had sorted their data into these categories. I suggested that we then explore Matthew's and Brandon's notions of what made speaking and listening difficult and easy. We quickly classified our data and developed two charts (see Figures 8–1 and 8–2, pp. 129 and 130).

SPEAKING IS . . .

Easy When . . .	Difficult When . . .
• you have a lot to talk about	• you have a set amount of time to fill
• the listener does not interrupt	• you get too excited
• the listener looks at you	• the listener doesn't seem to be listening
• you care about what you are saying	• you're tired
• you have time to get your thoughts together before you speak	• you're shy
• you don't have to speak for a long time	• you're in a new setting with new people
• you are comfortable with the topic	• you have lots to say but not enough time to say it
• you are comfortable with the audience	• topics are new to you
• you get to choose the topic	• you don't have much think time first
	• you're not sure if the listener really understands you

Figure 8–1. *When Speaking Is Easy/Difficult Chart.*

I then asked the students to independently reflect on these charts and record their personal generalizations about speaking and listening, especially in the classroom setting. David reflected upon what we had explicitly discussed numerous times, namely listeners giving their eyes, ears, and hearts to speakers.

LISTENING SKILLS

Give your eyes to the speaker which means to make direct eye contact and if they have something to show to the class then look at that also. Give your ears to the speaker which means to listen to the person and try to understand what they're saying. Give your heart to the speaker which means to really get into what the speaker is talking about and to face the person.

LISTENING IS . . .

Easy When . . .	Difficult When . . .
• you don't feel like talking	• you want to ask the speaker questions but can't
• the speaker is interesting	• the speaker does not appear comfortable
• the topic appeals to you	• what the speaker says makes you mad
• the speaker is expressive	• the speaker mumbles
• the speaker involves you	• the speaker is very funny
• the speaker uses good gestures	• the speaker talks very softly
• you care about the speaker	• the speaker seems to rush
• you agree with the speaker	• there is a lot of noise
• you know something about the speaker's topic	• you're tired
• you know your turn to speak is coming soon	• you're hot
• you are comfortable and can sit still	• the topic is new to you

Figure 8–2. *When Listening Is Easy/Difficult Chart.*

SPEAKING SKILLS

Effective speaking skills include talking loud so everybody can hear you. Talk in complete sentences so the class can understand what you're saying. Not to turn your back away from everybody.

As the students began to share their reflections, our conversation turned into a critique. Several students observed that certain characteristics of listening could be attributed to making it easy or hard to speak and listen, depending upon the situation. We then decided to try to list the qualities that would make a person an effective listener. We had discussed this concept during the first days of the school year. However, after students gathered and interpreted their data, this discussion became one in which they demonstrated much more of a personal investment and more deeply held convictions.

These charts became a central point for discussion for several weeks, as we continued to revise them in light of new data someone would bring to class. On the morning that we returned from Thanksgiving vacation, the students discussed how their families had spoken and listened to one another during Thanksgiving dinner. They all had been careful observers and were quite adept with their ethnographic field notes. Matthew noted, "It was so weird because everyone could be talking at the same time but then, it was like everyone just knew to stop for a second and let someone else talk. It was like, uh, they would just wait for silence and then someone else would speak."

Bryan shared, "Me, too! Nobody raised their hands, but they really didn't interrupt one another, either. They just kind of waited for a moment of silence."

Patrick added, "Yeah, same with me! It was like they'd just speak into the silence."

Several of the students giggled until Shannon added, "I think that's what a true community does. They wait until someone's finished talking and then they just speak into the silence."

The phrase "speaking into the silence" became somewhat of a touchstone for our classroom community. I'm not sure whether or not Patrick previously had heard this phrase that is usually attributed to the Quaker culture, but as we were reflecting on our data, it came to his mind and perfectly captured what we had discovered worked best. This phrase, along with our other findings from our inquiry into natural conversations, helped create a transformation in the ways in which we interacted with one another, moving the students away from raising their hands and waiting for me to decide who would share her or his ideas toward a more natural, relaxed manner of engaging in dialogue with one another. During impassioned class discussions, especially ones that dealt with issues of social justice and equity, several students often would attempt to speak at the same time. Inevitably, someone would say, "I'll wait until I can speak into the silence!"

Transforming Communication Patterns Throughout the Center

The simplicity and natural authenticity of the practice caused speaking into the silence to become the focal point of conversations at home between my students and their siblings from other classes at the Center. Meanwhile, the teachers at the Center were engaging in routine coaching sessions after school to discuss observations and insights from one another's classes. Speaking into the silence was highlighted to the faculty one day after my colleague, Michele Shamlin, had visited our fourth-grade class. While she was in the room, we were having a rather impassioned discussion about civil rights and the Trail of Tears. Several students were zealously sharing their thoughts about the travesties inflicted upon the Cherokee people. Overwhelmed by their emotional responses to the social injustices, many students often simultaneously spoke, resulting in a somewhat chaotic fervor in which the need to speak outweighed the responsibility of listening to others. I encouraged the students to listen to one another's comments by saying, "Friends, let's remember to speak into the silence." This reminder reestablished a more respectful, but no less visceral, conversation.

At the coaching meeting that afternoon, Michele shared her observations of our classroom and asked me to explain speaking into the silence. I shared the evolution of this practice and answered questions from my colleagues. As the teachers began excitedly discussing the possibilities of personalizing and implementing the practice in their classrooms, our discussion also quickly escalated into our own chaotic fervor, where our need to speak outweighed our responsibility to listen to one another. I smiled at the similarities between the intensity, intelligence, and investment of the adult conversation and that of my students. I then followed the lead that I had learned from students and suggested to my colleagues, "Friends, let's remember to speak into the silence," which seemed to explicitly illuminate the potential of this practice, as our discussion became once again focused and productive. I made a mental note to return to my students and share with them what had happened at the coaching session, validating that we were no less intense, intelligent, or invested in our Trail of Tears discussion than the teachers had been during curricular conversations. As the teachers carried their interpretations of our coaching session back to their classrooms, the phrase "speak into the silence" soon suffused the other classrooms at the Center and became a hallmark for their discussions, as well.

Our new style of dialoguing with one another allowed talk to flourish in our classroom community. Subsequently, this talk helped strengthen and expand our sense of community. As this talk united us as a community, it not only served to help us understand and appreciate one another better, but it also allowed deeper, more meaningful inquiries into numerous topics and issues that arose during the next year and a half in our classroom. Consequently, through our inquiry into conversation, my students and I realized that speaking into the silence was not just a technique to manage classroom discussions but a practice that could be effectively implemented in any group discussion.

References

Glover, M. K. 1997. *Making School by Hand: Developing a Meaning-Centered Curriculum from Everyday Life.* Urbana, IL: National Council of Teachers of English.

Merriam, E. 1991. *The Wise Woman and Her Secret.* New York: Simon and Schuster.

Short, K. G. 1993. "Curriculum for the Twenty-First Century: A Redefinition." Speech given at the annual meeting of the National Council of Teachers of English, Pittsburgh, PA.

Vygotsky, L. S. 1978. *Mind in Society: The Development of Higher Psychological Processes* edited and translated by M. Cole, V. John-Stenier, S. Scribner, and E. Souberman. Cambridge, MA: Harvard University Press.

9

Inquiry into Family Partnerships

DORI GILBERT, JENNIFER BARNES,
SUSANNE PENDER, AND HEIDI MILLS

So much of what we do at the Center for Inquiry grows out of and into our work with our colleagues. Parent communication strategies at the Center reflect our individual as well as collective wisdom. In this chapter, three teachers and the university curriculum specialist share stories and strategies that they have developed to invite parents into genuine partnerships. It has become increasingly clear and important that we work with parents as responsively as we work with their children. Therefore, the strategies that follow reflect what we are currently doing. We know that someone will develop something new in response to a parent's question, concern, or connection. And so it goes.

Each section in this chapter is written by an individual and, as such, portrays specific ways in which our stance regarding family partnerships gets operationalized. While they each focus on one moment in time in each classroom, they also illuminate the inquiry stance that is universal across classrooms over time at the Center for Inquiry. And it is the stance we take that makes a difference. Notice the multiple ways that children's stories and insights are woven into the communication strategies; notice the ways in which the teachers create engagements in response to parents' queries; notice the ways that parents are both informed and serve as informants throughout the curriculum. Notice.

Writing to and with Families: Insights from Dori Gilbert

As a kindergarten and first-grade teacher at the Center for Inquiry, I have made a commitment to invite parents into my classroom and introduce them to the philosophy of the school through my weekly newsletters. I have done so because I want parents to feel intimately involved in the daily life of our classroom; I want them to vicariously experience the ways in which their children live and learn together; I want them to understand why we make the choices we do, what we value, and how to make connections between home and school. I want them to appreciate their own children's growth and change while also celebrating the other children's thinking and work.

I have come to realize that my weekly newsletters reveal the essence of my beliefs and practices to parents while also serving as a retrospective portrait of my curriculum and evaluation strategies. In fact, I have been told that my voice and perspective come through most effectively when speaking from my heart and mind directly to the families with whom I work. And so it is that I have chosen to share my inquiry into family partnerships with you directly. It is my hope that the letter that follows will reveal how I establish relationships among the classroom, the community, and the children's families. Since I have come to know that our practices reflect our beliefs, I hope that the fundamental features of my philosophy emerge. In short, I have chosen to show them not simply tell them about my personal inquiry.

The Gator Gazette that follows was selected from one group of children I taught for two years. As you read the letters, imagine how lovely it is to loop with the same group of children, imagine how I intentionally and systematically help parents understand the philosophy of the Center; imagine how it feels for the children and parents to see their thinking, questions, and connections published for all to learn from; imagine how individual children and parents are validated for each contribution they make to the classroom community and world. Imagine. (See Figure 9–1, p. 136.)

Journal of Ordinary Thoughts

Weekly newsletters became a vehicle for consistent information about events that happened Monday through Friday at school. But what about all of the personal connections to school and the richness of learning at home on Saturday and Sunday? I had heard Bill Ayers talk about a teacher that used a journal to write down ordinary thoughts about teaching and learning. She had invited parents to share their ideas about their child's learning at home, and the Journal of Ordinary Thoughts was created. I had kept dialogue journals with parents before, but because of my growth as a teacher, I wanted more than I had accomplished in the past. I was at a new place as a learner myself and so transformed dialogue journals to reflect my current beliefs.

I was eager to find out what it would be like to have families become active researchers alongside me. What a wonderful historical documentation of

Gator Gazette

Dear Kindergarten Families,

What an awesome week for learning at the Center for Inquiry! Thank you for doing your Home Practice by writing your positive observations and goal for your child. The goals were varied and reflected what you feel is necessary for improvement this next nine weeks. The *strengths* mentioned in your parental evaluations included increased confidence, positive attitudes, enthusiasm, assertiveness, listening skills, mathematical concepts, vocabulary, and verbal skills. One goal for several children that we received was to . . . *please learn to tie shoe laces!* Parents' *goals* also focused on increasing sight word recognition; increasing 0–20 number recognition; improving reading, writing, and verbal fluency; becoming risk takers in learning; and increasing personal responsibility.

Thank you also for the positive comments regarding your child's love for school and learning. We strive to make learning as fun, productive, and contagious as possible!

Our walking trip to the neighborhood was healthy and very educational. All 42 feet made the long trek to Lot # 46 in the Hunter's Pond subdivision of the Summit neighborhood. There we were greeted by a realtor, Ann Shirley. She allowed us to go in the house that was under construction. We had to climb a makeshift ladder in the unfinished garage up to the foundation floor. The children thought it was the coolest thing, while Mrs. Belcher, Mr. Carlton, and I were silently praying that nobody would fall through!

Safely inside the house, we met a dry-waller and were escorted through all of the rooms. The children figured out where the light switches, ceiling fans, and outlets would be placed as they noticed the different colored wires protruding from the walls. Everywhere they looked they noticed patterns: the wiring, the caulking on the walls, the fireplace blocks, the stairs, the floorboards, etc. They asked a dozen questions, some which could not be answered. We did find out the house was 2,000 square feet at a cost of $167,000. Any takers? Vincent wants his aunt to move from Charlotte into the new house! We do plan to go back in late January to see the completed project and compare our field notes.

The children hauled their Journals of Ordinary Thoughts with them and recorded some sketches of what they noticed. The next day after our field study, we were astonished to find how much they remembered! Their sketches are improving not only in scale but with added details. *Thank you, parents, for writing in your Journals!

We compared different kinds of windows: rectangular, square, and semicircular. The building materials of the homes were varied as well. The results indicated that brick is the most popular type of building material in this particular neighborhood. Aaron pointed out that homes with backyard pools have fences *and* pool nets!

During art with Dr. Colbert and Mrs. Cato, the children sculpted clay into animals of their choice. They will add an environment or habitat for that animal this week. Ask your child what she or he created.

Please *continue counting by 1s, 2s, 5s, and 10s* with your child. They are really *into* this and consider it a big deal! We added play money that represents $1.00, $5.00, and $10.00 bills and pennies, nickels, and dimes to our restaurant for reinforcing number recognition, and value of 1, 5, and 10. Some are eager to add and subtract. We will play and practice with money before we actually begin writing simple algorithms ($1c + 5c = 6c$, $10c - 5c = 5c$). However you wish to reinforce this at home, please consider using real money (pennies, nickels, and dimes) in the context of authentic use. Which reminds me, a special thank-you to the O'Keefe family and the Grosso family for donating money toward our leopard gecko fund!

Our shared writing stories included Shelby's story about a toad, and Vincent taught us about snow owls. The next day he brought in information about owls that he found on his computer at home. He shared it with the class.

Later in the week we took a different perspective in which to view our world. We are now learning how to think like historians! Aaron, Andrew, and Baraka chose photographs of learning in October to begin our written history as kindergartners. They each thought of sentences that described a picture, what was being learned and a wonder question. We learn so much from five- and six-year old perspectives!

Rory's mom was our featured Royal Reader this week and she read a book *Mud*, and she taught us the chorus to a Woody Guthrie song about gardens "Inch by Inch." The children are so proud of their gardens outside. Our garden is beautiful with purple pansy flowers and yellow chrysanthemums in bloom. We also planted tulip bulbs, so cross your fingers! Mrs. Lusk spotted our lettuce sprouts on Friday. We were thrilled! *Grow, grow, reap what we sow.* Ask your child what that means. We hope you and your child are enjoying reading their *Pumpkin, Pumpkin* book. Be sure to talk about the sequence of the plant. It will help their understanding of our own school gardens.

The Center for Inquiry's Parent Advisory Board Grounds Committee requests that parents donate pine straw for Center Beautification Day, Saturday, November 15, at 8:00 A.M.

Mrs. Lusk came to share a book *Mother Earth Counts.* By using that book as a resource, we found an answer to one of our class' (Andrew wrote the I wonder. . .question on a sentence strip) inquiries: How many seas and oceans are there? We found out there are. . .well, ask your child to see if she or he can remember. Ask your child what we used a geographer's compass for and where the north, south, east, and west walls are in our kindergarten classroom?

Thanks to all of you for helping your child choose educational things to share. Each child is gaining confidence in speaking to our class community. You would be impressed!

Our *thought for the week* was: *Don't be afraid to let your true colors show.* Two favorite books read aloud were *Dandylion* and *Amazing Grace* which highlighted that thought. See if your child can retell those stories to you.

A special congratulations to the Shankar family, Priya is now a big sister! Her baby sister was born on November 6. She missed Andrew Draft's birthday by one day. A special thank-you to the Drafts family for donating another birthday book to our class library, *Arthur Writes a Story* by Marc Brown. Happy birthday to our third six-year-old. . .Andrew Drafts, November 7! Our new young friends are all growing up so fast. We love them so much and are enjoying viewing life through their eyes. Have a super week!

Mrs. Gilbert, Mrs. Belcher, and Mr. Carlton

P.S. Remember to illustrate the thoughts for the week and return it by tomorrow! We all want to share comprehension through our illustrations with one another. After the books are shared, we will send them home to stay and read over and over again!

Figure 9–1. *An Issue of the Gator Gazette Newsletter.*

a child's learning. I wished I were invited to do the same when my sons were younger; it might have made me take the time to write down what moments I treasured in their learning.

It was easy to initiate this collaborative venture. I extended the invitation for parent dialogue through journaling. During the first Curriculum Night, I asked parents to become researchers with me into their child's learning for two years. All it would take was a spiral notebook; careful observation of their child's personal connections to school, ideas, questions, or concerns, and time to write them down. Through my experience I had found that the journals serve as a communication log of written conversations between school and home. These Journals of Ordinary Thoughts would also serve as a tool for families' voices to be heard without using the telephone! Another advantage of this invitation for learning is that I can take the spiral notebooks home and respond to their families' ideas at my leisure. It is amazing how thoughtful one can be, if given time, in a setting away from school.

To initiate the first conversation during our first Curriculum Night, I asked the families to respond in writing to this question: If you could choose three qualities for all human beings to possess, what would they be? This is a question that has no right answer. The families sent their journals to school and I asked them to allow two days before receiving my written responses. This first initial response proved to be a bridge into deeper and more personal dialogue, which became the foundation for establishing stronger relationships. It became the link between home and school, and we could use these written opportunities to share ideas, personal connections, concerns, inquiries, or just springboards into future conversations. Taking the initiative to demonstrate reading and writing within this authentic engagement of family dialogue journaling allowed me as the tall teacher in the learning community to become a part of their home life. Paying close attention to what was written on paper and what was written between the lines broadened my understanding of what is valued in my students' homes. It helped us get to the heart of things right away.

As time went by it became easy for me to see patterns in the home-school communication process. Some families decided to share personal connections or content connections. One parent shared her daughter's progress in kindergarten at our school in relationship to her older sister who attended another public school kindergarten. I couldn't help but feel validation for the power of an inquiry-based curriculum and the importance of coauthoring the curriculum with the children.

A mother and father shared questions/concerns and some new ideas on a survey form we handed out during one of our Curriculum Nights. Just as we take our children's ideas seriously, so too we listen to parents' ideas.

The dialogue journals also helped me simply nurture individual children as well as the class. Being aware of the health problem of a student who was not eating breakfast at home gave me enough information to include a nutrition lesson as part of our shared reading. The class made individual books based on an innovation of *Huggles' Breakfast,* published by the Wright Group. Of course, I was grateful for the parent's appreciation and observation of my ability to teach responsively.

One family shared how their youngest child taught the oldest child by demonstrating the power of making personal connections to content. It is exciting to know how empowered five-year-olds can be when they believe in themselves as learners (see Figure 9–2, pp. 140 and 141).

Finally, the old-fashioned way of using blank paper and pen to express open and honest feelings about the children we love is a proven way to assure genuine communication. Dialogue journals helped establish, build, and nurture relationships between school and home. Put simply, our Journal of Ordinary Thoughts placehold stories and provide a safe space for new stories to grow out of the old. The journals have become as generative as my curriculum. Why? Because the parents and I focus on what matters most: the children.

Inviting Families into the Curriculum: Insights from Jennifer Barnes

Not only are the children involved in the life of the Center for Inquiry, but the parents and siblings are also invited into our community. From the moment a child is enrolled at the Center for Inquiry, many opportunities are made available for family involvement. A family picnic at the beginning of the year is one of the first opportunities to establish relationships between home and school. New families and veteran families exchange phone numbers and addresses to make contact with and befriend one another prior to the family picnic.

Once the relationships of our learning community have been established, we involve families in other more personalized ways. One is through the use of the beautiful newsletters that keep all well acquainted with the daily lives of the students. These newsletters are sources of information and education. Families are also encouraged to volunteer throughout the whole scope of life and learning at the Center. Family members take advantage of school life as Royal Readers, science experiment assistants, writing and math workshop volunteers, field study chaperones, and collaborators with children in completing home-study connections.

12/9/91

Mp Gilbert, I had to share this connection with you. On Thursday night (12/7), Lauren (my 3rd grade,) was having some difficulties with her 5-digit subtraction. Rather than borrowing from the ten's or hundred's column, she wanted to skip over to the thousand's column. Leslie hears the discussion and yells out,.....
"Lauren, Mp Gilbert said you always borrow from your neighbor house, if you don't have enough in the ones or tens column"! From that moment on, we started to re-iterate what Leslie learned in class and believe it or not, Lauren didn't have any more problems skipping over columns

Finally, on last night, Leslie told Lauren if you want to remember "greater than and less than, just remember the alligator's mouth! Take care and have a good weekend!

12/9/99

Ms Gilbert,

I had to share this connection with you. On Tuesday night (12/9), Lauren (my third grader) was having some difficulties with her five-digit subtraction. Rather than *borrowing* from the *tens or hundreds* column, she wanted to skip over to the *thousands* column. Leslie heard the discussion and yells out . . . "Lauren, Ms. Gilbert said you always *borrow* from your neighbor's house if you don't have enough in the ones or tens column!" From that moment on, we started to reiterate what Leslie learned in class and, believe it or not, Lauren didn't have any more problems skipping over columns.

Finally, last night, Leslie told Lauren if you want to remember "greater than and less than, just remember the alligator's mouth!" Take care and have a good weekend!

Figure 9–2. *Leslie's Mother Shares a Home-School Connection.*

One of our inspiring inquiries for my first graders in the fall was based upon a suggestion by fellow teacher Dori Gilbert. We discussed what a blessing our grandparents were and how their lives are similar and/or different from ours. We generated a list of interview questions and then designed a cover letter to send them via mail (see Figures 9–3A and 9–3B, pp. 142 and 143). The young authors created and addressed an envelope stuffed with a questionnaire for each of their grandparents. The process of writing the letters was authentic in and of itself, but we didn't realize the learning potential of the experience until we received letters in return.

A miraculous event occurred as the first of those letters started trickling back into the hands of the young authors. By reading their grandparents' letters together, we began to realize how unique and wonderful our grandparents are, what clever people our own parents are, and how our lives across generations are alike in several ways. Inquiring about childhood toys was a popular curiosity. It was amazing to discover the connections between family members' passions and expertise. One example is of a grandfather who was very intrigued by Lincoln Logs®. His grandson, Jonathan, is our Lego® expert! Another was a grandfather's hobby of making paper planes, so like his grandchild Allie's paper projects. This project revealed how similar the children were to their own grandparents.

Center for Inquiry

Dear Beloved Grandparents,

Grandparents are good for hugs and kisses, an extra bedtime snack, a fabulous retelling of a favorite book, and great stories of life long ago. We would like to add one more job description to your title of grandparent—that of curriculum designer! You, dear grandparents, are the keepers of our family stories. We look to you to learn of your values and lessons, your stories and dreams!

At this special time of year, we are reflecting on the best things in our lives. You are some of those best things! During this time of reflection, we are seeking information about you to share with our class at school. In this letter, your grandchild has included his or her very first "official friendly letter." (By the way, each child learned all the parts of the letter: date, greeting, body with indented paragraphs, closing, and signature. Each noted the uses of commas in letter writing.) In addition, we worked together as a class to compose a questionnaire of our inquiries to you. We want to know you better! We are enclosing some questions for you to document. We will be waiting patiently for your responses. Please mail them back to your grandchild as soon as possible.

Upon receipt of your letter, your grandchild will rush your letter back to our class, where we will work diligently. As mathematicians, we will graph the number of days in the mail, your favorite types of toys, and your special books. As geographers, we will pinpoint your homes on our map and discuss distance and directions. As historians, we will focus on newsworthy historical events—both nationwide and familywide! As readers, we will examine your favorite books and discuss your preferred genres of reading. As writers, we have already been busy starting this whole project!

What an impact you continue to make in our lives and now even in our first-grade classroom! We thank you—from the bottom of our hearts—for participating in our curriculum.

Very Truly Yours,
The First-Grade Students at the Center for Inquiry

Figure 9–3A. *Letter to Grandparents.*

Grandparents' Reflections

Grandparent Name(s):_____

Child's Name:_____

*Your Favorite Childhood Toy:

*Your Favorite Book as a Child:

*Your Favorite Book as an Adult:

*Describe how you spent your growing-up years (hobbies, sports, play, work):

*Write one story detailing an incident in which your child (your grandchild's parent) did something really good for someone else.

*Briefly describe the one historical event that had the biggest impact on your life.

*Reflect on some of your favorite holiday traditions, past and present.

*Your typical Thanksgiving meal includes:

Figure 9–3B. *Grandparents' Questionaire.*

But, even more special were their stories, stories that revealed their goodness and true character—stories about how Kylie's mother saved a child from drowning in a pool; how Shane's mother gave her entire collection of Barbie® dolls, clothes, and accessories to a child she deemed to be needy; and how Paxie's father has "always been there" for his loved ones.

My favorite stories originated from the responses to this task: "Briefly describe the one historical event that had the biggest impact on your life." Tears streamed down my face as I relived with Alex's Asian grandfather his best friend's death during the bombing of Japan in 1945. "Only two hours' bombing, more than 3,000 people were killed, and I lost my best friend." Reading the account of Stephanie's Filipino grandmother gave me chills: "One morning, in the autumn of 1944, we looked up and saw lots of planes, glistening in the sky. They formed the letter *V!* We cheered and jumped up and down." How special it was for me to see the narrative my own mother wrote to Zachary—my own child and student—about her days during the Second World War: "I cannot express how dark and dreary the days were— there were no dreams or hopes—no excitement even for holidays. People did not have a smile any longer. We looked forward to only one thing—the ending of the war and our boys coming home again." This sharing of their family stories and their lives with me made me feel closer to these students and families. Now I knew the children better as readers, writers, and people.

My life was changed immensely by that one inquiry event, and that was just the beginning of my growth as an inquiry-based teacher. Parents appreciated the personal engagement and, of course, begged for the treasured letters to be returned to them. Some parents told me how they had never heard the stories their own parents told in these written responses written to their grandchildren. What a valuable gift! I feel honored to have been a part of the historical investigation into their lives. To continue communication between children and families, one of our future inquiries will be to undertake a genealogical study of a family member. Many of the children will use their grandparents' special letters as springboards to help them get started.

Amazingly, those precious letters dramatically cemented a bond within the families of our first-grade class. Now it is not unusual for the grandparents to e-mail our classroom, to send a cute note, to schedule a visit, or to read a favorite book. One family brought our class a keepsake from their travels. We were touched to receive an artifact from New Zealand, a place well known to our children as author Joy Cowley's homeland! We are learning to read her delightful predictable books.

Our computer mailbox is full of letters from parents, too. In fact, the computer has been a communication tool and a great place for us to learn more about our world. We loved when Elizabeth's dad came and spent time helping us understand how computers work, how searches occur, and how we can create our own Website! We look forward to checking our e-mail from parents who have written to us each day. So far, we have received e-mail from parents who have written thank-you notes, sought additional information, congratulated us on our research strategies and behavior when conducting research in the public library, sent informative sites for us to check out on astronomy, and even sent some jokes. Occasionally, the children will e-mail our classroom's computer from their homes and delight in being discovered on the computer's mailbox!

All of these opportunities strengthen our relationships and extend communication with the families, children, parents, and grandparents. The investment is time well spent. Each investigation was easily integrated into our inquiry studies, from addressing envelopes to graphing responses; from practicing basic keyboarding skills to reading and writing e-mails; and from studying the past to understanding the present. Each of these authentic engagements has stretched us beyond our comfort zone and each has continually reinforced in families their dedication and commitment to the Center for Inquiry.

Responding to Parents: Insights from Susanne Pender

Newsletters

When I first came to the Center, I was amazed to discover a veiled truth had become strikingly clear. For years, I had understood and accepted my role as a teacher, but once I joined the CFI faculty, I began learning through my teaching. Once I recognized this role, I found myself constantly watching, learning, and using information gained from my students to make thoughtful and relevant instructional decisions.

I made this process more explicit when a parent asked about my decision to move away from weekly spelling tests. Although the words on the tests were generated by the class, and I attempted to make them low-stress events, I immediately noticed changes in the children, and so I devised alternatives to spelling tests. I needed to explain my observations on how the class was responding to this method, my resulting concerns, the discussion with the children, and our decided plan of action.

We chose to approach our spelling study by using problem-solving strategies rather than focusing on isolation and memorization techniques. Since this approach is much different than previous instructional techniques that many of the parents experienced while in school, it was essential that I keep them informed and up to date with our plan of study. While I used our first Curriculum Night to describe my shift, the newsletters were a necessary tool to keep an open line of communication with my parents.

Weekly Goal Sheets

During Curriculum Night and through subsequent newsletters, I shared the fact that most educators agree that children need to feel a genuine sense of accomplishment and success on a daily basis. I told them I believe my job is to provide numerous opportunities for each child to uncover a talent, work through a problem, or gain a new perspective on an idea or event. Children need a series of small and consistent successes in order to gain the confidence that is needed for larger, more sophisticated work. To accomplish this, I have developed a goal-setting strategy that helps parents understand what we do and why. Additionally, it promotes serious reflection on the part of my children, which has led to an increase in their sense of responsibility, understanding of content and process, and, finally, a sense of accomplishment. In short, goal setting has helped us look back, move forward, and grow and change.

We address setting and reflecting on our goals in a multitude of ways. Each section of our quarterly personal narratives ends with a goal for the child. The final section consists of a space for the student and parent to reflect and set new goals for the next quarter. Our classroom homework journals have taken goal setting a step further.

Along with an area to write daily homework assignments, there is a section that focuses on weekly, concrete goals. On the first day of the school week, the student, the parent, and I each set a detailed and personalized goal. The goals should be clear and specific and be something the student can accomplish and evaluate by the end of the week.

The following weekend, the child reflects and comments on the set goals, if and how they were met. The parent also reflects and responds to the child's performance. This process has been a powerful way to promote communication and increase a three-way dialogue between parents, teacher, and children that includes questions, concerns, and notes of encouragement.

Exit Slips

Another activity that encourages correspondence with parents and provides a brief glimpse of their child's day is called Exit Slips. We use this exercise to reflect on the day's events and explorations. I asked the children to create three statements that communicate skills, strategies, and concepts learned with specific details and examples. This activity allows the students an opportunity to revisit learning moments and celebrate growth that was demonstrated throughout the day.

The Exit Slip was originally developed in response to a parent's request for more information about our daily activities. I have found this and the other methods to be instrumental in helping keep parents informed of the direction of our learning. The parents have been very pleased to have this information and have used it to support the classroom learning.

Working with Parents Across the School: Insights from Heidi Mills

While the classroom teachers have devised elegantly responsive ways to work intimately with parents, we have also come to realize the importance of sharing consistent information regarding the spirit and structure of our school across classrooms. Amy Donnelly addresses the creation of the Parent Advisory Board in her chapter. Our PAB is central to the good work that occurs at the Center. The Parent Advisory Board is quite different from traditional parent-teacher associations. The members do much more than raise money for and promote the school. The organization runs much more like a lovely, tasteful bed and breakfast than a large, corporate hotel. The officers think carefully about every decision they make. I would imagine chefs in a fine bed and breakfast debate the merits of various ingredients when ordering supplies; so too with our PAB. They do not make large-scale decisions without first consulting with those who will be affected by them: the teachers. They are careful to preserve what is special about our school while also nudging us forward to consider new ways to raise money, publicize the goodness, and involve families, as well as address the tough issues that pervade our society such as equity and social justice.

While I am not a member of the PAB, I have played another role in schoolwide communication. I often conduct visitor debriefing sessions and parent orientations, write parent newsletters, and foster curricular conversations. Consequently, I have compiled a sample of the handouts that have been created and distributed to help parents decide whether or not they want their children to attend our school, to answer questions they pose, and to simply celebrate the promising practices that are infused throughout our school.

When asked the common question "What is inquiry?" I often refer to the definition in the preface of this book. While it works well for educators, it is a bit elusive for parents. Consequently, I have found the following statements work much more effectively when introducing our school to new families. I typically use this list in concert with videos that explicitly demonstrate each point. For instance, when arguing that inquiry is about teaching readers rather than reading, I often show a video of a teacher coaching a child and ask the parents to notice how she is making moment-by-moment decisions based on her knowledge of the reading process and careful kid-watching observations. While the range of responses she makes reflects her beliefs in general, when operationalizing the belief system at the level of a particular child, she is teaching the reader, period.

As you read the following statements, remember the stories that have come before this chapter and each point will come to life for you as it does for the teachers and children.

What Is Inquiry?

- It's about teaching readers, writers, mathematicians, scientists, historians, artists, and musicians.
- It's about fostering that sense of wonder and delight in learning that children bring to school.
- It's about preparing children academically and socially to take personal responsibility for their own learning while also making valuable contributions to the learning community.
- It's about truly respecting and celebrating diversity.
- It's about teaching responsively so that all children's needs and interests will be recognized and valued.

We implement an inquiry-based curriculum by helping children to do the following:

- learn the value of close, focused observation
- examine the world from different perspectives
- learn through active engagement in the process
- use skills, strategies, content, and concepts for authentic purposes
- understand the skillfulness of inquiry (how to learn)
- use reflection/self-evaluation to grow and change
- appreciate the integrated nature of life

While these principles and practices have served us well over the years, this year we found that parents wanted a more explicit explanation of the specific practices that were universal to the school. Since we have become a popular choice option in the district, we suspect that some of our more recent families selected us for reasons other than the philosophy that binds us together. So the chart that follows was created to provide a very practical overview of common practices at the Center for Inquiry. I intentionally took common curricular areas in elementary school and articulated how they look in our setting to help parents realize that we are not omitting important features of the curriculum, we are simply doing it differently.

TEACHING AND LEARNING AT THE CENTER FOR INQUIRY

The Center for Inquiry was established to implement promising practices in elementary education. The scope of the curriculum reflects the requirements set forth by Richland Two's curriculum standards in each content area. However, the order in which the standards are addressed and the instructional strategies used are determined by teachers after careful observation and documentation of students' needs and interests.

Decisions regarding curriculum development and evaluation strategies at the Center reflect:

- how children learn best
- principles on interdisciplinary learning established and endorsed by leading professional organizations such as the National Council of Teachers of Mathematics, the National Council of Teachers of English, the International Reading Association, the Council for Elementary Science International, and the Speech Communication Association.

As such, formal instruction and learning activities are devoted to helping children learn to think and work as readers, writers, mathematicians, scientists, artists, and historians. Children at the Center for Inquiry learn about reading, writing, math, science, art, and history while doing what strategic readers, writers, mathematicians, scientists, artists, and historians do.

Daily schedules across classrooms provide opportunities for children to learn about reading, writing, and mathematics during literature study groups, writing workshop, and math workshop/exploration. Reading, writing, and mathematics are also included as tools for learning and communication during interdisciplinary focus studies and/or expert projects on topics in the physical and social sciences.

Since our teachers devise learning experiences that are both interesting and congruent with how children learn, our students delight in learning. Historically, we thought the curriculum was rigorous if children struggled to learn it. We now know that curriculum can be just as challenging and learned quite efficiently and effectively when taught in ways that make sense to the learners. Consequently, children at the Center for Inquiry develop a solid knowledge base while also learning the skillfulness of inquiry. Most importantly, they learn to love school!

To appreciate how skills, strategies, content, and concepts are taught within the context of an inquiry-based curriculum, the following chart delineates basic curriculum areas and demonstrates how each topic is taught at the Center.

Topic	Center for Inquiry
Reading and Writing	Taught primarily using children's literature and writing topics generated by individual students, teacher, or class. Consistent with best practices in literacy instruction, children learn to read and write through real reading and writing opportunities. The teachers show children skills and strategies involved in reading and writing through whole-class or small-group mini-lessons and then coach the readers and writers individually during reading and writing workshops.
Vocabulary	Identified by individuals, small groups, or whole class through inquiry into language use by readers and/or writers. New words are placed in writer's notebooks or literature response journals for discussion of interesting language, effective language use, examples of parts of speech, and so on. Students are encouraged to placehold important words in their notebooks and to use them in their own conversations and writing.
Handwriting	Manuscript is taught in K–1 and cursive is taught in grades 2 and 3. Handwriting is practiced when publishing work. Students are encouraged to focus on the content of their writing during early drafts and to concentrate on handwriting during the production of their final drafts.
Spelling	Taught through use as part of writing workshop and/or language study. Emphasis is placed on helping children understand and use English spelling patterns. Spelling instruction occurs through mini-lessons focusing on spelling strategies and patterns.

	Spelling is also addressed with individual children when editing their work for publication.
Mathematics	Taught through mini-lessons or demonstration lessons. Focus of instruction is on skills and strategies—how, when, and why the math concept is used. Practiced through application during math workshop or as a tool for learning during a focus study unit. Emphasis is placed on effective strategies for problem posing and solving.
Science and Social Studies	Units of study are developed using the textbooks as one of many resources. Teachers create lessons that provide baseline information regarding the topic or concept under study and then have children work independently or in small groups to inquire further. All children are expected to learn the content standards and to develop special expertise through expert projects.
Classroom Management	The teacher and children establish a list of responsibilities that support student rights. The focus is on developing and implementing expectations for behavior that build a strong sense of community and establish healthy work habits for individuals and the class at large. Community-building strategies such as class problem-solving sessions and Friendship Circles promote respect and appreciation of all members of the class and enrich opportunities for children to learn from one another throughout the curriculum. (Mills 2000)

The parents have been receiving newsletters from the teachers from the beginning, but it was Linda Chapman, one of our charter parents, who took the lead by initiating parent communication through a series of newsletters she titled Parent Connections. This year Carla Bullard, our new Parent Advisory Board president, invited me to assume the responsibility. I must admit,

Linda was a hard act to follow, but with the help of Carla and input from teachers and parents, I took it on. I began with this piece:

PARENT CONNECTIONS

Greetings to all parents at the Center for Inquiry! I predict you and your children are in the midst of a thoughtful, productive, and joyful school year. I also predict that you will value the depth and breadth of information in your children's progress reports. As a parent of two children at the Center and a founding university partner, I am truly grateful for the time, thought, insight, and energy that goes into each individual report. When we read the reports of our children's growth and change, it is sometimes difficult to imagine how much careful observation and documentation needs to take place in order to share specific feedback about each child's strengths and needs.

For those of you who have grown accustomed to narrative reports, I hope you will remember how fortunate you are to have such detailed information about your children as readers, writers, mathematicians, scientists, historians, and community members. For those of you who are new to the Center, I hope this newsletter will help you understand why we have chosen to report progress in this way. We know it is more demanding and time-consuming than calculating grades for a report card, yet we know that the process reflects best practice in evaluation and are committed to nothing less.

Linda Crafton, a leading educator, describes what is currently considered best practice in evaluation this way:

- We used to think that evaluation only occurred at the end of instruction and learning. Now we know that evaluation occurs throughout the learning process.
- We used to think that evaluation was only the teacher's responsibility. Now we know that it is everybody's responsibility—something shared by teachers, students, and parents.
- We used to think that the primary purpose of evaluation was to uncover what was wrong. Now we know that the primary purpose is to find value in what we do.
- We used to think that evaluation occurred in isolation. Now we know that it needs to occur in supportive, social contexts.

These ideas reveal how the field of education has changed and why we have chosen narrative progress reports. As you reflect upon the traditional report cards that framed your childhood, imagine how nice it would have been to hear what your teacher noticed about your strengths and accomplishments.

Imagine how satisfying it would have been for your teacher to appreciate the strategies you used as well as your final products. Imagine how helpful it would have been to know his or her specific goals for you in each content area. Imagine the conversations that you would have had with your parents as they documented three pluses and a wish/goal for you. Imagine how much you would have learned by simply reflecting on your own work and making plans for improvement.

When we started the school four years ago, the teachers, principal, and university partners imagined what we needed to do to make solid instructional decisions that reflected the children's needs and interests. We imagined the kind of data we would need to collect and analyze each day to track children's growth. We imagined how we would effectively use the information we gathered through our notes, samples of children's work, audio- and videotapes of children reading and presenting expert projects, and so on. We imagined how useful it would be to turn classroom evaluation data into new lesson plans. We imagined how we could teach the standards across disciplines in ways that reflect best practice.

When Carla Bullard, president of the Parent Advisory Board, invited me to follow Linda Chapman's lead and write the Parent Connections newsletter this year, I imagine she did so because I am a parent who is devoted to the success of the Center while also having a background in the philosophy of the school. For these reasons, I accepted the invitation—although I must admit Linda is a hard act to follow! However, I know that I will only be helpful if you honestly share your connections, questions, and new ideas. So, please use the space below to share your reaction to the progress reports as well as other issues that matter to you. I have a box in the office and the teachers will be happy to collect your ideas and put them in my box. The teachers have taught me well—I will pay attention to your needs and interests and create Parent Connection letters throughout the year that address them. Enjoy!

—*Heidi Mills*

Connections:

Questions/Concerns:

New Ideas:

It seems only fitting to close with Linda Chapman's response to my request for parental feedback, since she started it all.

We thank all of those whose hearts and minds helped to create the Center for Inquiry and continue the educational mission. For we hold videos, narrative information, and project artifacts that have become the things we would go into a burning home to rescue.

—Chapman 1999

And so it goes. The cycle continues. Parents, faculty, and university partners live the model, and in so doing, grow and change alongside the children.

References

Chapman, L. 1999. Parent Connections. Columbia, SC: Center for Inquiry Newsletter.

Mills, H. 2000. Parent Connections. Columbia, SC: Center for Inquiry Newsletter.

10

Putting the Pieces Together

AMY NOVAK

Prologue: Some Things Never Change

The phone rings and I run to answer it before the machine cuts on. "Hello," I say, out of breath.

"Well, do you still love it?" my mom asks with a laugh. She's asking if I still love teaching half-day kindergarten at Rice Creek Elementary School.

"Oh, you wouldn't believe it!" I answer. "The kids were bringing in rocks from the playground, so we've been studying rocks, which, of course, led to dirt and mud. And then they discovered a worm in some of the garden soil I brought in and named it Elenia! It's great," I continued.

"Humph, well, some things never change," my mother said, laughing.

Later, as I smiled and thought back over the conversation, I realized that I'm doing the same things in the classroom that I did as a child. I've come full circle, back to where I was as a child and how I looked at things as a child. When I was a child, I marched off into the woods to "discover things." I spent hours digging in the soil, gathering rocks, and playing in the creek in my neighborhood. Now, I work with the children to help them uncover information and build on the knowledge they bring to the classroom.

As I look back now, it surprises me to see how much I have grown and changed by using inquiry as a framework for my own learning as well as that of my students. I believe having the opportunity to live and learn in the supportive learning community at the Center for Inquiry helped me make the connection between the wonderful texts I was reading and the classroom. I was immersed in inquiry—my own and that of the children.

In this chapter, I reflect on the experiences I had during my yearlong internship at the Center for Inquiry. My fall placement was in Michele Shamlin's

155

kindergarten class and my spring placement was in Tim O'Keefe's second-grade class. We all bring something of ourselves to our writing. In this paper, I write from a student intern's perspective.

The Puzzle

I scattered the puzzle pieces on the table. As I looked over the pieces, searching for an image, I thought aloud, "I think these pieces go together. No, not quite. Oh, there's a match! And, this one fits nicely with the pattern."

When I am putting together a puzzle, I usually spill out all of the pieces onto a large surface so that I can see everything at a glance. Then I shape and group together pieces I recognize as having similar characteristics. As I fit the pieces together, I recognize new patterns and regroup pieces accordingly. As I progressed through my internship, I often felt like I was putting together the pieces of an intricate puzzle. But sometimes, just when the pieces seemed to fit together, the image would change as my image of the education process changed.

Inquiry is a thread that has run throughout my experience in this program and I will use this chapter to share the process with you. I will discuss the different stages of my puzzle-building process as I fit together pieces of learning theory, alternate sign systems, knowledge domains, and lessons from the children along with my own knowledge, beliefs, and experiences to form my own image of how children learn and grow.

Spreading Out the Puzzle Pieces

Early in my internship, I found that I spent a lot of time searching for formulas to use in the classroom. I thought there was a secret to effective teaching. As I progressed through the program, I discovered that the secret, or foundation, for all learning in the classroom is community. Community in itself is more important to learning than any method or technique (Peterson 1992, 2).

In my fall placement in the kindergarten class at the Center for Inquiry, I saw a learning community develop over time. At first, I observed, and later, I participated. I observed the children working together in Friendship Circles to solve the problem of how to share learning centers. I listened and learned as they discussed multiple possibilities for solutions to the problem. Rather than telling the children what to do, Michele Shamlin trusted the children to develop their own solutions. Redirecting inappropriate behavior and encouraging children to consider alternate ways to solve their own problems allows children to make better choices in the classroom while maintaining their self-respect (Glasser 1986). I believe one of the goals of education in a democratic society is to help children become skillful, thoughtful, and concerned citizens who can work with others to solve their problems and reach common goals.

Later, as I observed and worked with a child in the kindergarten room as part of my kid-watching project, I realized firsthand the importance of creating a supportive learning community, one that encourages risk taking and exploration. During my kid-watching project, I worked with a child named Hutton, a thoughtful, insightful five-year-old. Yetta Goodman introduced the term *kid watching* in 1978. Since that time, many books and articles have been written on the topic. For me, kid watching involved watching children and making curricular decisions based on my observations. I observed Hutton during center time, field studies, reading sessions, schoolwide events, and more. I took careful anecdotal notes during this time.

In Hutton's earlier writing, he frequently asked teachers to write captions for him. Then Hutton began to use symbols in his work to signify meaning. He wrote dollar symbols on tickets he created for the puppet theater. Hutton was beginning to use writing for real purposes (Goodman 1996). I noticed that as Hutton became more comfortable in the classroom environment, he began taking risks in his writing. He wrote a cleanup song for the class using approximations of musical notes with circles in between to denote spaces. The classroom environment can be structured to accept children's approximations by creating an atmosphere where children can take risks (Fisher 1991).

My cooperating teacher offered the children lots of choices in the classroom. Allowing children choices communicates trust (Avery 1993). Children who are given choices eagerly take charge of their learning process. And this is what Hutton did. My role during this earlier time was primarily that of a cheerleader and a coach (Avery 1993). I celebrated Hutton's approximations, including invented spelling, and encouraged him to sound out words (phonics). I acknowledged his strategies and encouraged him to focus on meaning (semantics) in his writing. Hutton grew tremendously over the semester. I believe becoming part of a supportive classroom learning community encouraged him to become a positive risk taker.

I also experienced the power of community among colleagues and teachers during my yearlong internship. During this time, the interns working at the Center met weekly in teacher support groups to reflect on our classroom experiences with the children and offer suggestions and support for one another in our own explorations. We formed a close bond that will follow us out into our careers as educators. The bonds we formed with our cooperating teachers and professors also provided crucial support during the process. I know that without this support and collaboration, I would not have grown so much in this process.

Creating Curriculum with Children

Music fills the room. Children sit side by side with arms interlocked around one another's shoulders. As they sing "When I First Came to This Land," they smile and sway from side to side. Tim O'Keefe, their teacher, crouches near the center of the semicircle they form with their bodies. He smiles and sings as he holds one child's hand and sways back and forth. For a moment, I feel like I have intruded on a private moment, but Tim and the children beckon me to join them.

As I spent time researching in Tim's second-grade classroom at the Center for Inquiry as part of my teacher-researcher project, I kept returning to this image. It was near the middle of the fall semester and I wondered about the teacher's role in such a classroom. I wanted to learn how I could support children's literacy growth in the classroom, what I could do to facilitate connections and support outside of the classroom, and how I could integrate the curriculum to help children on their paths to becoming not only readers, writers, and mathematicians but responsible, thinking, feeling citizens. As this project progressed I realized that there is no set formula in an inquiry-based classroom because each year brings new students and each teacher brings personal beliefs, talents, and new experiences to the classroom. The elusive information I was searching for was not a stagnant formula, but instead an evolving curriculum. The classroom curriculum was evolving from the learners: the teacher, the children, and parents. "The power in process-oriented teaching and learning is that people in the classroom are creating the curriculum" (Hindley 1996, 97).

I experienced this process many times over the year, but my strongest memory is from a lesson in the kindergarten class during the fall semester. I planned and taught a lesson on showing two different types of information using a Venn diagram. My invitation had been for the children to create their own diagrams, and they did! I had prepared a follow-up lesson on how to show three different kinds of information for the following day, but when I noticed the children creating their own diagrams about various topics in centers, I put my original plans aside, and decided to follow the children's lead and use their plans instead. I facilitated as the children shared their diagrams and strategies. Other children commented on what they noticed and wondered about the charts. I encouraged the children to talk about what the charts showed and didn't show. The children followed my lead and asked their own questions. For example, Jonathan H. noticed Jonathan S. had included numerals on his graph. Jonathan S. explained that the numerals showed how many people had signed for each of their favorite things to do at school. He had included a key on his graph to show how many people selected each category. Jack created a graph to show whether children preferred painting, drawing, or both. He explained that a previous graph we had created about reading and writing didn't include these. It was obvious that this information was important to him. In his graph, Jack drew two circles side by side and connected them with two lines instead of interlocking circles, forming an interesting deviation from the original chart. Ali showed three different kinds of information in her graph by overlapping circles. She collected data on whether children liked cleaning up, playing, or dinosaurs. This led naturally to a discussion of how to show more than two types of information and how to show information in different ways. It was incredible! The children supported one another as they worked together to create new ways to show information. The open-ended nature of the assignment allowed children to pose problems, make decisions, and work at their own ability levels. This was a powerful lesson for me also because I trusted the children and myself enough to follow their lead. Harste, Woodward, and Burke refer to this as using the child as a curricular informant (1984). I watched the kids and followed their lead to help them build on their experiences and interests. The resulting lesson was much stronger than the one I had originally planned and carried over into the children's work in centers for weeks.

My view of curriculum evolved slowly over the past year as a result of my experiences in the classroom with the children. In my final curriculum model I presented in late spring, I defined curriculum as an ongoing process involving the interaction and collaboration of learners—both teachers and children. Curriculum is a negotiation in which the teacher builds on the knowledge and personal experiences of the learner by designing instructional invitations to facilitate learning. To illustrate this definition, I used a puzzle with learning at the center. The puzzle included the four sources of curriculum—the standards and district curriculum across disciplines, alternate sign systems, learning theory, and the nature of school in society—along with care, family, life experiences, and so on. I used water as the background image of the puzzle because water is constantly moving and changing. The end result was a familiar image that emphasized movement and change. Curriculum is difficult to define because it is constantly changing. Creating curriculum with your students creates an image you may not be able to name, but you recognize it when you experience it.

Alternate Sign Systems

Children use reading, writing, mathematics, and so on as tools to explore and make sense of their world. Short, Harste, and Burke (1996) define literacy as the use of language, art, music, movement, and other sign systems to explore and expand our world. When literacy is viewed in this way, inquiry becomes a natural way to view education holistically. I believe it is important to allow children to explore and learn using different sign systems. I encouraged this in the classroom during my full-time teaching. As part of the assessment for a science lesson I taught in the second grade, I asked the children to draw a picture illustrating the changes in the seasons. I asked the children to include the tilt and position of Earth in relation to the Sun during each season. I also asked them to write a brief explanation. The results were intriguing. Several children had difficulty showing their understanding using a drawing yet were able to write a detailed description of the process. Other children struggled with the writing but drew elaborate illustrations demonstrating their knowledge.

Howard Gardner (1983) refers to seven multiple intelligences. The current curriculum in most schools focuses on only two of the seven, the linguistic and logico-mathematical. In *The Challenge to Care in Schools,* Nel Noddings (1992) questions whether the current curriculum is the best for all children. Since the current curriculum focuses on only two areas, the children who have strengths in areas other than language and mathematics are left to do the best they can in a system that will not help them reach their full potential or that leaves them out all together. I believe children need lots of opportunities to succeed in the classroom and encouraging children to express their understanding in different ways offers more opportunities for success as well as a deeper understanding of the topic being explored. In addition, children develop an appreciation for the talents of others.

The Power of Inquiry

Short, Harste, and Burke (1996) refer to education as learning, outgrowing ourselves through inquiry. One way to actively involve children in the classroom is through the curriculum. An inquiry-based curriculum encourages children to ask questions. By inviting children to ask questions, you involve them in the learning process, and as a result they develop ownership of the process and benefit from the outcome. Children who have these opportunities become seekers of knowledge and develop a love of learning. When we allow children to direct their own learning, they become genuinely interested in what they are learning and their inquiry reaches beyond the confines of the classroom.

In the fall semester, I met with Tim to discuss my topic of inquiry for my interdisciplinary inquiry unit. We talked about district requirements and what the children had been studying in class. Tim mentioned that the class had studied some elements of space earlier when they studied time. Since then, space had continued to be a topic of interest in the classroom. Space was also a topic of interest to me, so the topic for my unit grew out of district guidelines, standards, the children's interests, and my own expertise.

Inquiry doesn't just happen. You have to plan for it by gathering resources to support learners' questions. As I gathered information for my inquiry unit,

I gathered lots of resources about space, read books, looked at movies, joined a local astronomy group, and visited the local planetarium. Through this process I followed my own questions about space and tried to anticipate questions the children might have. I went through the process of webbing what I know and wonder about space just as I would with the children in the spring. This helped prepare me for my full-time teaching. I planned invitations and mini-lessons to build on children's knowledge and address standards in context. While I gathered many, many resources for this topic of study, I realized that I would have to do this on a much smaller scale on a daily basis in the classroom because of time constraints.

In the spring, I started our unit by capturing the children's interest. I used a "Bill Nye, the Science Guy" videotape to generate conversation about space, and then the children worked together in groups to generate lists of what they knew and wondered about space. I introduced the idea of science focus groups to the children. I explained that we would be working together in groups to determine topics to explore in more detail. It was powerful to see the children sharing what they knew and wanted to learn about space. They had so many questions! It helped me see how children learn from observing, questioning, and searching for answers. The children connected with what they knew about space. This process helped the children develop ownership of their own learning, which I believe is very important.

I allowed the children a week to discuss and formulate questions for inquiry. Giving children time to uncover their questions and areas of interest allowed their questions to become more focused. To build on the social nature of learning (Vygotsky 1978), I planned time each day for the children to meet in science groups to share their questions. After these meetings, we met as a whole group to share our thoughts with one another and the children made insightful comments. For example, Amanda said, "I'm glad we had time to ask questions and talk about them with people." Another group functioned as scientists and used this perspective to explore their questions. Overall, our work in groups enhanced the learning process.

There were difficult moments. I noticed that I planned more open assignments during the afternoon when the children were more active, which caused some problems in classroom management. As a result, I monitored and adjusted my plans to include more structure when needed. There were also difficult moments for the children. They had worked together in groups before but had never worked together on an inquiry project. They had to learn how to share ideas and responsibilities while working in groups. I think it's important for the children to have these types of experiences so that they can learn to work with others. My cooperating teacher was impressed with how well the groups worked together. This helped me realize how high my expectations of the children were and how high their own expectations were for one another.

Nel Noddings (1992) discusses schools' emphasis on producing an end product rather than focusing on the active learning process. I believe a focus on product results in a competitive environment. Unfortunately, this is also an environment in which many children lose. Instead, I believe we need to allow children the opportunity to work together in cooperative groups. This gives children the opportunity to learn from peer interaction and gives children an appreciation for the skills and talents of others. In a cooperative group, each child can excel in his or her own way. And children will learn and grow at a higher level through the support of others (Vygotsky 1978).

Evaluation

It is important for evaluation to focus on the process as well as the products. For the evaluation to support learning, it must be meaningful to the learner. As a result, I worked with the children to develop several evaluation instruments for our inquiry unit. My goal was for the children to reflect on the learning process during and after the focused study. We developed a science group project evaluation form to provide feedback during science group presentations (see Figure 10–1). This form used the three pluses and a wish format the children were familiar with and included a rubric to evaluate AV (artwork, audiotape, videotape, etc.), effort, creativity, voice, length, interest, writing mechanics, and group connection. We also developed a form for science group reflections (see Figure 10–2, p. 163). It allowed children to reflect on the process of working together in groups and offer advice to other children and teachers

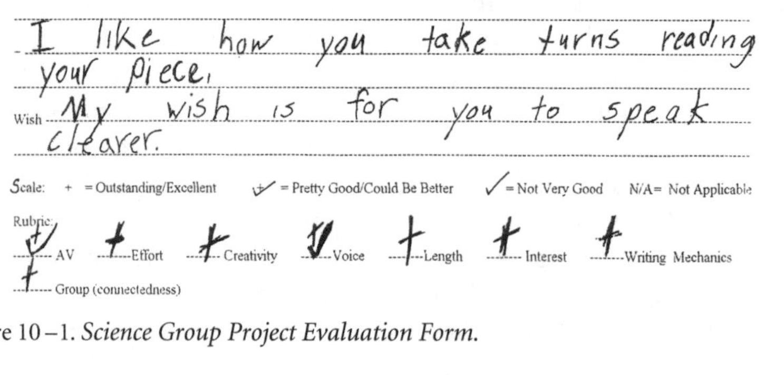
Science Group Project Evaluation Form

Group Members: Robert, Richard, Thomas, Reginald, Brian

Topic: Space shuttle Date:

Evaluator: Kyle

Nice Facts about space shuttles.

Nice artwork. Nice qustions.

I like how you take turns reading your piece.

Wish My wish is for you to speak clearer.

Scale: + = Outstanding/Excellent ✓+ = Pretty Good/Could Be Better ✓ = Not Very Good N/A= Not Applicable

Rubric:
✓+ AV + Effort + Creativity ✓+ Voice + Length + Interest + Writing Mechanics
+ Group (connectedness)

Figure 10–1. *Science Group Project Evaluation Form.*

Name: _____   Date: _____

Science Group Reflections

1)   List 3 ways you helped your science group.

     1. _____

     2. _____

     3. _____

2)   How did your group's presentation show what you learned?

     _____

     _____

3)   What did you like about working in science groups? (What worked well?)

     _____

     _____

4)   What was hard about working in science groups? (What didn't work well?)

     _____

     _____

5)   What advice do you have for other children working together in science groups?

     _____

     _____

6)   What advice do you have for your teacher? How can he or she help kids working

     together in groups?

     _____

     _____

Figure 10–2. *Science Group Project Reflection Form.*

on how to support children working together in groups. In addition, I took anecdotal notes, photographs, audiotape, and videotape throughout the process. Children kept detailed notes in their science journals and saved products they created throughout the unit. This included stories they wrote and published, artwork, reading logs, and math stories they created.

Assessment must support the learning process. An interdisciplinary approach to evaluation allows children to vocalize, interact, and build on their previous learning experiences as well as those of their classmates (Martinello and Cook 1994).

Doing What the Kids Do

As I read through my field journals over the past year, I saw a journey unfold and I saw the puzzle pieces dropping into place. Reflecting on my entries allowed me to look at where I've been and how far I've come in the process. I noticed several patterns. For example, in the fall semester my entries included lots of observations as I tried to make connections between the readings and theory in practice. This raised new questions as I explored ways to support children as readers, writers, mathematicians, and scientists in the classroom. I noticed patterns of kid watching and risk taking occur as I actively participated in the classrooms with the children. My confidence grew as I continued to learn, grow, and take risks.

The most exciting part of the year was during the late spring semester when the patterns of kid watching and risk taking reemerged much stronger as I made the shift to an active full-time participant and coexplorer in the classroom. During this time, I volunteered to do an expert project along with the children during our ocean study. (My cooperating teacher had done one during the previous unit of study.) I knew it was important to do what the kids do but I wasn't sure how I was going to balance taking anecdotal notes, teaching, and researching for my expert project. In addition, I decided to use Hyperstudio, a computer program that I had never used before, to present my project, so this was quite a challenge.

I spent many hours outside of the classroom learning Hyperstudio, making many mistakes and losing documents along the way. Finally, with the help of two able fifth graders and a book I purchased, we figured it out together. Then, I was so excited about my coral topic and about using Hyperstudio that I got carried away. I ended up with more than twenty display screens, or cards, in my presentation, including original artwork, pictures from the Internet, a voice recording, and buttons linking to other screens for additional information.

It was when I developed my own expert project and was evaluated by the children that I realized I had truly become a member of that classroom community. In the class evaluation sheet created by the children, Lindsay evaluated me using functional spelling. She wrote in a way that made sense to her. In caring supportive classroom communities, the teachers do what the kids do and that involves taking risks. That's tough, but the children were very supportive of me. They were excited that I was going to share and they were interested in hearing about what I had learned. Don Holdaway (1979) and Brian Cambourne (1988) both talk about the importance of demonstrations in the classroom. I believe it is important for the children to see us as readers, writers, and coexplorers in the learning process.

Making Connections

The lack of care is one of the biggest problems in our society today (Noddings 1992). Children need care and encouragement to learn. Children also need to care for others and for their world. Bronfenbrenner (1979) emphasizes the importance of social interconnections between the child, the school, and other settings in society. Everyone wants to belong and every child deserves to belong to a supportive classroom community. Educators need to encourage connections between our classrooms and children's families, communities, and the environment. One way I tried to do this in the classroom was by involving parents as much as possible. I sent home letters each week explaining what we had been working on in the classroom and providing an opportunity for the parent to work with the child on a homework project, something I learned from one of my cooperating teachers. In addition, I encouraged parents to come in during writer's workshop several days a week during my full-time teaching. The parents shared strategies they noticed children using during workshop and actively supported the children in their writing and exploration.

Another way I encouraged connections outside of the classroom was through use of the computer as a tool to communicate and aid research. During our space inquiry unit in second grade, I forwarded some of the children's questions to an astronomer at Midlands Tech. He was so excited to work with the children that he sent replies to some of the questions and continued to communicate with us outside of class via e-mail. Since the Center was not online yet, (it is now) I printed e-mail messages at home and brought them in for the class. As a result, I received e-mail from a child in class who noticed my e-mail address at the top of the handout I had given out.

Over the past year, I frequently used the Internet to reserve books at the library, communicate with subject matter experts, and research topics for class. I researched ways to integrate technology into the curriculum and realized that it will be an ongoing process. As a professional educator, it will be essential for me to use the tools available to me, share my knowledge with others, and stay informed about new developments. At this point computers are the newest tools available to learners—both teachers and students—in the classroom. Of course, this will change as new products are developed. That's what lifelong learning is all about!

There are so many possibilities for teachers to use technology to support learning in the classroom. The Internet can serve as a vehicle for student inquiry. Interactive programming such as The Nine Planets can be used to support astronomy study. Students can enhance their communication skills by participating in Web-based projects and explorations such as Mayaquest. Students can publish their work online through Web pages, online magazines, and other sites. In the future I hope to see children in the classroom using the Internet to talk to children in other countries and consider viewpoints, cultures, and ways of living other than their own.

The Big Picture

Inquiry is a thread that has run throughout my experience in this program. I've learned so much over the past year by following my questions. I've learned there are no formulas for an inquiry-based classroom. Each year brings new students and each teacher brings personal beliefs, talents, and experiences into the classroom. The curriculum in an inquiry-centered classroom is constantly evolving and changing as the learners change and grow.

It takes time to build classroom structures and rituals and to create classroom community. But the time is well worth the effort in establishing an open, nurturing learning environment for the children, one where miscues are seen as an important part of the learning process. Children feel safe talking, learning, and taking risks in an open classroom community. And when choices are offered, they eagerly take charge of their learning process.

Teachers have many roles in the classroom. One of the teacher's most important roles is that of supportive coach, encouraging and celebrating the child's learning process. This involves helping children develop as readers, writers, mathematicians, scientists, and so on by valuing their work and acknowledging and sharing their strategies. Good teachers notice what children are good at and help them build on what they know. Good teachers encourage children to explore information from different perspectives using different sign systems to deepen understanding.

We are all learners. Teachers are coexplorers, actively involved in their own learning and discovery as well as that of the children. Teachers and children have stories to tell. All of our voices are important in the classroom.

Like the person who spreads the puzzle pieces on the table, I looked at or reflected upon the information and experiences I brought with me to this internship as well as what I learned from my classes and from the children. As I reflected, I tried to put together the pieces that appeared to match, but I couldn't always envision the final product in my mind. Perhaps that is because learning is a process that has no end. The important part of putting this puzzle together is the process and the certainty that the pieces will continue to shift and move throughout my career as a professional educator. In order to continue to learn and grow, I need to be flexible and open to change and new inquiries.

As I contemplate beginning my first year in my own classroom, new questions come to mind. I wonder how I will build and maintain community in my own classroom over time. I have lots of good examples to learn from at the Center, but I need to find what will work best for me and the children. I am also interested in looking more closely at the types of talk—conversation, dialogue, and so on—in the classroom. My head is full of the wonder about the past year and I am eager to learn and grow along with the children as we begin the process anew in the classroom.

Epilogue: The Friendship Circle

As I closed my chapter, I wondered how I would build and maintain community in my own classroom, and that's where my thoughts were at the beginning of the school year. As I sat in the middle of my empty classroom in September and contemplated the year ahead, I remembered what Tim had once said to me: "It doesn't matter what kind of teacher you are—inquiry, traditional, or whatever—if you don't care about those kids."

Tim inspired me through his words and actions to share my life with the children, to let them get to know me as I got to know them. I learned about community in the classrooms at the Center and I knew for my children to be successful risk takers, I needed and wanted that feeling of community, of having a family in my own classroom. During the first few weeks, I planned experiences and opportunities for us to get to know one another by sharing family pictures and stories. We sat in our Friendship Circle and I listened as children shared their stories and listened to one another. We put our pictures on display in the classroom and soon it began to feel more like our own place. We took time each day to talk about good things that had happened that day and things we wanted to work on. For example, we discovered that we needed a special time on Mondays for everyone to share news from the weekend. We called this Headline News, adapted from Bobbi Fisher's book *Joyful Learning* (1991).

Over time, we developed classroom rituals. I didn't always know they were rituals until a child would say, "Mrs. Novack, you forgot to . . . ," and then I knew! Our morning message became a favorite ritual after the children took it over. I write a message to the children each day, as many teachers do. Each morning, we read the message together and talk about what we noticed—letters, words, patterns, and so forth. I also use the message to communicate which learning centers are open during the morning and/or to ask the children to complete certain tasks. One morning, Tyler asked me if he could write the morning message. I said, "Sure!" Tyler was thrilled. He quickly wrote,

"GD MNG BoYS ND GrLs P.S. SNTS R oPN." When Tyler got up to read his message in front of the class, he had our undivided attention. Tyler pointed to the words and read, "Good morning, boys and girls. P.S. Centers are open!" Everybody clapped and Tyler beamed. Tyler had opened all of the centers and in the process demonstrated the power of writing for real purposes! We talked about what we noticed in Tyler's message just as we had done with my own. Each morning children tried to be the first one to school so that they could write the morning message. We met and decided as a group to use a signup sheet so that everyone would have a turn.

When we sat in our Friendship Circle and discussed the death of a classmate's grandfather, I remembered sitting in the Friendship Circle in Michele Shamlin's kindergarten room, and I knew we were in good company. I feel I am sitting in a circle of friends that reaches far beyond the confines of the classroom, a circle that stretches out to include my colleagues, friends, and the children at the Center.

"What would you like to do for our friend Grace?" I asked the children.

"We could write a letter," one child suggested.

"And we could make it a heart and we could all sign it," another child suggested.

"Mrs. Novack, we could make one of those paper chains, but make it like a circle, like a friendship chain," Shakayla suggested. Everyone quickly agreed. Many of the children put their arms around one another's shoulders and swayed from side to side. "This is it!" I thought. "Classroom community." I wanted to freeze that moment in time. And that's about how long it lasted. A few seconds later, giggles broke out as one child leaned back too far and we all went sprawling on the carpet. But, that's what it's all about—community comes from the heart.

Scientists at Work

As it was at the Center, kid watching has continued to be an important part of what I do in the classroom. When we care about people, we listen to them, and kid watching helps me get to know the children better. "Hmm, how did you figure that out?" and "Tell me more about that" have become familiar comments to the children. They know that there are many ways to solve problems because they listen to their classmates share their strategies.

Early in the school year, Hollis chose the categories for the attendance count as we began our Morning Business. "If you have on brown shoes, stand up," he said. "One, two," he counted. "Okay, if you have on black shoes, stand up," he continued and counted five children. I wrote the numbers on the board as he continued. "If you have on white shoes, stand up," he said and grinned. "You know what? I think it's going to be seventeen," he said, still grinning. "How do you know that?" I ask with a smile. "Well, because yesterday we had seventeen and we have seventeen kids without the teachers, so I think it's going to be seventeen," he explained. "Sounds like a good theory," I added. "Let's test it out." Hollis counted the remaining children and added the categories using the number line. "See, I told you," he said. "Seventeen!" We all clapped. Often these lessons the children teach are the strongest.

By trusting the children, I've learned to lead from behind. I listen to their questions and interests and plan and adjust my lessons to meet their needs. For example, an accidental discovery in the classroom led to a rich study of earthworms. We were in the middle of examining different kinds of soil when a group of children discovered an earthworm. Cries of "Mrs. Novack, Mrs. Novack, come and look! What is it? What is it? It's a worm!" rose from a table where a group of children were working.

For about two weeks, our housekeeping area was vacant because our scientists were at work observing earthworms. "I want to draw a picture of it so I can recognize it next time," said Grace as she demonstrated why scientists record their ideas. During our earthworm inquiry we observed earthworms, recorded our observations with drawings, and shared our ideas like scientists do.

Inquiry as a Way of Life

Now, I am a teacher who realizes that while it is magical, it is not magic that occurs in successful classrooms, but thoughtful planning based on effective kid watching. My experiences at the Center helped me make the connection between the texts I was reading and projects I was completing because I lived these lessons in the classroom with the children. I learned about the heart of good teaching and the importance of building community in the classroom by living in a supportive learning community. The experience at the Center has changed me. It has reminded me of who I am. And it has taught me about possibilities, what I can be, and what children can become.

"Look! His ears look like mine!" Tyler says as he lifts a floppy ear.

"He has smooth stuff on his feet," Kashaad adds.

"I think it's to protect his feet or something," Alisa theorizes.

We are observing Tip, my brother's twelve-week-old beagle. Our inquiry into earthworms has led to a broader study of animals and we are forming questions and exploring different types of animals as we begin our study. I wonder about introducing expert projects. Does anyone know where I can borrow a snake? I guess some things never change, and I'm glad because there is so much to discover and learn!

References

Avery, C. 1993. *And with a Light Touch: Learning About Reading, Writing, and Teaching with First Graders.* Portsmouth, NH: Heinemann.

Bronfenbrenner, U. 1979. *Ecology of Human Development: Experiments by Nature and Design.* Cambridge, MA: Harvard University Press.

Cambourne, B. 1988. *The Whole Story: Natural Learning and Acquisition of Literacy in the Classroom.* New York: Ashton Scholastic.

Fisher, B. 1991. *Joyful Learning: A Whole Language Kindergarten.* Portsmouth, NH: Heinemann.

Gardner, H. 1983. *Frames of Mind.* New York: Basic Books.

Glasser, H. 1986. *Control Theory in the Classroom.* New York: Harper & Row.

Goodman, K. 1996. *On Reading.* Portsmouth, NH: Heinemann.

Harste, J. C., V. A. Woodward, and C. L. Burke. 1984. *Language Stories and Literacy Lessons.* Portsmouth, NH: Heinemann.

Hindley, J. 1996. *In the Company of Children.* York, ME: Stenhouse.

Holdaway, D. 1979. *The Foundations of Literacy.* Portsmouth, NH: Heinemann.

Martinello, M. L., and G. E. Cook. 1994. *Interdisciplinary Inquiry in Teaching and Learning.* New York: MacMillan College Publishing Co.

Noddings, N. 1992. *The Challenge to Care in Schools: An Alternate Approach to Education.* New York: Teacher's College Press.

Peterson, R. 1992. *Life in a Crowded Place: Making a Learning Community.* Portsmouth, NH: Heinemann.

Short, K. G., J. C. Harste, and C. L. Burke. 1996. *Creating Classrooms for Authors and Inquirers.* Portsmouth, NH: Heinemann.

Vygotsky, L. 1978. *Mind in Society.* Cambridge, MA: Harvard University Press.

11

Visual Arts as Inquiry in Elementary Education

CYNTHIA COLBERT

My questions for my own inquiry-based learning began to form following the meeting where I accepted the challenge to return to the elementary classroom after nineteen years in higher education. My questions were numerous, but several of the more global questions stayed with me and made it into a journal I began keeping prior to my work at the Center. They are:

- How does art instruction fit into an inquiry-based school setting? Will my desire to teach art in units that are interdisciplinary in nature be well received?

- Can I still do it? After nineteen years of teaching in higher education with only short, research teaching stints in art classrooms, can I still handle a classroom full of children and effectively teach art?

- Will I be accepted as the art teacher? Will the children accept me as their teacher? Will the faculty accept me as a teacher and not as a dilettante professor who is dabbling in teaching?

- Will the work be meaningful? Can I make art instruction meaningful for the children enrolled in my classes? Will this experience be personally meaningful to me?

- How will teaching children impact my graduate and undergraduate teaching at the university? How will my teaching impact my own research program?

- How different will the children be when compared with those I taught almost twenty years ago?

Art as a Vehicle for Inquiry

When teaching the visual arts, most art educators consider mainly the cognitive domains that may trigger multiple forms of learning in their students. Art students are generally engaged in long-term, open-ended units of study that integrate the production of art with inquiry into cultural heritage, aesthetics, and criticism. What art teachers also know deep in their bones, possibly from their memories of being the class artist when they were in elementary school, is that the affective domain is also very important. I find that my students need to feel capable, welcome, and respected to perform well in the visual arts. For some students, the affective part of art learning comes easy. These students are confident and capable and see art class as an adventure. For others, learning to believe in their own capabilities is more difficult. In teaching at the Center for Inquiry I have found that a few students are needy in the affective area. I try to engage these students in some activity that allows them public success within the first five to seven minutes of class each day. For one student, in particular, I find that a smooth transition into the art room with the successful answer to a question or comment about a work of art makes a marked difference in the productivity of the fifty minutes he spends with me.

In each unit of study in the visual arts we look at works of art and discuss specific qualities that are related to our lesson. With each instructional unit, students are exposed to one or more artists. Usually we use large art reproductions to accomplish this part of the lesson, but sometimes we use small, colored or black-and-white photocopies that put the work in the hands of students. Sometimes the focus of discussing the work is based on the formal qualities of the reproductions. Sometimes students focus on the content, the themes, or the styles of the work. Students often compare and contrast the works of different artists. In the discussions of the works of art, students use their perceptual skills to describe, analyze, interpret, and judge works. Students also use their verbal skills to convey their perceptions and often to argue a point with another student.

In the creating part of the lesson, our dialogue about the nature of the problem and the many possible solutions to it continues as students begin to work. Students have been told and shown repeatedly that there is no single solution to art problems and that diverse, individual, and creative ways of solving problems are best. Involved in the hands-on part of the unit of study, students travel in diverse directions, feeling free to take risks. Some students prefer to work in materials and with processes where they have control, while others like to experience new ways of using materials and techniques. Trying to help students gain mastery of a material or technique is in constant conflict with wanting students to try new and innovative solutions and ways of working. This is a constant dance for me as the art teacher. It is difficult to know when to nudge a student who is stuck in a rut, as it is very difficult to distinguish when a student is working in the groove and when he or she is stuck in a rut.

During art instruction we try to think like artists, do what artists do, and see the world through the artist's lens. Students learn how hard artists work and that very little of what they do is easy. Sometimes we play roles in art class. I become the art director, rather than the art teacher. My students become designers and illustrators who must submit their work to me for what I call "negotiated criticism," or criticism that is negotiated between the teacher and student, with each having an equal voice.

Students' inquiry into art is in part prescribed by my curriculum beliefs that we need to touch on ideas, concepts, forms, media, and processes that are important to the discipline of art. These are generally set up as open-ended problems to be solved. Students' inquiry into the visual arts is also dependent on the risks they are willing to take, the amount of work they are willing to do, and how far they are able to submerge themselves in their work. Individual students are simultaneously predictable and surprising in their solutions to problems. Some try to take the easy route, creating solutions that are often elegant in their simplicity, but not simple to accomplish. Others immerse themselves in materials, barely coming up for air and often going far afield from the original problem. Some children have characteristics in their work that I can see in almost each piece they create during the year. Others jump around, using different ways of working, as if trying on a new persona in every unit.

Our units of study make interdisciplinary connections with themes used by the classroom teachers. Oftentimes I follow a teacher's unit on a nature theme by using the specific species studied as subject matter for a unit I want to teach on space and depth. There is a continual exchange of ideas between the classroom teachers and me concerning upcoming themes and special events. Collaboration on interdisciplinary instruction has, I believe, made the visual arts more important and more connected to the children's interests and skills. When students create expert projects in the classroom, we often follow up with an art unit using the same theme. Seeing the enthusiasm of children who are putting to use the information they already have and seeing it translated into an art form tells me this is the way art should be taught.

In viewing the accomplishments of my students, I find the work of Gallas (1994, 1998) and Hubbard (1989) supportive of my views. I see children as individuals, whose work is kept in portfolios and whose progress is compared to their own prior work, not the work of classmates. The solutions to problems in the visual arts may require writing, sketching ideas, drawing and writing plans, collaborating, discussing, and defending work in verbal and written form. I see students who are strong writers, drawers, painters, and sculptors. One student who is a strong writer consistently writes two to three times as much as his classmates on any written assignment I give. I appreciate his careful thinking and writing and respect him for these efforts. I make him aware that I recognize his strengths as a writer and tell him that I am also a writer of books and articles, as well as someone who creates art. There are others who are very excited by one unit of study and seemingly left uninspired by others. One child, whose progress I have charted for the past four years, seems to alternate from being totally involved and committed to his work, to showing only surface involvement, to returning to total involvement. It is as if he is exhausted and can't summon up the energy for the unit that follows one to which he has completely committed himself. Another student created work that reminded me of Chagall's paintings. I found a book at her reading level on Chagall's life with some good color illustrations of his work and offered it to her. I told her that her work reminded me of Chagall's and that I thought she might be interested in reading about him and seeing some of his paintings. She was so pleased that I had connected her fifth-grade work to the work of an accomplished artist. She took the book and brought it back to me the following week, eager to discuss her ideas about Chagall's life and the hardships he faced just to be allowed to make art.

My History at the Center

I spoke with my graduate research assistant, whose job had been to collect materials from journals in the library for me. I asked if she would be my partner, assisting in teaching art at the Center. She agreed that it would be a good experience for her, so she joined me. Soon, another graduate student asked if he could work with us. So, the Center had three art teachers. I still planned the lessons and the graduate students assisted in one-to-one and small-group instruction.

I taught in front of my two students with just my plan for instruction. There was no script, no net to catch me if I fell. I felt that I was in part teaching and in part doing performance art. In the beginning, I was very conscious of the presence of my two students. I was careful not to violate any of the standards or practices I had taught my students in class. Sometimes having them in the room made me nervous and made me behave unnaturally. At some point before the end of October, I had become comfortable with having my students as spectators. We talked a lot after the classes ended, hitting the highs and lows of the day and considering how we could have done things differently to improve the students' experiences. We agreed that the schedule was just too tough, so in early November, I requested a schedule with more time between classes.

Our principal at the Center was an assistant professor from the College of Education, one of the two professors who wrote the proposal for the school. My students and I found her to be a wonderful and warm person who encouraged us in numerous ways. Best of all, she understood us. She could enter the art classroom, look at our students' work, and understand the layers of concepts and skills that went into the work. She appreciated the interdisciplinary instruction and loved the writing our students did with their artwork. We were pleased that she "got it." She was the first person at the Center who offered us praise. Praise is especially important for people who are not being paid for their work.

My students and I became a team. We had bonded. I could give a certain look to one of them, and he or she was able to "read me." We began to try more innovative lessons. Our administrator found some money for better materials. We were gaining a lot of support from the classroom teachers and the administration. The teaching was beginning to go more smoothly. I offered the fifth-grade class to my graduate students. They could plan the lessons and teach; I would assist. They did well and we worked together well. During the spring semester, my research assistant had an opportunity to take a long-term substitute job in an elementary art classroom. My volunteer assistant became my paid assistant. Several other art education students came to see the school we talked so much about. They helped and taught classes along with us.

In our second year, Richland School District Two funded an art education graduate student to assist in all aspects of instruction. I nominated several candidates and they interviewed with our principal for the position, just as any teacher would. A woman who was approximately my age was chosen for the position. We worked well together from the beginning. Because of her presence, I taught three classes on Mondays and three teams of two graduate students taught one class each on Wednesdays. My assistant was present on Mondays, assisting me in teaching; on Wednesdays to teach one class and assist graduate students teaching two classes; and on Fridays to offer special help and catch-up sessions for students who were absent or lagged behind for other reasons.

Our parent group gave us one hundred dollars to assist in purchasing supplies. We bought clay, good papers, and printing inks. Our school and parents shared the cost of purchasing portfolios so that we were able to keep the year's production intact for every child. We were asked to speak at Curriculum Night to explain the new portfolio practice and received wonderful feedback from the parents and children who attended. At the end of our presentation, we asked if there were questions and a kindergarten student raised his hand. We encouraged him to speak and he said, "I love you." We took that to mean he loved art class as well as each of us. I will always remember that moment. I don't get responses like those in higher education.

In addition to my assistant, we had another art education student on campus on Tuesdays and Thursdays. She served as our artist in residence. This was a wonderful added dimension for art instruction. She began and completed several of her rich, layered, oil stick drawings while working at the Center. The work in progress was displayed in the art room. Children were fascinated with how hard she worked, how much time it took to create a work, and how good her work was. On nice days, she often worked outside. Children passed her on their way to lunch or recess and admired her work and questioned her. She also visited classes to talk about the artist's point of view and assisted in finding direction for visual arts portions of the expert projects children did in class.

The children were noticeably more comfortable with the school and with the art program by the second year. We were able to do so much more because we knew what they had been taught the prior year, so we were able to revisit some skills and concepts and take off from there. The extra resources we were given were a boon to our program. What a difference from the first year when we were borrowing and begging supplies. In our second year we were not lavishly supplied with materials, but we had the basics and could do more than before. We began to push the envelope a bit and plan more complex, more involved units of study. Our students, administrator, and classroom teachers responded well.

One problem I found still vexing was that there was no place at our school where students could see their work displayed. The hallways found in school buildings did not exist for our cluster of portable classrooms. Charming as our school was, I longed for a place where work could be displayed and admired by all. I felt that was an important element lacking in our program. The principal for the adjacent middle school, where our children eat lunch, agreed to give us one bulletin board in the cafeteria and a portion of a wall that our children passed on their way to lunch. I appreciated his understanding and his offer. We began to display small numbers of works in these two spaces and were happy to have them. Still, it did not seem like enough display time when we compared what our students were getting to what students in schools with hallways had.

My graduate assistant wanted to offer our children the experience of having an art museum similar to those held by the schools our children attended in another district. We approached our principal, who was ever-supportive of this plan. She approached the parent organization for funding and found a rental tent with side flaps and clear plastic windows on the sides to let in light. We rented it. The parent volunteers were wonderful in delivering the tent to the school and pitching it. The district loaned us the plywood flats used to display work at our Youth Art Month Exhibit and elsewhere. We spent several days mounting work and making sure that every child had two pieces to show in the museum. We encouraged the younger children to review their portfolios and place sticky notes ranking their work. We tried to include what they chose. In some classes, we displayed everyone's work from a particular lesson. We displayed all of the Prismacolor pencil illustrations of an African folktale for fifth-grade students, all papier-mâché puppets from the first grade, and all clay seated figure sculptures and drawings of those sculptures by kindergarten students. All of the art education graduate students contributed to the mounting and selection of work from their classes and with the hanging of the exhibit. The experience was positive for us and very useful for the art graduate students, who will do this three to four times each year as art teachers.

Many families came to our museum opening, as did several school board members, art teachers from other schools, and faculty from the university. Even with temperatures in the high nineties, and much hotter inside our tent, we hosted a good crowd. We used the museum as a teaching tool, taking each class through the display during its designated art period, and celebrating the students' accomplishments. We distributed postcards to students and instructed them to use their art criticism skills to write to a child in another class about a specific piece of work, giving specific comments about the work. We delivered the postcards to various classes and wrote many cards ourselves, trying to make certain that every child received a note.

In our third year, I began the semester with a new assistant. My former assistant still works at the school two mornings each week and is in charge of our fund-raising activity. With our parent group and administration's approval, we are doing an art fund-raiser that incorporates children's artwork that is printed onto mouse pads, sweatshirts, mugs, key chains, and writing paper. Each child's work can be printed on as many items as the family wants to purchase. The art program will have use of the money raised to purchase materials.

My new assistant was a good choice. He has a natural way with the children and is getting to know them quickly and with ease. He has taught several classes and encountered few problems. He is an enthusiastic participant in our visual arts programs at the school and has taken time to observe several of the classroom teachers at work. Since I am now more comfortable in working in front of my students, he benefits from what came before. He has stayed for a second year and will leave to do his student teaching at the end of this semester.

In the following sections, I address the questions I posed at the beginning of this chapter.

Can I still do it?   I have to answer yes, I can still teach children about the visual arts. I look forward to my work with the children and I think about our plans for class all during the week. Although I can still teach, I need to say that

I would not do it nearly as well if I did not have the expert help from my graduate students. Having three adults in a class of kindergarten students allows us to do much more painting, work with clay, and other material-driven lessons with greater ease than with just one teacher.

When I taught six classes a day during our first year, I went home and took a nap on the couch on Monday afternoons. My family and I went out to dinner consistently each Monday, as I was too tired to cook. I called several of my elementary art teacher friends and told them just how difficult I thought teaching art all day was. I do not recall feeling as tired when I taught twenty years ago. Work at the university is mentally intense, but not nearly as physically demanding as teaching art in an elementary school all day. When I came home tired from teaching, I felt that I had done an honest day's work. I also found that I slept very well on the evenings after teaching children.

We have been interviewing children to find out how they feel about what we do in art class and how they feel about the skills they are developing in art. Our children have told us they look forward to art and are comfortable there. They are very specific about what they have done in the past year that they enjoyed and what they hope to do during this academic year. Students are engaging in self-assessment of the work in their portfolios, ranking their work and writing assessments at the end of many lessons. I find myself writing responses to many of the comments made by children who are so honest and are putting their feelings on the line.

We consistently get outstanding artwork from every age group. I am sure that every art teacher feels this way about his or her students, but I get very excited about the successes of our students. I love to look at the work from an entire class and savor the individual qualities in them while I search for attributes that come from my objectives. I never tire of teaching the kindergarten children. They are so wonderfully naïve, and their work is expressive and bold. I am enjoying seeing the growth of last year's kindergarten group now that they are first graders. I have taught students in our fourth-grade class since they were in second grade. This group and I have a history. We understand each other and can get more done because of this.

Will I be accepted as the art teacher? The children were quick to accept me as the art teacher and they were also generous in accepting my assistants as coteachers. The children came from different elementary schools within the district. When questioned about the art teachers they had worked with prior to coming to the Center for Inquiry, the children seemed happy or relieved to know that I knew their former teachers. I also had a good idea of what experiences they brought with them to the class.

In the second year, we took several new students in each grade level (in addition to our new class of kindergarten students) and my students and I worked hard to make them feel comfortable. Since the returning students and I had a shared experience, I wanted our new students to feel welcome and accepted in art. One of our most interesting students was a young man who had been schooled at home prior to his third-grade year. When he joined us, he was very quiet and careful to follow instructions in art class. He wrote numerous notes to my assistant and me, telling us how much he liked art or liked a particular thing we did in art that day. He always ended his note by telling us that he hoped we would come back next week to teach art again. He seemed to think that we might not. We received many notes and drawings from children affirming our place in their hearts and in their school week. Parents, too, told us that their children never wanted to miss school on art days, that they anticipated art class with high expectations.

I suspect that I was more worried about being accepted by my teaching colleagues than by the children. My first impression of several of the teachers was that they did not place much value on art instruction, nor were they particularly interested in having it. Of course, that challenge made me want to show them the importance of art. I was also concerned that teachers might see me, the university professor, as a dilettante. During the first year, several teachers stayed with their students during art class and tried to create work along with them. We enjoyed having them, as it showed they were interested and that they cared. Since art instruction is one of the few breaks the teachers get each week, they usually needed to use that time to do other things. We found that most teachers were like-minded and did come to appreciate the way art was taught.

We made every effort to offer interdisciplinary connections to what was being taught in the classroom. Teachers gave us lists of the major units they planned to teach and we planned our instruction to connect with their themes without diminishing the content of the art instruction. The opportunity to teach art in an interdisciplinary setting is one of the things that attracted me most about the teaching experience at the Center. I had spent the past two years working on an interdisciplinary elementary art program, so I was excited about the possibilities of teaching my lessons with these students. What I found, however, is that I enjoy inventing new lessons far more than teaching what I've already developed. Now that I have taught many of the lessons in the new program, I want to push the envelope further.

The classroom teachers were pleased to see the connections we made in art class to the units they taught. Several of them noticed the individual qualities of the students' work, done with the same materials, with the same instruction, and with the same theme. Several of the teachers wanted to know more about how we taught to get such individual results. We appreciated their notice of that aspect of our instruction. One of our main goals is to champion the work of the individual, to encourage individual style and use of materials.

We are very flexible and open to individual interpretations of our lessons, encouraging children to find their own way. We find that under these circumstances, children produce very creative and unique work. Our program does not endorse the make-and-take mentality of many other elementary art programs. We rarely spend as little as two class periods on any lesson. Our lessons are designed around concepts and skills that build as the children master them. Our classroom teachers recognized that we were perhaps different in our approach to teaching art in some of the same ways they were different from many of the teachers in their former schools. I suspect they found that we were philosophically very much alike.

Faculty at the Center for Inquiry enjoy reading professional materials together and discussing them during scheduled meetings. For one such meeting, I was invited to choose two articles on visual arts education. I suspected that one colleague who used a coloring sheet approach to some class projects could be offended by information contained in an article on interdisciplinary approaches to teaching art (Colbert 1997). I did not expect the reaction I received to my work. The teacher said aloud that if my article was correct, then what she did in the classroom was wrong. We discussed the issues professionally. I suggested that she give herself permission to try more open-ended ways of working to see if her children could handle it. What resulted were some increasingly creative approaches to classroom projects that were more open-ended than before. I was careful to observe the production from her class and praise her whenever the work allowed children to be individuals.

Will the work be meaningful?   After reading this far, you must know that my work in teaching children at the Center is meaningful to me. After talking with my art education graduate students who contribute their work to the school, I can attest that it is meaningful to them. I am pleased to have new, fresh stories about teaching art to tell in my university classes. I have to be careful that I don't say too much, as those who have not been to the Center feel left out. Many students, both graduate and undergraduate, come to the Center for Inquiry just to see what I have talked so much about. I learn something new each day I teach. Often I relearn things I already knew but did not pay attention to in my practice. This year I have two grants related to my work at the school. With one, I purchased release time from the university to do a yearlong study of what and how the children learn in art and how they feel about what they learn. We have been in the process of interviewing children for several weeks, asking them to reflect on last year's art class and to offer suggestions for this year.

Our children have shared with me some very interesting insights about our art program. When asked if they had stomachaches, fear, or anxiety about coming to art class, no child has answered "yes." Several have told us of times when they did feel scared or had stomachaches in relation to other activities. Students say they look forward to art class and love to create. Several have shown preference for specific materials and activities over others, and several have shown preference for a particular teaching style. One boy told me that he "loved it when I read myths from other countries and they got to illustrate or write their own." Two other children said that they "didn't like it when I read to them, as it made it too much like their other classes." So far, no child has told me that looking at and talking about works of art is her or his favorite part of each lesson, but it is a part of every lesson. No child has complained about looking at and talking about art.

Through my interviews and my observations of children who are fully engaged in the work they do in art class, I have come to believe that art instruction is meaningful for them. There are several students in the upper grades who have excellent abilities but for whom focusing on the work for long periods is a problem. We also have several students who are detrimental to those by whom they are seated. We try to solve this by reassigning seating for those who create problems for others or seating them in isolation. One child who is seated in isolation often told me that he realized he gets more work done when he sits alone.

I want art to be a positive, important part of every child's week. Going back to Lowenfeld's work in 1947, I want to see emotional, intellectual, physical, perceptual, social, aesthetic, and creative growth occurring in art class. That is why it is difficult to isolate students; I want to see them learn to work within the social framework of the art class, cooperating and sharing with others.

How will teaching children impact my undergraduate and graduate teaching at the university? First, and most importantly, teaching children in a school setting while teaching preservice teachers keeps me honest. I am quicker to tell preservice teachers how very difficult it is to teach—something I may have forgotten—and not rely on twenty-year-old stories of my glory days as an art teacher. My reactions to what we read in class are more critical and honest than before. I am, perhaps, becoming far more practical in what I teach and less esoteric. In my graduate research class, I teach more about being a teacher-researcher, something I believe is more useful to my students than a heavy coverage of the history of research in art education. We get to the historical research as a way of supporting what students want to do for their own studies. This way, students are discovering those great historical studies from which they can develop research studies of their own.

I have become a better listener because of my work with young children. I listen to what is said and to what is omitted. For example, when a child recently said to me, "This work isn't really that good," I'd had to consider many possibilities before I replied. Was the child looking for a compliment, for me to differ with him? Was he seeking my criticism on how the work could be improved? Was he dismissing his responsibility in making the work by separating himself from the work, by saying the work wasn't good rather than saying he did not do well in making the work? In situations such at this, I try to ask a few questions so that I can discern what the child is really saying prior to having a conversation about the work. After working with children and developing a more sensitive ear to discern their needs, I have found that my undergraduate and graduate students use some of the same techniques to involve me in discussions about their ideas and their work. I was not as aware of some of the needs of my adult students until I reconnected with the elementary students.

In listening carefully to children as they talk with one another about their work and about the process of working, I have heard comments and stories that I will always remember and that I share with my university students to make certain points I am teaching come alive for them. At the completion of a papier mâché unit in which third graders made fantasy creatures, one child said, "I like this so much, I think I'm going to keep it and give it to my own children someday." Another child said to me, "Oh! Paint! I'm so happy when we use paint in art." Still another child in fourth grade said to me, "I like to draw, but I don't like to paint what I draw." From children's statements, I can learn what they enjoy and what dilemmas they are experiencing in art class. I might take the child's comment about preferring drawing to painting to my university class so we can debate the pros and cons of letting a child go in his own direction, allowing him to continue drawing, using values with graphite while his classmates work with values in paint. The combination of working with children while I work with those who will teach children makes what I do much richer.

I hope that if someone compared my teaching from six years ago with my teaching today she would notice that a windstorm of fresh air has blown through my pedagogy, changing my approach and making me more personal, honest, and accessible to students. Because I am spending two days a week this year at the Center for Inquiry, I have encountered some criticism from several university colleagues about the impact of my teaching art at the Center on my work at the university. I have colleagues who do not understand the connection between my teaching children and my teaching preservice teachers how to teach children. For them, teaching children is something I shouldn't be doing at my level.

My art education students do not seem to have a problem with my work off campus. I have a note written to students who are trying to meet with me, explaining my work assignment for this year and giving them several ways of reaching me. I use e-mail more in corresponding with students about ideas for papers, use an answering machine in my office to record messages, and return them promptly when numbers are left. During the next semester, I have scheduled my university classes on days when I do not teach at The Center for Inquiry. Perhaps my presence will be felt more within the department when I teach morning classes next semester.

How different will the children be when compared with those I taught almost twenty years ago? I find very few differences in the children I teach now and the children I taught years ago. I prefer the ethnic mix I have at the Center for Inquiry to the lack of mix I had when I taught twenty years ago. However, the elementary school in which I worked long ago was similar in many ways to the Center. We had just one class for each grade, so there was no grouping of students by ability levels. I began teaching art from a media cart and worked my way within a year to having a room of my own.

The children at the Center are perhaps quicker to speak out in class when questions are asked than the children from my early experiences. I suspect that is in part because of the way most classroom teachers work in our school. Children are encouraged to share insights and opinions. One of the rights of children at our school is the right to be heard. I like this difference. I enjoy a spirited discussion with many contributors. There is a sense of independence and a lack of dependence on the teachers to do things for them that I also appreciate. This may come from my own expectations of children based on my experiences as a parent in the intervening years, rather than from the children themselves. Perhaps in my early teaching, I babied the kindergarten children rather than requiring them to take care of their own needs.

Children at the Center respond well to the interdisciplinary connections we make in art instruction with subjects the classroom teacher is presenting simultaneously. Children's faces light up when they make the connection that we are using knowledge they have and putting it into a new form. They enjoy putting what they have learned into an art form. In my previous teaching, I did less connecting in my instruction with the classroom instruction. Yet, I recall one of my most meaningful units was designed to connect with the fifth-grade teacher's study of Colonial America.

I do not find the big differences in children today that I read about and hear about in the media. I have just one or two children with whom I have repeated behavior difficulties in art class. I expect I had more problems twenty years ago because I was a young, inexperienced teacher. I demand more respect now and I expect much more from the children. They seem to rise to the occasion.

I do see a difference in the attitudes teachers have about working mothers, and the availability of early and after-school care. I see these as positive. As a working mother, I often felt that my child was viewed by her teachers as being more needy in some ways than those of stay-at-home mothers. I recall wondering at the time if those teachers realized that homemakers were also working mothers. I do not sense that kind of prejudice in our school.

Postscript

The size of our school, with approximately 132 students, 6 teachers, and 13 university students working as student teachers or in other practica, allows us to know all of the children. Staff and teachers show a feeling of responsibility for everyone. My daughter went to two excellent elementary schools, both with about 1,200 students. When she has had inservice holidays on days when I teach at the Center for Inquiry, she has assisted me in the art room. Her impressions of our school are that it is "such a nice, small school, where people seem to really care for each other." I agree with her appraisal. It is a place where people—teachers and students—care for one another and work hard for one another. Our school is a place that encourages individuality and assertiveness in children. We are very child-centered, respecting the rights of children as a group and individually. I suspect that if my daughter had been a student at our school, where she would have been given "rights and responsibilities" instead of rules and where her individual gifts could have been better recognized and encouraged because she could have received more individualized attention, she might have developed her academic self-confidence much sooner. My one disappointment in working in such a wonderful school environment with caring faculty and staff is that my child did not get to experience this kind of schooling.

Author's note: My research assistants during the four-year period were Audra Holcombe, Richard Coatney, Candace Catoe, and Kevin Pettitt. Our artist in residence was Laura Meester. I would like to express sincere appreciation to the National Art Education Association's Foundation. This grant provided release time for my teaching and research activities at the Center.

References

Bruner, J. 1986. *Actual Minds, Possible Worlds.* Cambridge, MA: Harvard University Press.

Cadzen, C. 1988. *Classroom Discourse: The Language of Teaching and Learning.* Portsmouth, NH: Heinemann.

Colbert, C. 1997. "Visual Arts in the Developmentally Appropriate Integrated Curriculum." In *The Integrated Curriculum and Developmentally Appropriate Practice,* edited by C. H. Hart, D. C. Burts, and R. Charlesworth, Albany, NY: SUNY Press.

Gallas, K. 1994. *The Languages of Learning.* New York: Teachers College Press.

———. 1998. *Sometimes I Can Be Anything: Power, Gender, and Identity in the Primary Classroom.* New York: Teachers College Press.

Hubbard, R. 1989. *Authors of Pictures, Draughtsmen of Words.* Portsmouth, NH: Heinemann.

Lowenfeld, V. 1947. *Creative and Mental Growth.* New York: Macmillian.

12

Living the Model

AMY DONNELLY

What the best and wisest parent wants for his own child, that must the community want for all its children. Any other ideal for our schools is narrow and unlovely: acted upon, it destroys our democracy.

—DEWEY 1938

Those who wish to reap the blessings of liberty must undergo the fatigues of supporting it.

—THOMAS PAINE

You've come to understand our conception and you've visited our classrooms in the preceding pages. Let us turn toward the part of the story that examines our actions in light of how our shared philosophy of learning informed the creation of a culture rooted in inquiry, a culture in which I served as principal for three years. We brainstormed each structure described in the previous pages so that our individual voices were always visible within our community. From our children and their parents we have gained new perspectives and the Center faculty continues to build on what it learns. We soon felt at home in the ambiguities of the complex process of moving inquiry practices from the classroom level to the level of an entire school. We let our questions become the lanterns that pointed us toward the answers waiting to be illuminated. We were ready.

Ways of Living and Learning in a Community

At 7:30 A.M. children in Tim O'Keefe's third-grade classroom were already playing checkers, sharing books, playing chess, and working at the computer.

"Good morning, Hutton," I said.

"Hey, did you know that echolocation is how bats use sound waves not to bump into things and find their prey? Remember, I learned that about bats when I was in Miss Shamlin's first grade? Here's the way it works," he said, as he pointed to the diagram on the computer screen.

"Hutton, what do you guys call this time of day when everyone is coming into the class and finding something to do?" I asked. He looked puzzled.

"Well, we don't call it anything. It just like when you go home from school and tell your Mom the cool things you're thinking about and that's what we're doing."

Rituals such as this settling in in Tim's room are predictable time frames that help children make the transition from home to school in a caring way. They also nurture a mindset that says this classroom is a place where your interests and ideas become a part of what we accomplish here. Hutton was right. Rituals become second nature.

Ralph Peterson's book *Life in a Crowded Place* (1992) helped us look closely at the underpinnings and value of establishing rites and rituals both schoolwide and in our classrooms. Since we were a small community of six classrooms, we wanted a ritual that would connect us one to the other and communicate to each individual that he or she was part of a larger community. Morning Gathering now occurs on the first Monday of every school week with individual classes and their teachers taking responsibility for orchestrating it.

Music played softly that morning as everyone found a seat in our outdoor arena. Several parents who walked their children to their classrooms found seats around the periphery and joined us for the opening of our school week.

"Good morning, everyone!" Catlin said into the microphone, smiling.

"Everyone, please stand for the pledge," announced Mylan.

After the pledge, Susanne Pender, our second-grade teacher, took the microphone and asked if everyone had had good weekend.

"My father and I went fishing and I caught three bass!" came Brad's voice from the back.

"My aunt had a baby girl," said Jessica.

"Did you know that Kentucky, where my cousins live, is getting flooded?" asked Tori.

"It sounds like a lot happened this weekend and we'll all have to find Kentucky on our classroom maps and watch the newspapers to find out if the weather clears up. Are there any announcements?"

I reminded everyone that the teachers would have a business meeting after school and that Eric and Taylor's dad needed everyone's input for our Earth Week Extravaganza.

Robert announced, "Our thought for the week is 'Celebrate new beginnings.' Please bring your class examples of your new beginnings in math, reading, and everything to share at Learning Celebration Friday."

It was calming and energizing to hear the birds chirping as one of the students dismissed each class, row by row. The children responsibly led the way, and the faculty eagerly followed.

Sharing songs, announcements, the Pledge of Allegiance, celebrations of birthdays, special family events, whole-school events for the week, and the Thought for the Week helped us keep our focus on who we were: a group united in common purpose, learning and working together. Morning Gathering kept us all organized and aware of events in our classrooms and families, yet it did so organically, much like in family life.

Monday Morning Gathering spawned Friday afternoon Learning Celebration. This ritual draws closure to the week. Students and teacher share what they have learned and wish everyone a good weekend. The same class that organizes Morning Gathering organizes Learning Celebration. Often Learning Celebration includes a song and a demonstration of learning from that classroom as well as a participatory celebration of ways individuals and groups have enacted the Thought for the Week. The Learning Celebration ritual highlights exciting information and artifacts generated in classrooms during the week. It also serves as a way to separate from one another for the weekend with a feeling of joy and accomplishment.

Other community rituals include the use of playful language, such as "Ding," "Well, there you go," "Send the whammie." All these invented terms and phrases were coined to express a powerful emotion of the moment; because the phrases concisely express complex emotion, adults and children began repeating the language. In this way, personal codes became the shared codes of an intimate learning community. Those codes—our community fun language—however trite and meaningless they may appear to outsiders, are powerful ways of communicating within our school community.

Rituals often involve marking rites of passage (Peterson 1992). One rite the school performs is closing the school year with a solemn celebration that marks classes moving to the next grade level. Since classes sit together on the wooden benches in the outdoor arena for Morning Gathering, Learning Celebration, and other schoolwide events and are organized by grade with the kindergartners in the first row, the staff uses that arrangement to tangibly honor and celebrate their grade-level progression. For example, the first graders are asked to stand and recall significant events that occurred during their year together. Then they march in a line to the second-grade row and remain standing while the rest of the school applauds their accomplishments, welcoming them as second graders. And so the rite continues in the same manner for each grade level, leaving an empty row for our incoming kindergartners.

Another rite of passage is the Promotion Ceremony for the fifth-grade children. This ceremony is the most formal of the year and occurs during the last week of school. Children dress in their finest clothes and the outdoor arena is decorated simply yet elegantly with live plants. Children parade onto the outdoor stage to music they select, and one by one they state their names and the most important learning memories they will carry with them to middle school. After everyone is seated, the principal welcomes the parents, shares a few words of wisdom, and invites the fifth-grade teacher to share comments about each child. Certificates of promotion are awarded, and numerous photographs snapped. Most of the napkins at the ensuing reception are used to dawb adult tears.

A favorite rite of mine was hugging each and every child on the last day of school before he or she crossed the street to parents and caretakers who waited to transport the children home. These seemingly small acts created a personal and shared history that we hope will influence what these children will carry with them through life.

Responsibility in a Community

In a democratic learning community, discipline involves holding others responsible to exercise their right to participate. Of course the level of responsibility and the degree of participation vary with age level and curricular engagement or invitation. In a democratic community we don't talk about management or managing children because our instructional responsibility is to help children develop responsibility, not to regulate or control them. We believe that most children are capable of knowing how to behave and participate in any given context. Our responsibility is to create "autonomous citizens who can think for themselves in all kinds of situations" (Kamii 1985, 39). This is best accomplished by employing the power of demonstration and by designing numerous and varied opportunities for children to act autonomously. Many of the opportunities to create autonomy come into play during routine learning activities. Teaching discipline in a learning community is about looking for opportunities to encourage participation and foster responsibility, enabling neophytes to discover their capabilities and in doing so, develop autonomy.

Every routine at the Center for Inquiry is established with the thought of facilitating autonomous behavior in children. Children are put in charge of the learning community, while teachers act as guides. Morning Gathering and Learning Celebration are led by the children, as are morning announcements from the office. Children greet visitors and show them around the school while explaining learning at the Center. Older children earn the responsibility of keeping their peers safe by serving the community as a Safety Patrol.

The school district requires each school to have an established Discipline Plan. In a democratic way of life, individuals have rights and responsibilities. Just like the educators at the Manhattan New School (Harwayne 1999), we believed that it was our responsibility to provide experiences for children to learn the meaning of participating in a democracy. Consequently, we established the Center's Rights and Responsibilities. As part of the school behavior plan, parents are asked to talk with their child and complete an Individual Responsibility Contract that details the responsibility her or his child has in guaranteeing that student rights are maintained.

CENTER FOR INQUIRY RIGHTS AND RESPONSIBILITIES

I have the right to work and play in a safe and organized environment.

I have the right to be happy and to be treated with kindness and respect.

I have the right to learn new things.

I have the right to be myself and express my opinions.

I have the right to hear and be heard.

For example, having the right to be treated with kindness and respect means that each and every person, child and adult, must treat others kindly and respectfully. Parents are encouraged to help their children be as explicit as possible when describing their responsibilities. For example, to be heard, they must guarantee that they will demonstrate their responsibility through actions such as looking at the speaker and listening attentively. Respectful audience members also think about what the speaker is communicating and ask questions to demonstrate that they have heard and thought about what the speaker is saying.

As teachers, we believed in the most natural and immediate consequences possible. If a child chooses to hurt another child's feelings, then, in addition to being asked to verbalize the responsibility that was breached, he or she might be asked to find a way to perform an act of kindness for the child she or he hurt. If a pattern of problem behavior emerges, the child is often sent to the office to have a conversation with the principal. While children are rarely sent to the office, when children visit the principal for this purpose, they understand that this is a very serious consequence of their irresponsible choices. I chose to enact my role as judge with dramatic flair demonstrating my disappointment through facial expressions and eye contact. At the same time, I consistently treated each child with kindness and fairness. Most often their visits to the office include a quiet time for reflection. Next the child writes about the responsibility he or she did not uphold, what rights or privileges she or he feels should be lost as a result, and what steps the student will take to prevent this behavior from occurring again. Then the principal and the student use this writing as the basis of a discussion on the pattern of behavior that is emerging and reach a decision regarding the consequences.

A visit to the principal for inappropriate behavior is serious and warrants parent involvement. Depending on the nature of the behavior, several actions might be taken. Parents might be called in for a three-way conference that includes the child, or the child might be asked to telephone the parent while in the principal's office and participate in a conference call. Another option is sending home the Behavior Plan—the written reflection described previously —for the parent to sign. The important outcome of all these actions is that the child understands that the adults in his or her life

- hold him or her accountable for his or her decisions
- help her or him devise a plan to change that behavior
- support him or her in becoming responsible to make necessary changes

Coaching as Model of Community Responsibility

As a democratic community of learners, all learners, tall and small, hold themselves accountable to do their personal best. In order that we might provide a demonstration of the process of continually revising our thinking and behavior, we implemented coaching not only as a problem-solving model but also as a model to push us theoretically and instructionally.

At the Center, this model operates simultaneously on two levels: the teacher/instructional level and at the child/behavioral level. Both levels involve the processes of observing and recording information, reporting observations, conducting group discussion and analysis, and providing suggestions. Teachers visit one another's classes for any short period of time. The teacher takes notes while participating in the class activity at hand. Immediately after school, the faculty meet for a short fifteen-minute sharing session that includes a description of the teaching environment, the instructional episode, and engagements or invitations available for the children. The observer shares his thoughts in the form of three pluses and a wish, and the discussion is then open for general feedback (Mills and Clyde 1990). Feedback gives teachers and administrators yet another opportunity to examine their beliefs by reflecting on what they each pay attention to while observing. And these conversations link theory to practice, as they wonder aloud why something happened, discuss learners that they are concerned about, and share and validate their successes. While they make their pluses and wishes meaningful and thoughtful enough to push one another's thinking and practice, they always agree that they learned simply by seeing one another in action.

One day, quite by chance, a child accompanied his teacher to observe another teacher's room. The teacher invited the child to coach as well, only the child's task was to watch the children in the class and record his observations regarding their behavior and learning. During our coaching session that afternoon, the teacher enthusiastically shared the child's insights with us. We immediately saw potential in the spontaneous event as a way to create a venue that would encourage our children to learn from one another just as we were learning from one another. We decided to try having children coach children for the following reasons:

- Coaching would give children the practice they needed to become keen observers of their world.

- Coaching would help children reflect on and name what they know and are able to do in relation to others.

- Coaching would be a useful strategy to push behavior and content expectations by learning from another class.

The teachers and interns have continued to develop the children-coaching-children model. Recently, our fifth graders were playing soccer each recess. Each day for a period of several weeks, an argument broke out that disrupted the game. Since everyone had a different version of the disagreements, the USC intern, Brent Petersen, decided to videotape the recess activity. He then invited the class to watch the video and make observations. To everyone's surprise, it appeared that the majority of the arguments were related to boundary lines, and the class appointed a task force to research the dimensions of a soccer field. This information was put to good use, as the class designed a regulation soccer field on our playground.

In this way, we are all learners and take an active responsibility for our own growth. Coaching provided an open model to learn from one another, try out new ideas, get our colleagues' feedback, and outgrow ways of acting that didn't resonate with our beliefs.

Parents as Partners

We knew from the onset that we didn't want our students' parents to be reduced to the role of volunteers only. Forming a real partnership between parents and school would best serve the children's needs. We reasoned that parents must have a wealth of information about what they wanted for their children in the name of education as well as many great ideas about how to turn their needs into realities. Opening a school of choice opened the door for a totally new and different level of participation by parents. The very nature of choice implies that parents are making the decision to participate. And participate they have!

In August, before the school opened for the first year, we sent a general information letter to all parents regarding school hours, fees, transportation, and so on. In that letter, we invited them to attend a parent leadership session if they were interested in designing a model for parent participation at the Center. We were delighted that approximately eighty parents attended that meeting. The group was very quiet as I welcomed them and invited them to introduce themselves to other parents at their tables and explain why they were interested in having their children attend the Center for Inquiry. The conversation started in hushed tones but was soon very loud. I asked parents to share some of their reasons for enrolling their children at the Center for Inquiry. Their responses were varied:

- Some said they had received recommendations from teachers at other schools.
- Some said they liked the idea of a small learning community.
- Some said they wanted to be part of a school that was in a university partnership.
- Some said the classrooms they saw on the videotapes were fascinating and they wanted that kind of classroom for their children.

Heidi Mills and I brainstormed several areas of leadership needs in which parents' assistance would be helpful. Some of those areas included technology, landscaping, classroom support, content expertise, public relations, and social events. We asked parents to each choose an area that he or she was interested in and to brainstorm ideas together. Additionally, we asked that they record their names, addresses, and telephone numbers as well as recruit a chairperson that would agree to attend an initial meeting to create an advisory board of parents.

One woman's hand went up in the back and she asked, "Are you planning on having homeroom parents?" I smiled and said, "Of course we are. Anyone who wants to assist by being a homeroom parent, please join your new friend at the back table." Silently, I thought, "Oh my." In our quest to move beyond the notion of parent volunteer and construct curricular partners, it would be imperative to begin that endeavor with what the parents currently defined as 'working' in and with the school, and from that place, grow. We knew from studying the authoring cycle (Short, Harste, and Burke 1996) that learning is best supported by starting from the known. This would be no different for parents in our community.

The Parent Advisory Board Is Born

Under South Carolina statutes (1977 SC Education Finance Act, 1984 Education Improvement Act, and the Early Childhood Development and Academic Assistance Act of 1993), school boards in each district have the responsibility of establishing a School Improvement Council (SIC) at each school in its district (School Improvement Council Assistance 1989). The responsibilities of such a school improvement council include planning, implementing, and monitoring the school's efforts toward achieving its stated mission as well as the district and school goals. Two dilemmas were immediately visible: the Center for Inquiry's small size restricted the possibility of meeting the state's recommended membership, and our small size necessitated a serious fundraising initiative. Fund-raising is essential to the survival of contemporary schools and it is an area of responsibility typically held by parent-teacher organizations (PTOs). This dilemma was the first topic raised at the meeting of seven parents who originally volunteered to serve as chairpersons for their areas of interest several weeks before. The group reasoned that it seemed irrational to try to form two distinct groups, given that we were so small. Our entire group of parents and teachers could form a body called the Parent-Teacher Partnership. It seemed to make sense to start with that organizational structure.

In May of that same year, the Parent Advisory Board requested that I contact our district office to seek its assistance in developing a strategic plan to lead us into the next five years. The following is a newsletter that explained the development and outcomes of the strategic planning process to the entire Center community

Strategic Planning Newsletter

What Is a Strategic Plan?

Every teacher, the elected Parent Advisory Board, as well as parent representatives from each grade level, participated in the two-day process led by two district representatives. It was through this process that our mission statement was developed.

Every school in South Carolina, as a result of the school improvement act of N 135, is required to create a strategic plan and review it annually. A strategic plan differs from the standard long-range plan in that it is constantly updated and revised. It is a living document designed to re-create and renew an institution.

A strategic plan consists of a mission statement, goals that support the mission, strategies for reaching the goals, and action steps to support the strategies.

The Center for Inquiry's Strategic Plan

On May 15 and 16, 1997, parent volunteers and Center faculty met over a two-day period to begin the process of creating our strategic plan. Those present included the following:

Tammy Ballard	Rob Chapman	Michele Shamlin
Amy Donnelly	Dori Gilbert	Diana Stout
Norm Ivey	Tim O'Keefe	Shelly Dunphy
Claudia Johnson	Babette Renfro	Rick DuVall
Deborah Basnight	Mary Bias	Linda Chapman

The strategic planning process was led by Debbie Hamm and Dale Holden from the RSD2 district office.

During the two days we created a mission statement, established goals, and developed strategies. The next step is to create action plans and establish time lines for those actions.

Mission Statement

The students, parents, and staff of the Center for Inquiry, a genuine collaboration between the University of South Carolina and Richland School District Two, are responsible for developing ourselves as more thoughtful, caring, and intelligent people who delight in learning and are committed to creating a more compassionate, equitable, knowledgeable, and democratic world!

Goals

The students, parents, and staff of the Center for Inquiry will:

- competently and confidently demonstrate their growth as inquirers and teachers through multiple perspectives
- value diverse perspectives and commit their knowledge, skills, and attitudes to create a better world
- demonstrate habits of mind and heart that compel them to be thoughtful, caring, and intelligent
- delight in learning and actively enhance the educational experiences of others

- have the knowledge, skills, attitudes, and resources necessary for a healthy and responsible lifestyle
- meet or exceed all national, district, and school standards of achievement
- have a vision of excellence for self and the global community
- be artistically and technologically literate

Strategies

In order to achieve these goals we will:

- obtain funding and resources from public and private sources sufficient to accomplish our mission
- expand and enhance usable space
- provide an optimum professional environment for our faculty
- refine and expand an integrated inquiry-based curriculum
- continue to expand the curriculum choices for students, parents, and other professionals with an emphasis on technology and the fine arts
- define and strengthen partnerships among the following stakeholders: University of South Carolina, Richland School District Two, Summit Parkway Middle School, families, businesses, and public agencies
- increase our visibility and success in the community
- identify, practice, and reflect upon respectful attitudes and behaviors

What Now?

The next step in our strategic plan is to create our action plans. An action plan is a list of specific action steps that we will take in order to enact our strategies. These action steps establish priorities, responsibilities, and time lines.

Now we need your input. The Center, because of its small size, needs help from every family. Action plans can be established in just a few meetings. Please read the strategies carefully and choose which action plan you would most like to be involved in. Your ideas and input will give the Center for Inquiry its direction for years to come.

Working on an action group is not difficult. Each group will meet regularly and report on its progress to the Parent Advisory Board. Don't be intimidated by this process. It is a rewarding and useful experience. If you are unsure of which area you would best be suited to, or if you simply need more information or guidance, please talk to Norm Ivey.

If you volunteered for an action group at either spring's picnic or the back-to-school picnic, we have your name, but please volunteer again just to assure that we have the information right.

The Parent Advisory Board, a Parent-Teacher Partnership, meets on the first Monday of every month at 7:00 P.M. in the Center's teacher work room. All parents with students enrolled at the Center are members of the Parent-Teacher Partnership, and are encouraged to attend and participate in all board meetings.

Remember the lone parent who first raised the concern regarding homeroom parents at our initial meeting in the middle school? She ended up organizing a cadre of parents and other friends of the Center to assist the school in sixteen different areas! See below for a sample of those areas.

Welcome Parents, Grandparents, and Friends of the Center for Inquiry!

The Volunteer Program or Parents as Partners at the Center for Inquiry needs you! Come and share your special interests, talents, and time. There is a volunteer activity for each of you! The time that you volunteer at the Center is very important and does not go unnoticed. All volunteer time is recorded and sent to the district office. This data is used to assess our school for state and national awards. A sign-in sheet is located in the CFI Office for volunteers to record all their hours.

We have compiled a list of events and activities for the coming year. Select those activities that match your talents and schedule. Please return this form to your child's teacher by FRIDAY, SEPTEMBER 4, 1998. This will help us get organized for a fun-filled year!

Thank you in advance from two of your volunteer coordinators,
Pat McLaren and Karen Colburn

I / We can help with the following events:
_____ **Fall Festival** on November 6, 1998
     _____ Food _____ Paper Goods _____ Activities
_____**Teacher Appreciation Luncheon** on November 20, 1998
     _____ Coordinator _____ Food _____ Assist in classroom
_____ **Winter Celebration** on December 18, 1998
     _____ Food _____ Paper Goods _____ Activities
_____ **Valentine Celebration** on February 12, 1999
     _____ Food _____ Paper Goods _____ Assist in Classroom
     _____ Activities
_____ **Sparkleberry Fair** on April 17, 1999
     _____ Setup _____ Cleanup _____ Volunteer to work hourly shifts

In fact, one parent was solicited to share his expertise in the area of science and technology with a group of second graders. He had so much fun that, in turn, he organized a clutch of volunteers from his workplace, Dupont, to work with children and teachers in the areas of electricity, energy conservation, water and air pollution, wetland conservation, and recycling. Parents sharing their expertise, their talents, and their financial resources remain the sustenance of the entire program.

Center for Inquiry   200¹/₂ Summit Parkway ♦ Columbia, S.C. 29223

Dear Parents of the *Center*:

Take a moment to walk the school campus. Feel the excitement and energy coming from the classrooms. Experience the professional excellence. Listen to the information shared and see everyone working hand in hand. As parents we are a vital part of this exciting time in our children's lives.

To show our support, the Parent Advisory Board is sponsoring our first Center for Inquiry Fund Drive. We are asking parents, grandparents, friends and neighbors to make financial contributions to the CFI-PTO. 100% of the money donated will go directly educational resources for our children.

We are proud of the initiative the children have shown in organizing a loose change drive to purchase a basketball goal. We need more than loose change to ensure educational excellence for our first year school. Consider the time and money you have spent in the past on fundraisers. Can we count on you to make a financial contribution to our school PTO by the end of November?

_____   Enclosed is my contribution of: _____.

_____   My employer has a matching funds program.

          Company name_____.

Please make checks payable to CFI-PRO. An envelope is attached for your convenience. Thank you, your contributions are greatly appreciated.

Sincerely,

Brian Dunphy
Parent Advisory Board
Center for Inquiry

Figure 12–1. *Fund-Raising Letter.*

Fund-Raising

During our first three years, fund-raising efforts included a letter requesting donations, book fairs, school T-shirt and sweatshirt sales, and children's art (see Figure 12–1, p. 198). Our initial group of parents felt strongly that they did not want their children selling door-to-door and competing for prizes that would go in the garbage the next day. Thus the model of buying a useful item such as a T-shirt or donating an amount that seemed appropriate was honored. Our fund-raising initiatives have furnished our children with musical instruments, physical education equipment, and classroom books. Our most substantive fund-raising initiative was realized when parents were able to support a salary for a technology teaching assistant to work directly with small groups of children in the areas of keyboarding, Internet research, and multimedia presentation skills.

Parent participation in the school and ownership in the process of creating a successful school was crucial to our healthy, vibrant climate. Parents who were partners acted as buoys through the rough times and as cheerleaders shouting about each success. Our parents have been our strongest supporters. They chose this school and they have been committed.

Life as an Administrator

I've always considered myself a teacher and it's the role in which I feel most comfortable. I delight in helping others uncover their talents and in sharing in their quest to inquire. And I delight in learning. The opportunity to create and participate in a community where a principal could be a teacher and a learner was absolutely irresistible! I chose to open this school to enact theory, "to publish" with the greatest degree of integrity and responsibility, so that my future practice and that of my colleagues would be one of creating theory to push current thinking in our field.

Whoa! Pushing theory? Not yet! We didn't even have a state access number to order textbooks. We had a budget of $5,000 and the copy machine cost $4,398. Our school site was landscaped but we didn't have an irrigation system to keep the plants alive. These were the regular, everyday stresses that most principals face. In fact, I'd dare say that none of these items would make a seasoned principal blink twice. But responsibility for the welfare of a school of children in portable classrooms might make even some veterans take notice. Given the kind of weather conditions that exist in South Carolina and the national attention to school safety, school life in portable classrooms requires special attention. Weather concerns necessitated evacuation to the middle school building at least three times one year. Then, too, stresses such as working extraordinarily long days week after week, days in which you witness teachers taking work home with them in an effort to support a pioneer endeavor, was excruciatingly painful. Being reduced to the role of technocrat sometimes left me feeling exhausted and joyless. Our inspirational colleague, Shelly Harwayne, aptly summarized our efforts, "Curriculum heaven is exhausting!"

Yet each morning the sun rose and the cars pulled up to the school with those smiling faces and those warm greetings from parents and children alike. Teachers gathered in my office to share their latest kid stories and messages from children, teachers, and parents inspired me or nudged me back into the role of learner that I so loved. Still, my days often consisted of responding to the moment. It seemed that no matter how early I arrived or how late I stayed, I couldn't escape the mundane tasks that seemed to be so important and so urgent to someone else. I had to do something. So first, I changed my perspective because I knew that I could not change events. I began to expect never to be able to totally plan a day and I started consciously slowing down enough to enjoy what was going on around me and indulged myself in being with the children as often as I could. Secondly, I acknowledged that I could not successfully manage full-time university responsibilities and adequately manage all the district responsibilities. With the cooperation of our school district, I hired an extremely competent and experienced doctoral student, Jane Ness, to assist with the administrative duties of the school. Together, we further developed the role of administrator in an inquiry-based community. With the help of Jane's insights and through our conversations, I was finally able to stop long enough to think about what was going on around me.

My daily plan became one of participant observer. I treated everything like data. At the end of the day, I searched for connections and patterns that were emerging and I strategized on how to move forward the next day. I found my way back to being a learner again. This stance helped me retain my vision.

I came to believe that leaders must live their vision. While living the vision of our small school collaborative, the main areas that captured most of my time included planning how to use time and space, seeking and managing funds, maintaining the facility, and listening to students, parents, and teachers.

Using Time and Space

First of all, we had such space constraints that there was no private space for any conversation at the Center. Often private conversations were held outside under the guise of "taking a walk." We had one portable the second year that we were able to use as a multifunctional space. That room served as our PE space on days the weather would not permit outdoor instruction; our music/movement space; a storage space for equipment; a USC classroom one day a week; and a group conversation area, if it were empty. Benches and the outdoor arena added additional space for collegial gatherings as well as for instruction. We all grew to expect the outdoors to be part of our work environment, weather permitting.

Since so many different groups of people—music staff, art staff, seven parent committees, weekly visitors—had to share space, it was always a rare and valued commodity. Often we looked at an empty classroom, while children might be out to recess or on a field study, as our most prized meeting location. As with our multipurpose classroom, we soon came to know that every space in the school must serve several purposes. One teacher even turned to old issues of *Apartment* for inspiration on utilizing small spaces to their maximum potential. My semiprivate office space was used by speech therapists and for volunteer meetings, and when I wasn't there, everyone understood that he or she was welcome to use it.

Time was a resource that I was determined to use differently than other schools. Maybe because it worked with space, we tried making one meeting serve multiple purposes, but that strategy made the meetings last way too long. So we began breaking down meetings according to purpose. Business meetings concerning schedules, budgets, and district requests were held every other Monday after school. Every meeting began with a "read only" handout and a time to share stories of the day, voice concerns, and ask questions. I tried to revise the agenda according to needs raised. Thursday afternoons were reserved for inquiry study meetings. Heidi Mills orchestrated this block of time, and it usually involved a focal topic such as literature study groups or assessment, in which one or two of the teachers' classrooms would be featured while we explored the topic through our own observations. Usually a powerful discussion ensued; this was the way we'd all envisioned time during the school day to be used. During this time, the USC interns took the children to lunch and orchestrated an instructional engagement for the time after lunch. While our Thursday curricular conversations were growing experiences that sustained us, teachers still struggled to find enough time to plan instruction for their classes and time to plan with their looping partners. It still remains a dream that teachers will be able to complete the bulk of their work during the school day.

Seeking and Managing Funds

A district that is among the fourth largest tier of districts in our nation has very complex procedures for tracking the use of funds. Luckily, we were blessed with a secretary/bookkeeper who knew how to use our district's complex system. Once a month we would review the printed statement sent by the district office and discuss any adjustments that needed to be made in the categories of funds.

Since we were so small and the majority of our funds were generated per pupil, it was necessary to look outside our regular budget for funds. Our after-school care program generated some monies that could be used for curricular materials and supplies. Also in our first year we were awarded three small seed grants via USC's Professional Development School initiative. These funds started our school's Publishing Center with bookbinding machines and purchased a multitude of children's literature in the area of mathematics. In our second and third years, we sought fuding from several outside agencies. One of USC's benefactors was duly impressed with our curriculum and understood that hands-on experiences meant having a variety of materials and tools if children were to do what real mathematicians and scientists do in their professional lives. In order to sustain our dream of an integrated, experience-based curriculum, we devoted a substantial amount of time to seeking development subsidies. We remained alert to any possibilities to access funds to enhance our curriculum supplies, our professional library, or our professional development fund.

Maintaining the Facility

Maintenance concerns never end. Most of those concerns were easily handled, and custodians from the adjacent middle school were often willing to lend a hand. Once a year, each school in the district is able to submit budget requests for capital improvements, and those requests brought canopies over our sidewalks this year, which certainly shield a large part of the rain.

Maintaining the grounds was also a time-consuming task. Luckily, a group of parents work diligently weeding, replacing pine straw, and even planting seasonal flowers. The school district contracts with an agency to keep our grass mowed and shrubbery trimmed. Often, however, our parents mow and trim before the landscaping maintenance crew is able to attend to our small setting. Controlling fire ants and changing light bulbs are other tasks that I am quickly becoming adept at.

Listening to Students, Parents, and Teachers

Listening to children was a joy, and quick chats with them between classrooms happened naturally. Through listening time in the classroom I experienced the pride a child feels about publishing in a new genre, the concern about Angela, the class turtle, not eating, or the excitement of the birth of a new sibling. Listening is at the heart of all that is done in the name of teaching, because in focusing on just one child we allow ourselves as educators to wonder, to hypothesize, and to consider what is essential to the development of one child.

Parents' life stories were interwoven in the concerns and dreams they shared about their individual children. Listening intently allowed me to understand parents' points of view. Frequent early morning and afternoon conversations took the place of many formally scheduled conference, and in a small community where serendipitous conversations happen, people begin to know me beyond my formal role. When that happened, sharing new ideas, gathering advice, or seeking information was just as easy as picking up the telephone. In numerous tiny conversations I discussed the nature of schooling in our society, beliefs about learning, and contemporary family life. Many of these issues are probably the same issues that parents in many schools around our country talk about with one another. The difference at the Center was that parents felt that their concerns were both heard and honored in this intimate context.

It was time to listen to teachers that took preplanning. One task of a principal should be that of helpmate. This kind of collegial support can be provided by listening to teachers' concerns, their dreams for the future, and their current accomplishments. Creating time for a variety of professional conversations is essential: one-on-one, between and among looping partners, and among the whole faculty. It is such a satisfying experience to participate in a conversation in which your colleague shares his or her visions for instruction in the classroom and ideas for ways that our school could grow and change. It is an honor and an inspiration to review student data with a teacher and hypothesize about the kind of instruction that would best support a particular child or group. In fact, this act demonstrates the kind of professional respect and trust that has the potential to move the role of principal in a new direction. Our grand conversations happened twice a year, once in the fall after school started, and once in the spring. Most conversations revolved around the major questions such as:

- What have I learned this year?
- What contributions have I made to the school this year?
- What instructional innovations am I especially proud of?
- What areas would I like to develop?
- What are my plans to reach my goals?
- What materials or resources will I need next year?
- What are your concerns and ideas to help us grow together?
- What suggestions do you have for me?

If time were not such an endangered commodity in a small school setting where teachers have a mind-boggling number of roles, I would recommend that having more time just to talk frequently about whatever issue was most pressing at the moment might have been more effective than two grand conversations a year. While the teachers and I talked often, these grand conversations gave us an opportunity to summarize, to reflect, and to plan ahead. Through these conversations, we found ideas for staff development, saw connections between our areas of interests, discovered ways to play together, began the budget planning process, and identified children who needed our collective expertise to help them grow. Listening is a tool to facilitate teacher empowerment. Conversations foster teacher ownership of their professional development, responsibility for quality instruction, and a willingness to take risks that is often the only way to move instructional moments toward excellence. Conversations are extremely powerful professional development tools. Creating enough time for conversation and silent time for reflection remained a constant challenge.

The Terrorism of Testing

I am proud, as are the CFI teachers, that our test scores on the Palmetto Achievement Challenge Test were at or above the district average. It stands to reason that if good teaching is happening and students feel responsible to share their learning in a variety of ways, then the test scores should reflect those learning processes. There is no single best practice that will be the silver bullet for raising test scores. The only best practice is responsive teaching. That is the kind of teaching that seeks to understand and support each child.

As all schools today seek to develop skillful test takers, Karen Smith, elementary director for the National Council of Teachers of English (NCTE), suggests we look closely at tests as a genre of literature. Our children certainly felt comfortable interrogating a topic from a variety of perspectives and this strategy seemed like a natural fit. Using commercially published practice test materials, our children set out to examine test formatting, testing terminology, the concept of multiple choice, and the influence of time on test completion. Of course, we also just practiced as the commercial materials advised, and we all agreed that the often-lengthy debriefing sessions that followed were invaluable! In these sessions we discussed why a particular answer was chosen over another, the reasoning that was used to eliminate some choices given, and strategies to complete a test within a time limit. We played strategy games to find the distracters within a test question and discussed the implications of placing superfluous or confusing information in the text of the test.

In a small school setting, test scores can be problematic when a single score evaluates teaching and learning. In addition, a very low score can skew the class results significantly. Standardized test scores only represent one dimension of what a child is able to do and not even what he knows, but rather how well he takes tests. In small settings like the Center for Inquiry, standardized tests can hang individual teachers out to dry or coerce them into a kind of status quo teaching from a text that promotes high test scores. In larger settings, grade-level scores are averaged so that individual teachers' scores are reported as a group achievement. At the Center for Inquiry, teachers act accountably in the area of testing; it is their professional responsibility to confront the testing issue with courage and professionalism.

Walking the Tightrope Between Two Institutions

The Center for Inquiry is one shining example of collaboration between institutions. Yet this collaboration, with all of its contracts and agreements, is full of ambiguities and unanswered questions. The vision for teaching and learning in this setting involves a commitment to simultaneous renewal of teacher education and K–12 schools as well as lifelong learning for all stakeholders involved.

Collaboration is rooted in trust. Trust is the force that propels groups through ambiguity toward greater insights. Differences viewed from a collaborative stance are assets to be used to stretch our current understandings. Boundary lines become more flexible and resources more easily shared when contrasting perspectives are understood and valued. Trust is extremely difficult to develop and sustain when collaboration menus bring two historically entrenched cultures together. Commonly held views declare that excellence in practice is the domain of public schools while theory belongs to the academicians in universities. The dichotomy is overly simplistic. Experience offers daily evidence that practitioners do act as theory makers and academicians can enact good practice. Collaboration calls for the roles of all educators involved to be fluid.

I recently received a card from a colleague who routinely brings her preservice teacher classes to the Center. In the card, she quoted one of her students as saying, "Being at the Center for Inquiry was like walking into one of our books!" Preservice teachers need firsthand experiences to live and learn in classrooms where practices reflect the philosophy being demonstrated at the university. In fact, six preservice teachers live and learn at the Center during their yearlong field placement. Other preservice teachers work in classrooms during the fall as a part of their graduate method's course that is taught on-site.

Still other preservice and inservice teachers visit the Center as a part of Visitor's Day.

Visitor's Day was established as part of the Center's commitment to simultaneously renew K–12 teaching. In this way, teachers have an opportunity to see what theory looks like in practice and are then more likely to feel supported in their efforts to transform their own teaching. Because the Center is a Professional Development School, many interns from various colleges and programs as well as university faculty are involved in the curriculum there. USC faculty members from art and music are providing special-area classes for the Center children and in the process are implementing the apprenticeship model for their preservice students. They teach courses on-site and involve their students in planning and implementing instruction on a weekly basis. The following list details the extensive USC faculty involvement at the Center for Inquiry:

- Cynthia Colbert, College of Liberal Arts, Department of Art, supervises interns, designs art curriculum, and teaches children as well as offering summer art classes.
- Wendy Valerio, College of Music, and interns design music curriculum and teach music as well as offering piano lessons after school.
- Earlene Walker, College of Education, teaches a wellness fitness program to children.
- Diane Stephens, College of Education, Instruction and Teacher Education, supervises students in an after-school Literacy Club to support struggling readers and writers.
- Laurie Ford, College of Liberal Arts, Department of Psychology, supervises Ph.D. interns and collaborates with the district to provide social and emotional support for children and parents.
- Pam Wills and Janet Mason, College of Education, Departments of Instruction and Teacher Education, supervise education minor students who assist in our after-school program under the direction of Natalie Scipio and Jaretta Belcher.
- Louise Jennings, College of Education, Departments of Educational Foundations and Psychology, documents the growth of one group of students over six years.
- Robert Johnson, College of Education, Department of Educational Psychology, supervises graduate students in designing and conducting research surveys that assist us in gathering data related to parent perceptions.

Looking Toward the Future

Karen Smith, the elementary director for NCTE, was commissioned by the school district to direct an extensive review of the Center during the second year of operation in the spring of 1998. The design Karen developed for the review grew out of the work of Linda Darling-Hammond (1997) and was adapted from New York's State School Quality Review. Karen explained to the group of expert practitioners and representative stakeholders, "The review process generates tensions between ideals and reality. Peter Senge describes this process as essential for organizational learning: 'The juxtaposition of the vision (what we want) and a clear picture of current reality (where we are relative to what we want) generates what we call "creative tension": a force to bring them together caused by the natural tendency of tension to seek resolution'" (Darling-Hammond 1997, 286). School goals (see the Strategic Planning Newsletter) and national standards were used to reveal what is actually occurring in the name of learning in the classrooms, how learning events are affecting children, and how events enact or fail to enact the school's mission and professional practice. The four major lenses for examining the total school habitat included: school environment, teaching and learning, curriculum and assessment, and schoolwide inquiry and development. The group, representative of all stakeholders in the school, spent one full day interviewing faculty, parents, and staff; reviewing artifacts; and observing instruction. While the final report highlighted many commendations, the group's recommendations point the way to the Center's future.

School Environment

- The Center for Inquiry would benefit from improvement in physical facilities.
- Some improvements in staffing would be beneficial, such as certified media/computer specialist and guidance counselor.
- The Center could be better suited to students with special needs.

Teaching and Learning

- The strategies that teachers are already effectively using should be continued and further enhanced.
- The school district should look into allocating additional State of SC Act 135 funds to support meeting the needs of academically at-risk students.
- The establishment of an appropriately supplied media or resource center is an essential and urgent need.

- Commitments by parents for volunteerism and community relations are essential.
- The Center for Inquiry should continue to provide professional development activities and opportunities for collaborations for teachers and staff.

Curriculum and Assessment

- A media center and the continued use of technology as an instructional tool would greatly enhance the Center's emphasis on inquiry.
- Assessment is well done. Narratives were very extensive, yet teachers should consider reporting a variety of data.

Schoolwide Inquiry and Development

- The university and school district need to work together to resolve immediate resource needs.
- Teachers need the opportunity to build on the strong foundation they have established.
- The Center for Inquiry should explore scheduling options to provide more time for teacher planning and collaboration.
- Intensive staff development should be provided to teachers who enter the school without a clear understanding of or commitment to inquiry-based instruction.

The report summarizes, "The strong cords of commitment and the shared learning that binds teachers and students to one another at the Center for Inquiry provide a strong foundation for continued growth and development."

Creating a community and culture of inquiry was both an operational and inspiration goal. A democratic community was the nonnegotiable tenet underpinning our definition of good schooling. We wanted children to fall in love with learning, to access their potentials, and we dreamed of furthering our professional knowledge in the process. As I reflect on our first three years, I see that we tried to tackle too many difficult issues at once. We were carried by the strong current of the powerful river of Status Quo toward becoming similar to all the other schools in our district in terms of staffing, committee work, facility resources, and organizational structure. Yet we knew that we vied for the privilege of building our own boat and so we rowed with a euphoric work ethic. And then in our weariness and scarcity of resources, our vision blurred, and we stumbled over issues of personal autonomy and spent our most valuable resource, time, trying to reach consensus through lengthy discussions that left us feeling more depleted than energized. Then we were reenergized and found focus in our semiregular curricular conversations. Yet, we remained a group of exceptionally strong personalities that were used to doing it our own way and that fact made it very easy to beach our boat as we struggled to collaboratively define our school. As is predictable, in all things that are meant to be, our shared teaching philosophy and our commitment to children contributed to the rising tide that again buoyed our boat and kept us steadily rowing toward new possibilities.

Measuring Our Success

We measure our success by the fact that we, as professionals, used the concept of choice to celebrate what was best in public education. We used our professional knowledge and talents to make a difference in our world. In doing so, we provided a vision for many. We created a school where learning is "cool" and where diversity is valued as potential for greater learning. We created a school where questions are valuable and multiple solutions are expected. We created a school where parents are active participants in teaching, learning, and cocreating the culture. We created a school that will live on in the habits of the minds and hearts of all who have lived and learned with us.

References

Anthony, R. J., T. Johnson, N. Mickelson, and A. Preece. 1991. *Evaluating Literacy: A Perspective for Change*. Portsmouth, NH: Heinemann.

Barth, R. 1990. *Improving Schools from Within: Teachers, Parents, and Principals Can Make the Difference*. San Francisco: Jossey-Bass.

Darling-Hammond, L. 1997. *The Right to Learn: A Blueprint for Creating Schools That Work*. San Francisco: Jossey-Bass.

Dewey, J. 1963. *Experience and Education*. New York: Collier Books.

Dorn, L., C. French, and T. Jones. 1998. *Apprenticeship in Literacy: Transitions Across Reading and Writing*. York, ME: Stenhouse.

Freire, P. 1972. *Pedagogy of the Oppressed*. New York: Herder and Herder.

Fullan, M. 1997. *What's Worth Fighting for in the Principalship*. New York: Teachers College Press.

Greene, M. 1995. *Releasing the Imagination: Essays on Education, the Arts, and Social Change*. San Francisco: Jossey-Bass.

Harwayne, S. 1999. *Going Public: Priorities and Practice at the Manhattan New School*. Portsmouth, NH: Heinemann.

Hubbard, R., and B. Power. 1999. *Living the Questions: A Guide for Teacher-Researchers*. York, ME: Stenhouse.

Ivey, S. 1996. *Starting from Scratch: One Classroom Builds Its Own Community.* Portsmouth, NH: Heinemann.

Kamii, C. K. 1985. "Autonomy: The Aim of Education for Piaget." In *Young Children Reinvent Arithmetic: Implications of Piaget's Theories,* edited by C. K. Kamii, 29–51. New York: Teachers College Press.

Kohn, A. 1996. *Beyond Discipline: From Compliance to Community.* Alexandria, VA: ASCD.

Lindfors, J. 1999. *Children's Inquiry: Using Language to Make Sense of the World.* New York: Teachers College Press.

Meier, D. 1995. *The Power of Their Ideas: Lessons for America from a Small School in Harlem.* Boston: Beacon.

Mills, H., and J. A. Clyde. 1990. *Portraits of Whole Language Classrooms.* Portsmouth, NH: Heinemann.

Oglan, G. 1997. *Parents, Learning, and Whole Language Classrooms.* Urbana, IL: NCTE.

Peterson, R. 1992. *Life in a Crowded Place.* Portsmouth, NH: Heinemann.

Rogoff, B. 1990. *Apprenticeship in Thinking: Cognitive Development in Social Contexts.* New York: Oxford Press University.

Schockley, B., B. Michalove, and J. Allen. 1995. *Engaging Families: Connecting Home and School Literacy Communities.* Portsmouth, NH: Heinemann.

School Improvement Council Assistance. 1989. *Effective School Improvement Councils: A Guide for South Carolina Schools.* Columbia, SC: University of South Carolina, College of Education.

Short, K., J. Harste, and C. Burke. 1996. *Creating Classrooms for Authors and Inquirers.* Portsmouth, NH: Heinemann.

Vygotsky, L. 1986. *Thought and Language.* Cambridge, MA: MIT Press.

Wells, G. 1986. *The Meaning Makers: Children Learning Language and Using Language to Learn.* Portsmouth, NH: Heinemann.

Wortman, B., and M. Matlin. 1995. *Leadership in Whole Language.* York, ME: Stenhouse.

13

The Center for Inquiry as a Professional Development School

RICHARD E. ISHLER AND HARVEY A. ALLEN

Public School-University Partnerships

One of the guiding principles underlying the blueprint for the Center for Inquiry was that the Center would be aligned with the University of South Carolina Professional Development School (PDS) Network. From 1990 through 1996, the university had eleven PDS sites included in the network. By the time the Center for Inquiry, which represented a unique and very significant partnership between the University of South Carolina and Richland School District Two, became a partner school, the USC PDS Network had increased to seventeen schools. The partner schools of the USC PDS Network consisted of one university preschool–K site; two high schools; two middle schools; eleven conventional elementary schools; and the Center for Inquiry, a small, six-classroom K–5 public school of choice.

The Center for Inquiry was well suited to be a PDS site because it represented a unique opportunity to establish an inquiry-based approach to teaching and learning. From the outset, it was conceptualized that district educators and students would collaborate with university researchers to investigate processes of inquiry teaching and learning and curriculum development at the Center.

The Professional Development School approach has proven to be an effective change agent, which enables the renewal of education and improvement of teacher education to occur simultaneously. Educational change cannot take place unless the two basic institutions that educate the young collaborate to bring about changes in the educational process. Public schools and universities must work together on educational problems. Partnerships between public schools and universities are being established throughout the

211

country and are rooted in the belief that the two institutions need each other to achieve the goals that they hold in common. In communities where these partnerships have operated successfully, the education programs have been enhanced. Education in these communities operates on a continuum from preschool through college and is recognized as a joint responsibility.

Blending Professional Relationships

Historically, colleges and universities have assumed the major responsibility for the preservice education of teachers. To some extent, this responsibility has been shared with public schools, especially in providing clinical and field-based experiences for preservice teachers. However, control and responsibility for teacher preparation have largely remained with the colleges or universities. By the same token, public schools have not assumed operational responsibility for the education of teachers, except to make pupils and classrooms available and to provide teachers to supervise student teaching and other required field experiences. Thus, educators have staked out certain professional boundaries: colleges and universities have viewed teacher education as their responsibility and public schools have regarded the education of children as theirs. Factors of tradition and professional status have made existing educational boundaries understandable, but not acceptable. The concept that universities produce and the public schools consume teachers is no longer operationally feasible. With the societal pressures facing both public school education and higher education, it is necessary to build cooperative relationships among all members of the educational community. Once teacher education becomes a shared enterprise, numerous opportunities will emerge whereby university faculty and public school teachers and administrators can work together to improve the educational programs offered in the public schools and colleges. Such partnerships will also result in students who are better prepared to face the challenges of higher education and college students who are better prepared to become teachers.

Creating Professional Development Schools

Teacher education programs cannot survive and flourish by providing preservice teachers with theory on the college campus and practice in a brief student-teaching experience in the public schools. The PDS approach eliminates this artificial dichotomy by distributing theory and practice throughout the teacher education program. Clinical and field-based experiences must be extensive and continual, culminating with student teaching and a full-year internship in a

Professional Development School. In the Center for Inquiry, classroom teachers would assume roles as school-based teacher educators because they play an important part in shaping the future teaching behaviors of preservice teachers.

Research clearly indicates that one learns to teach by modeling or patterning the teaching methodologies of others. More specifically, cooperating teachers greatly influence the teaching behaviors of their student teachers during the relatively short student-teaching experience, thus performing the role of teacher educators. Classroom teachers in the Center would need to identify and understand clearly this aspect of their professional responsibility and they must be prepared to carry it out effectively. The Center would provide an exemplary venue for fulfilling the critically important roles of public school teachers in shaping teaching behaviors of novices.

In its capacity as a PDS, the Center became part of the laboratory school tradition in education because such clinical schools have existed in some form since the late nineteenth century. John Dewey recognized that teachers need a professional development laboratory, as do scientists and medical practitioners. Public schools in the USC PDS Network differ from traditional laboratory schools in that a PDS serves a diverse population of students in a public school setting, while a laboratory school serves a more targeted population of students in a university campus setting. The Center for Inquiry is a contemporary evocation of the laboratory school approach in a vital professional development school context. The Center combines the best elements of traditional laboratory schools and conventional professional development schools in that inquiry is the driving force of the school and that collaboration among students, parents, and faculty in the school, and students and faculty from all disciplines of the university as well as school district and community leaders is emphasized. The Center for Inquiry, with roots in the time-honored progressive education tradition of inquiry, child-centeredness, and learning by doing and problem solving has extended beyond Deweyian theory and practice. The Center has transplanted the laboratory model from the prescribed setting of the university campus to a public school setting. As a school of choice, the Center serves a diverse population of students from throughout Richland School District Two. Additionally, through the direct relationship between USC and the school district, district teachers, administrators, and parents, and faculty and students from education and other university disciplines have been involved in the development of the rich educational program of the Center.

When the Center for Inquiry determined that it wanted to seek association with the USC PDS Network, it followed the formal process outlined in the Guidelines of the University of South Carolina Professional Development School Network, which included an application and self-study. The Center satisfied the various criteria required of all PDSs, such as a commitment to: (1) the improvement of the education of children and the education of educators, (2) university-school agency partnerships, (3) a level of USC faculty support, and (4) inquiry-based teaching and learning. The activities and practices of the PDS Network were derived from principles and postulates of national education reform/renewal groups such as the Holmes Partnership and the National Network for Educational Renewal. Additionally, the USC Network adheres to the set of standards governing professional development schools, established by the National Council for the Accreditation of Teacher Education (NCATE). There are several basic premises that give direction and dimension to the partner schools in the network, which coincided with the goals and objectives of the Center. Some of those commonly shared PDS beliefs are (1) teaching for understanding, (2) organizing schools into learning communities, (3) making inquiry and reflection the focus of the school, (4) demonstrating essential best practice in teaching and learning, and (5) providing opportunities for preservice teachers to develop the skills needed to become teachers and for inservice teachers to continue their professional development.

The Center for Inquiry PDS is a new kind of school in many respects. It embraces democratic values and uses the full range of knowledge and skills of classroom teachers, school administrators, future teachers, and professors to shape the teaching and learning processes of the school. The CFI PDS is a school in which professors, teachers, administrators, parents, and prospective teachers and administrators work together to build a learning community. This community has as its primary goal the intellectual engagement and development of all its members—students, teachers, administrators, parents, professors, and future educators.

Beginnings

The decade of the 1990s witnessed a clarion call for better teachers and improved teacher preparation. The College of Education of the University of South Carolina has answered that call for reform and renewal through its leadership in establishing professional development schools. Through commitment to the USC PDS Network, the college/university has moved beyond the confines of the campus and has collaborated with these schools to improve the education of schoolchildren and the education of educators.

The Center for Inquiry has benefited from its partnership in the USC PDS Network. On the other hand, the university, Richland District Two, the other partner schools in the network, and countless other schools have been influenced by the successful implementation of inquiry-based teaching and learning at the Center.

During the last one hundred years, educators have been occupied with efforts to develop inquiry-based approaches to teaching and learning. The philosophy of a student-centered school has challenged the elementary school. Through the collaboration of the university and Richland School District Two and the vision and energy of two resourceful professors, the "unheard of" has happened in education—the creation of a "new" place called school. The exciting story of the Center for Inquiry is that this new school is dedicated to the proposition that school is for children and that the business of the school is the celebration of learning. The Center for Inquiry represents an exciting new beginning for inquiry-based teaching and learning. Great strides have been made in creating a culture of inquiry in a public school, but there is still much to be done to make the promise of inquiry-based education a reality for more children and young adolescents.

Epilogue

HEIDI MILLS WITH AMY DONNELLY AND FACULTY

What are we to make of the teacher's sense that she is giving some-thing up when she takes children's inquiry seriously, even to the extent of making it the fundamental shared expectation in collaborative in-quiry genres such as discussion and science talks? What does she lose? I submit that what the teacher is giving up is control *but not* power. *Indeed in exploratory classroom genres, the measure of her loss of con-trol may be precisely the measure of her gain in power, for if her goal in such events is to better understand the children's thinking, then the more that the thinking can reveal itself, the more fully she reaches her goal . . . collaborative inquiry events such as discussions and science talks, I hear empowered children. I also hear empowered teachers.*
—JUDITH LINDFORS 1999, 174

The previous chapters written by the children and teachers capture the essence of Judith Lindfor's position. The more the teachers learned to truly collaborate with their children when creating curriculum, the more they all learned from one another. The more they learned to slow their teach-ing down to make space for children to learn, the more the children amazed them. The more the teachers fostered community within their classrooms, the more the children revealed essential insights and posed perceptive questions. The more teachers empowered the children, the more they became empowered as professionals.

This unique relationship between power and control promoted inquiry within the context of the Center classrooms and our professional development experiences. However, the relationship between power and control looked quite different outside of the classrooms. The relationship between the district and the university, as well as the school and the district, was much more frag-ile than we originally realized. These tensions promoted inquiry as well. How-ever, we have found that knowing a great deal about theory, kids, and cur-riculum can only get you so far. We have learned that we need to redirect our

217

energy to better understand the politics of education; the ways in which the state laws are translating the standards movement; and the culture of the school board as well as district offices.

We learned that we needed to ask new questions of ourselves and of the profession. Instead of asking how we might change our practices to improve our standardized test scores, we asked: How might we foster test literacy? How might the inquiry stance that serves us well across disciplines be translated as inquiry into test-taking strategies? Instead of asking how we should approach grading, we devised narrative progress reports and student-led conferences. Instead of letting the standards movement and accountability legislation interfere with our teaching, we maintained a focus on the children and met standards using inquiry-based instruction and assessment strategies. In so doing, we allowed our children to develop incredible confidence and genuine competence across disciplines while our test scores also remained well above the district average. Instead of asking how to develop integrated thematic units, we learned to ask: What are the universal concepts that cut across sign systems and disciplines (e.g., diversity, systems, growth and change, cycles, relationships, patterns)? How might we plan with and for children to promote a solid conceptual understanding within and across the curriculum?

From Reflection to Action

Asking our own questions was not enough. After three years of framing our curriculum development initiatives around issues that mattered most to us, new state accountability legislation pushed us to directly answer questions framed by others. Suddenly we were faced with new requirements to document that we were teaching the standards. While we knew we were doing so, our authentic assessment strategies did not make them visible enough for outsiders to see. At the same time, many teachers across South Carolina were being asked and/or forced in some places to identify the individual standards they intended to address in their daily lesson plans. However, one of the reasons we had worked so hard to start our own school was to have the freedom to focus on doing what made sense for teachers and children. And the standardization of curricular planning to prove we were teaching standards simply didn't make sense. It didn't make sense in our school culture because of the following facts:

- Our teachers begin with intentional and systematic kid watching. The teachers determine the ways and the order in which the standards are taught based on their assessment of children's needs and interests.

- Our teachers and children work together to uncover rather than simply cover the curriculum. In so doing, they bring the standards to life through authentic engagements, through thoughtful conversations, and through interdisciplinary inquiry projects.
- Our teachers believe that the original intent of the national standards was to give teachers more power and insight, not less. So they use the standards. They don't let the standards use them.
- Our teachers organize curriculum through broad concepts or units of study that are comprehensive, not discrete. Additionally, multiple standards representing different disciplines are woven into reading, writing, and math units of study and workshops day in and day out.

While such a stance made perfect sense to us, we were confronted with the reality that we had to do more to show as well as tell how we were teaching and assessing the standards. With the freedom to create curriculum came the responsibility to make the standards explicit in a way that would not violate our model.

With Freedom Comes Responsibility

After several curricular conversations about the standards dilemma, we did what we have always found works best—we turned the problem into a new inquiry project. We spent several weeks sharing how we document the standards using rubrics, student artifacts, and anecdotal records. We also took a close, hard look at how well we were communicating the standards via our narrative progress reports. Initially we discussed ways to revise our narrative reports to make the standards more visible. But it became crystal clear that the intimacy and beauty of the current reports would be lost in the changes we were devising. While the reports are incredibly time-consuming, we are always pleased about how much we learn about the children when writing them and how much parents value the portraits we paint of their children with words.

Everything came together during one study group meeting. We suddenly remembered that we had choices. We didn't have to revise what we valued, we could simply devise an alternative. After four years of writing four extensive narrative reports on each child, some of us were growing tired even though we knew it was the right thing to do. So we negotiated a compromise, a compromise that the Richland School District Two Office supported and one that also met our needs. We decided to use the original progress reports as they were designed for the first and third grading periods and create a standards-based report for the second and fourth periods. By doing so, we could give parents explicit information regarding their children's growth and change in relation to the standards as a summary of each semester. We are in the process of fine-tuning the new report now. At this point in time, we plan to list the major strands in each discipline and then identify whether the child is *developing, accomplishing,* or *extending* the major strands across content standards. To be honest, we know others will devise more brilliant ways to explicitly address the standards, but at this moment in time in Columbia, South Carolina, this works for us.

A Moment of Honesty

It has been four years and we still have not fully actualized our dreams for the Center. We started with a critical mass of remarkable teachers; the superintendent and chief academic officer in the district had made a real commitment to the venture, and several university partners devoted as much time, expertise, and resources as they could to the Center. It seemed as if all of the people and procedures needed to soar were in place. To be perfectly honest, however, there were days we hardly got our feet off the ground. We can honestly say it was more difficult than we ever imagined to start a school; establish and maintain a university-public school partnership; find teachers who had a solid knowledge base and who could also operationalize the theory day in and day out; and live the model of inquiry we created. It was *more difficult* yet *better.*

Looking Back to Move Forward

As we looked closely and listened carefully within classrooms, it became clear that the children had internalized the processes and practices that pervaded the Center. They understood what they were learning, why it mattered, and when the information or strategy could help them investigate or solve a problem. When we started the Center, we simply *imagined* what would be possible; now we *know.* And because we know what is possible, we could never go back, we could never settle for what is typical again. The power of a shared philosophy, the integrity of a school based on democratic principles, the intimate and respectful nature of the small learning community, the collaborative relationships with parents and university partners all contributed to the strengthening of our hearts and minds.

We have a new professional dream now. Now that we have been blessed with the opportunity to make new connections between Richland School District Two and the University of South Carolina; connections within and across classrooms; connections with parents; connections with distant teachers; and connections with visitors from across the state and country, we hope our story will inform and inspire others to make their professional dreams come true in their own ways and in their own contexts.

It has been good, so good that we feel a sense of urgency to share it with others. Forrest Carter (1976) reminds us in *The Education of Little Tree*, "Gramma said when you come on something good, first thing you do is share it with whoever you can find; that way, the good spreads out where no telling where it will go. Which is right" (Preface).

References

Carter, F. 1976. *The Education of Little Tree*. Albuquerque, NM: University of New Mexico Press.

Lindfors, J. 1999. *Children's Inquiry*. New York: Teachers College Press.

Appendix A

Original Proposal for the Center for Inquiry

SUBMITTED BY HEIDI MILLS, AMY DONNELLY, AND RICHARD ISHLER

What

- Richland District Two, in collaboration with the University of South Carolina, will develop a small school of choice for parents who desire an inquiry-based curriculum for their children.
- The university-public school partnership, or Professional Development School relationship, will operate as an "ideal" or model elementary school. In so doing, it will enhance learning opportunities for everyone involved. It will also function as a demonstration site for educators in Richland Two, the state, and the nation.

Who

The school will strive to accommodate a population representative of the greater Columbia community.

- A stratified random lottery will be employed to ensure that the student population will portray academic and cultural diversity.
- A diverse student and faculty population (age, ethnic, cultural, and economic backgrounds) make classrooms rich, interesting places to live and learn.

Curriculum and Instruction

An inquiry-based curriculum is by nature interdisciplinary as it reflects the ways in which scientists, mathematicians, authors, historians, artists, and musicians learn. The Center will be devoted to helping children develop a knowledge of and appreciation for traditional content areas by engaging them in rigorous units of study that require an understanding of the concepts, skills, and strategies inherent in individual subjects, as well as the interrelationship between content areas. Since subject areas are naturally integrated in the real world, classroom experiences will reflect the holistic nature of knowledge. The children will not simply learn about science, mathematics, history, reading, and writing but will do what scientists, historians, authors, and mathematicians do. This will be accomplished through individual, small-group, and whole-class inquiry projects, strategy lessons, and direct instruction. The staff will work together to develop, implement, and evaluate a truly supportive, meaningful, and challenging inquiry-based curriculum.

To accomplish this goal, the staff will create curriculum following the guidelines set forth by *The Consortium for Interdisciplinary Teaching and Learning*. The guidelines were devised and endorsed by the National Council of Teachers of English, the International Reading Association, the National Council of Teachers of Mathematics, the Speech Communication Association, and the Council for Elementary Science International. Early childhood and elementary curricula should:

- be authentic and worthwhile
- maintain a balance between student-initiated and teacher-initiated experiences
- cultivate a learning community in which students develop both independence as investigators and the ability to collaborate with one another and teachers to raise questions, investigate issues, and solve problems
- foster interaction among diverse learners to promote learning for all students and to enhance attitudes toward others and toward learning
- encourage active learners who can effectively use a variety of learning strategies
- teach students to use a wide variety of sources, including primary sources, oral communication, direct observation, and experimentation
- use language, art, mathematics, music, technology, and drama as tools for learning and communication
- encourage application of knowledge through real-life problem solving

Standards

The scope of the curriculum will reflect the requirements set forth by Richland District Two's curriculum guides in each content area (language arts, the arts, mathematics, science, social studies, physical education, and occupational studies). The order in which the objectives will be addressed, and the instructional strategies that will be used to do so, will be determined by the individual teachers after careful observation and documentation of the students' needs and interests.

The curriculum will also reflect the standards set forth by national organizations such as the National Association of the Education of Young Children, the National Council of Teachers of English, and the National Council of Teachers of Mathematics.

Since all of the teachers will be operating from a shared vision and use consistent teaching strategies, there will be continuity across learning experiences and grade levels. Children will work with the same teacher and group of children for two years. This will further promote continuity of learning experiences and will also build strong classroom communities.

The instructional day will be balanced among large-group, small-group, and individual activities. Also, a balance will exist in curriculum and content areas, as well as teacher-directed and child-initiated experiences.

Although each content area features unique skills, concepts, and learning strategies, the general teaching and learning process will be consistent across the curriculum. The framework for the curriculum will reflect a workshop format. As such, instruction in reading, writing, mathematics, science, and social studies will involve the following experiences each day:

- Demonstration: Teachers will create formal demonstration lessons that highlight skills, strategies, content, or concepts in context. The lessons will demonstrate how to apply the ideas and why the issues matter. For example, teachers will feature phonics, print concepts, and language conventions as well as effective reading and writing strategies during reading and writing workshops. During math workshop, teachers will feature strategies for problem solving, important mathematical concepts, and computational skills during demonstration lessons. The same format will be applied in all content areas and during theme cycles.

- Engagement: Teachers will create opportunities for children to think like readers, writers, mathematicians, scientists, and historians. Children will apply the skills, strategies, and concepts they are learning in each content area daily. Teachers will provide a significant block of time each day for genuine reading, writing, mathematical, scientific, and historical investigations.

- Reflection: Children will be encouraged to reflect upon their own learning in each content area. They will self-evaluate their progress, gain greater control over learning strategies across subject areas, and determine future goals to be accomplished. Teachers will build formal reflection time into the fabric of each school day.

- Celebration: The teachers will highlight children's accomplishments by providing opportunities for them to share their work with others. The children's learning will be enhanced through opportunities to teach others while receiving recognition for their efforts. They will exhibit their work in the classroom, education center, and community at large.

Assessment and Evaluation

Evaluation strategies will determine the benefit of the educational experiences provided at the Center for Inquiry. However, in regard to learning, the main purpose of assessment should be to inform instructional practices and make decisions that will lead to continued growth and learning. In addition, assessment should provide teachers, children, and parents with information related to the question "How am I doing?" Assessment and evaluation will be viewed as dynamic and integral parts of the curriculum and should be consistent with the goals of the curriculum.

Assessment and evaluation will consist of examining the processes involved in learning as well as the products. To accomplish this, profiles of student achievement will be developed to paint a comprehensive portrait of the child's growth. The profiles will provide detailed descriptions of students' learning. This detailed description of learning will occur over time and will consist of multifaceted data including standardized test scores and classroom examples representing discipline-based competencies. Standardized test scores will be one of many indicators of learning that will be used to document individual growth over time. A complete profile will also include observations from teachers, parents, and the learner.

Gathering and Interpreting Information for Evaluation

The framework for gathering this kind of diverse information related to each student's learning consists of four categories: observation of the process of learning, products that communicate learning, classroom measures, and measures outside the classroom such as standardized tests. This framework is best represented by a circle with four quadrants such as the one in Figure A–1 on p. 227.

Observation of the process allows patterns of behavior that contribute to student growth to be uncovered. When a teacher tries to understand the general pattern of learning exemplified by a child, he or she can design meaningful plans for future instruction. Products demonstrate performance competency and encourage learning to be viewed from multiple perspectives. Classroom measures are the most familiar examples of classroom learning and they include scores from student work, such as projects and pieces

Evaluation and Assessment
Data-Gathering Profile

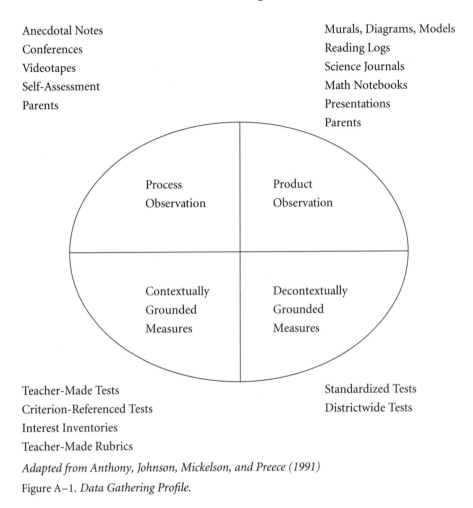

Anecdotal Notes

Conferences

Videotapes

Self-Assessment

Parents

Murals, Diagrams, Models

Reading Logs

Science Journals

Math Notebooks

Presentations

Parents

Process Observation

Product Observation

Contextually Grounded Measures

Decontextually Grounded Measures

Teacher-Made Tests

Criterion-Referenced Tests

Interest Inventories

Teacher-Made Rubrics

Standardized Tests

Districtwide Tests

Adapted from Anthony, Johnson, Mickelson, and Preece (1991)

Figure A–1. *Data Gathering Profile.*

of writing. Decontextualized measures are developed outside the classroom and include standardized tests such as California Achievement Test (CAT), Metropolitan Achievement Test (MAT), and Basic Skills Assessment Program (BSAP).

Information related to a student's learning will be gathered systematically to create a portrait of growth. All content areas will be included in this individual profile of achievement. Some information will be gathered on a weekly basis, some monthly, while other information will be gathered on alternating years. Once the information is compiled, it will be interpreted so that evaluative conclusions can be drawn. The student, the parent, the teacher, and the administrator will all have questions that will be answered by reviewing the information in a child's learning profile. Of course, all four parties' concerns overlap, but the difference lies in their unique perspective and level of specificity. The students and parents will be concerned with individual progress. The teachers will be concerned with how each child is doing as well as the success of the instruction at the classroom level. The administrator will be concerned with the learning of individual children. Additionally, the administrator will review evaluation data to analyze the success of the entire instructional program. Aggregated profiles will be especially helpful in addressing instructional reform at the building level.

Reporting

Individual student achievement will be discussed and reported through evaluative conferences that include the parent, the child, and the teacher. A narrative report that communicates an individual child's progress in relation to a continuum of competencies in each given content area will be written. The profile reports will reflect a continuum of standard skills and concepts in each content area. In addition, this continuum will reflect Richland School District Two's high standards and rigorous curriculum. Profiles of student growth will be useful in charting learning for all students, including those described as academically gifted, those who are in need of remedial instruction, and those with identified special needs. Profiles of student growth will document and encourage all children to reach their fullest potential.

Why

Educators, children, parents, and business leaders all recognize the need for educational reform.

- The Center for Inquiry will employ teachers and administrators who are knowledgeable in current educational research and can transfer that knowledge into outstanding instructional practices.
- Preservice teachers from the University of South Carolina will function as instructional assistants while pursuing MAT degrees. The inservice teachers' and children's lives will be enriched by opportunities to work with instructional assistants with extensive background in early childhood and elementary education. The selection process to become instructional assistants will be very competitive.

- The Center for Inquiry will make a commitment to locating and securing outside funding sources in this time of dwindling resources available to public education.
- The Center for Inquiry will capitalize upon the strengths of children. The teaching/learning process will be viewed as a responsibility shared with children, rather than merely one imposed upon them, in order to produce responsible, thoughtful, lifelong learners.
- The Center for Inquiry will view parents as true partners in their children's education and will utilize their areas of expertise throughout the school.
- The Center for Inquiry will incorporate current and future state and national educational initiatives such as Goals 2000, national, and state-level standards when planning and evaluating the curriculum.
- The Center for Inquiry will recognize the need for productive, intelligent citizens in the twenty-first century identified by business leaders. *The South Carolina Chamber of Commerce Education Study* will be utilized when designing and implementing the curriculum.

How

The administrative structure is expanded to include both instructional as well as managerial responsibilities.

- District Two will specify commitments of each institution for a five-year period. National standards for Professional Development Schools will grow out of the operation of this Center.
- The focus of the administration will be to facilitate and empower reflective practitioners who engage in systematic, collaborative, and continual inquiry about teaching and learning.
- Since individuals learn more effectively when they learn together, a collaboration will be fostered within the school and across traditional role boundaries.
- Shared decision making will take place in the context of weighted but not distinct responsibilities appropriate to different roles and strengths of individual faculty/staff.

What We Are About

The Center for Inquiry is about making classrooms exciting places for teachers and children to be. It is about the sustaining of children's successful learning strategies that they bring to school with them. It is about helping all children become thoughtful, intelligent people who care about others and who delight in learning. It is about helping preservice and inservice teachers recognize what is possible in elementary education. It is about genuine collaboration with families and the community. Put simply, it is about good teaching.

Reference

Anthoney, R. J., T. Johnson, N. Mickelson, and A. Preece. 1996. *Evaluating Literacy: A Perspective for Change*. Portsmouth, NH: Heinemann.

Appendix B

Proposal for the School Board (December 1995)

DEBRA HAMM

Introduction

The Center for Inquiry will be a collaborative educational program of Richland School District Two and the University of South Carolina. It will be a small school of choice that will serve approximately 140 students in grades K–5. Its small size will foster a sense of community, and the school's programs will emphasize close relationships among the school, students, and parents. A shared philosophy of active, interdisciplinary learning coupled with high standards will ensure continuity across learning experiences and grade levels.

The Center will be a professional development school—a site for students to learn from exemplary instructional practices and for preservice and in-service teachers to learn effective teaching strategies. While traditional courses and workshops will be held at the school, it will also offer a unique opportunity for professionals from the district, state, and region to see theory put into practice. The school will employ an inquiry-based model for learning and will serve as a demonstration site for that approach. Inquiry-based programs teach students traditional content but in the context of units of study that are interdisciplinary and of high interest to the children.

Key Features
- small school
- inquiry-based, interdisciplinary curriculum
- shared teaching philosophy
- professional development school
- collaboration with University of South Carolina
- school of choice

Location and Facilities

The Center for Inquiry will be located on the campus of Summit Parkway Middle School in a cluster of portable classrooms. It will be distinguished by

231

an attractive awning, which will identify it, and it will be surrounded by a fence to ensure the security of the students. A communication system will further enhance the security and flow of work among the classes.

The facilities will be located in an area convenient to the main Summit Parkway school building but sufficiently distant to preserve their own identity. The portable classrooms are already in place but will be supplemented with an outdoor stage and playground. Each grade level will have its own portable, equipped with a restroom. An additional doublewide portable will serve as a multipurpose administration and large-group instructional site.

Students will follow the normal elementary school schedule, which will result in their arrival and departure times being different from middle school students. This will minimize elementary students' contact with middle school students and will improve traffic flow.

Student Selection

All Richland Two students in grades K–5 will be eligible to apply for enrollment at the Center for Inquiry. The goal of the selection process will be to have a student body that is approximately representative of the district's elementary population and to achieve that representation through a process that is fair to all.

Students will be selected using a method that is technically referred to as stratified random. Stratification refers to dividing the applicants into groups. Students are then randomly chosen from each group in a proportion that is representative of the population as a whole. These groupings will be based on race, sex, free/reduced lunch status, and aptitude scores. For example, if 55 percent of the district's students score above average on aptitude, the students selected for the center will reflect the same percentage. The selection method will include provisions to keep families together. Special-education students who are able to learn in a regular classroom setting with assistance from a resource teacher will also be eligible to attend.

Because of the overcrowding in the Rice Creek and North Springs attendance areas, preference will be give to students from those zones.

Organizational Structure

The school will consist of self-contained classrooms. The class sizes will be typical of those in Richland Two—approximately 24:1 for kindergarten, 22:1 in grades 1–3, and 25:1 in grades 4–5. There will be one class per grade level. Teachers will stay with the same group of students for two years to ensure the continuity of their learning experiences and to minimize time lost to transitions between grades. This practice is referred to as *looping*, and will be a standard feature of the instructional program.

The school will be supervised by a lead teacher who is jointly employed by Richland Two and the university. The teaching staff will also take a leadership role in making decisions about the school and its programs.

Staffing

The core staff will consist of one lead teacher (program coordinator), one secretary, six teachers, one teaching assistant (for kindergarten), and one part-time curriculum, research, and development specialist. Additional staff may be employed if the enrollment or characteristics of the school warrant.

The school will be staffed by employees of Richland School District Two who are mutually agreeable to the district and the University of South Carolina. The lead teacher and a secretary will be employed jointly by Richland Two and the university. The part-time curriculum, research, and development specialist will be funded by the university.

Because it will be a Professional Development School, many interns and university faculty will be on campus. The school will select teacher interns from early childhood and teacher education programs at the university who will serve as teaching assistants at the school. They will also be mutually acceptable. University of South Carolina professors will provide advice and consulting services as needed. At least one faculty member will receive released time from the university to serve as a liaison and to assist in instructional planning.

Curriculum and Instruction

The Center will be devoted to helping children develop a knowledge of and appreciation for traditional content areas by engaging them in rigorous units of study that require an understanding of the concepts, content, skills, and strategies inherent in individual subjects, as well as the interrelationships among the subjects. Since subject areas are integrated in the real-world, classroom experiences will also be integrated and reflect real-world applications of knowledge. The children will learn the basics about science, mathematics, history, reading, and writing but will also learn to do what scientists, historians, authors, and mathematicians do. This dual task will be accomplished through individual, small-group, and whole-class inquiry projects, strategy lessons that focus on skill development, and direct instruction.

The scope of the curriculum will reflect the requirements set forth by Richland Two's curriculum standards in each content area. Consistent with the inquiry approach, the order in which the objectives will be addressed and the selection of instructional strategies that will be used will be determined by teachers after careful observation and documentation of the students' needs and interests.

Technology at the Center will be used as an everyday tool to support thinking and learning. For example, uses of technology might include students extending their classroom research by using telecommunications to participate in national and international research projects, using computers to solve mathematical and scientific problems, preparing multimedia reports, using e-mail to communicate with scientists and authors, and using word-processing programs to facilitate writing. In addition, teachers will continually explore the possible roles of technology in the instructional program of the Center.

Publicity

It is important that Richland Two families receive adequate information about the Center for Inquiry so that parents can make an informed choice for their child. Printed materials including brochures, information in newsletters, and news releases will be distributed. The brochures will be mailed to each family with elementary-age children along with a letter indicating the names of district personnel to contact for additional information and the availability of orientation sessions that will be held at Summit Parkway. The orientation sessions will provide detailed information and a forum for questions and answers about the program.

Benefits

The Center will relieve some overcrowding at the elementary level. Preservice teachers from the University of South Carolina will function as instructional assistants while pursuing MAT degrees. This will lower the student-to-adult ratio and give students the benefit of working with instructional assistants with an extensive background in early childhood and elementary education. The selection process to become an instructional assistant will be very competitive.

As resources are limited, the Center will make a commitment to locating and securing outside funding sources. The district-college partnership will enhance the ability to attain grants. The prestige of a successfully implemented program will provide a competitive edge for recruiting students and teachers to Richland Two.

The Center will give parents an enhanced partnership opportunity in their children's education and its small size will allow it to better utilize their expertise throughout the school.

The Center will provide a special sense of community for its students and teachers that will foster successful learning.

Accountability: Assessment, Evaluation, Reporting

Students in the Center for Inquiry will be expected to learn the same curriculum as all other Richland Two students and will also participate in the same testing programs. The school will embrace high standards for academic excellence.

Evaluation of the Center will focus on its benefits to students and its usefulness as a professional development school. Assessment of the program should provide teachers, children, and parents with information related to the question "How am I doing?"

Assessment and evaluation will examine both the learning process and products. To accomplish this goal, profiles of student achievement will be developed that show each child's growth. The profiles will provide detailed descriptions of students' learning over time and will consist of a variety of data including standardized test scores; observations from teachers, parents, and students; and classroom examples representing discipline-based competencies.

In addition to student profiles, individual student achievement will be discussed and reported through conferences that include the parent, student, and teacher. A written narrative report will communicate the child's progress toward the competencies in each given content area. These competencies will reflect the standards of Richland Two's curriculum.

The school will have an advisory panel of parents, community-business partners, district office personnel, and USC faculty. Once a year, the faculty of the Center will present evidence of the program's achievements to this advisory group. A summary report will be sent to all parents and to the board of trustees.

Appendix C

Center for Inquiry Interview Materials

Center for Inquiry Interview Procedures

During Step 1, an interview team will be designed to reflect the collaboration between the university and Richland School District Two necessary in implementing the PDS philosophy outlined in the proposal for the Center for Inquiry.

The interview team will consist of two employees of Richland School District Two and two employees of the university. This will facilitate support for each agency as well as allow expertise from both agencies to be accessed.

Candidates will be initially screened through an individual interview that will include submission of a videotape illustrating an instructional segment from their classroom. Top candidates will be sent a letter inviting them to participate in Step 2 of the interview process.

Step 2 will include screening files and calling individuals back for a group interview. Since one unique feature of the Center is to facilitate philosophical congruence between and among faculty, a group interview should ascertain the degree to which this goal can be met with certain individuals. In addition, this will allow the team to observe interpersonal skills and provide an opportunity for applicants to meet one another.

Group Interview Questions

Make introductions and talk about the current interest: "This interview is designed to give us an opportunity to get to know more about you and to allow you to learn about others who are interested in the Center. We're going to ask you questions and will give each of you a chance to respond to each question. You can take turns being 'first,' but we'd like you to think of this as a conversation among people interested in inquiry, instruction, and professional development, rather than a question-and-answer session."

Next, watch the video and discuss insights and recommendations: "Stories and reports about schools are often in the media. Talk about something you have heard, seen, or read about recently that you think is important for teachers to think about."

Finally, ask the following questions:

"What sort of things do you hope to learn at the Center?"

"What do you expect to be the biggest challenges you will face if you become a part of the Center?"

Center Interview Evaluation Form

Philosophical Congruence

Questions

1. Give applicant the Center proposal to read as he or she waits, and then ask him or her to describe experiences that he or she has had that makes him or her a qualified candidate for this type of school and instruction.

2. You realize that it is important to consider the subject matter, the classroom environment, and the individual when designing instructional experiences. Describe your classroom and instructional practices in relation to each of these elements and discuss the significance of viewing these elements simultaneously.

3. Talk about curriculum—what is is, how it should be organized and developed, and what components are essential.

4. One of the purposes of the Center for Inquiry is to create a setting where like-minded colleagues can work together to create a school where their professional learning would be supported and extended. Describe experiences that you would expect in such an environment and possibilities that might exist there for professional educators.

Components (Check all that apply)

Articulates how children learn.

_____Describes learning as a transaction among the content, the instruction, the environment, and the learner.

_____Describes learning as a recursive process.

_____Describes learning as a social process.

_____Talks about the zone of proximal development and the implications for instruction.

_____Describes learning as a natural process.

_____Talks about the capability of all children to learn.

_____Discusses learning in relation to thinking.

_____Describes the importance of intrinsic motivation to learn.

_____Describes learning as the teacher instructing the student.

_____Describes learning as mastery.

_____Talks about motivating the students to learn.

_____Describes learners as learning in different ways.

Defines inquiry-based instruction.

_____Talks about the importance of creating a sense of wonder.

_____Describes integrating curriculum.

_____Discusses restructuring time to create larger blocks necessary for thinking.

_____Describes the process for negotiating the standard curriculum with children's interests.

_____Explains that the use of certain materials or strategies, such as big books, units of study, and journals, do not necessarily imply that the curriculum operates from an inquiry perspective.

_____Describes the importance of academic strength.

Describes characteristics of an inquiry-based philosophy.

_____Choice.

_____Freedom with responsibility.

_____Talk as an instructional tool.

_____Using children as curricular informants.

_____Teachers trusting the children to learn.

_____Describes reading and writing as tools for learning.

_____Discusses the value of reflection.

_____Describes risk taking as essential to the learning process.

_____Describes an academically rigorous curriculum.

Gives examples of translating theory into practice.

_____Talks about using the children's questions to structure a unit of study.

_____Talks about journal writing to capture children's thinking.

_____Talks about the value of kindergartners writing and reading from the first day.

_____Describes the physical environment.

_____Talks about strategic instruction.

_____Describes rituals such as class meetings or opening or closing class-room routines.

_____Talks about alternative assessment.

_____Talks about professional publications.

_____Talks about professional presentations.

_____Discusses the value of parental contributions.

_____Describes learning from colleagues.

Describes the significance and possibilities related to philosophical congruence of a faculty.

_____Describes continual learning personally and professionally.

_____Describes curriculum as a dynamic, evolving product.

_____Describes risk-taking benefits for children.

_____Describes risk-taking benefits for teachers.

_____Describes benefits for children related to similar learning expectations and instructional processes.

Describes how theory is developed.

_____Discusses data-collection techniques.

_____Discusses informed instruction.

_____Discusses creating instructional strategies.

_____Discusses looking for patterns of growth over time.

_____Describes the cyclical nature of data collection, creating instructional strategies, and revising instructional strategies.

Philosophical Congruence Rating *(Circle one number for each category)*

Category					
Learning	5	4	3	2	1
Inquiry Instruction	5	4	3	2	1
Inquiry Characteristics	5	4	3	2	1
Theory to Practice	5	4	3	2	1
Faculty	5	4	3	2	1
Develop Theory	5	4	3	2	1

Experience

Questions

1. Tell us about the professional experiences, schools, and grade levels you have taught. Please include curriculum and assessment as you discuss these experiences.

2. Tell us what you like or dislike about the assessment measures you use in your classroom and school and how those measures relate to your instructional goals.

3. Imagine a colleague observing your teaching and then meeting with a group of teachers to discuss the strengths of your instruction and collaborating to make suggestions to improve instruction. Describe your feelings and expectations related to this scenario.

4. Describe how you think the Professional Development School initiative is vital to the success of the Center. Could you talk about ways in which you have best supported the profession through work with a student teacher, new colleague, or inservice teachers?

5. Given that parents should be partners in their child's education, describe what you do now and what you envision.

6. Given that inquiry-based instruction is innovative, how do you integrate curriculum standards and measures?

Components *(Check all that apply)*

Diversity of school/grade-level/professional experience

_____ Taught in different school districts.

_____ Taught in different schools.

_____ Taught in the following grades:
   K_____1_____2_____3_____4_____5_____

_____ Taught in a multiage classroom.

_____ Other: _____

Implementing elements of inquiry

_____ Has designed integrated units of study from an inquiry perspective.

_____ Describes process of integrating standard content, disciplinary perspectives, and ways to communicate learning.

_____ Describes designing experiences from the children's interests.

_____ Describes the importance of creating a sense of wonder.

Alternative assessment *techniques*

____Describes various assessment tools developed and used.

____Describes how these tools are used to evaluate students' growth.

____Visualizes a system for assessment and evaluation that includes standardized test scores.

Peer *review*

____Describes experiences with peer review.

____Discusses ideas for improving process.

____Talks about the concept in a positive light.

Experience with PDS *initiative*

____Defines PDS.

____Explains the USC PDS initiative.

____Discusses specific ideas related to the Center as a PDS.

Experience with parents *participating in the curriculum*

____Shares way parents are now involved in his or her school.

____Shares ways parents are now involved in his or her classroom.

____Discusses ways parents can become true partners through field studies, alternative assessment strategies, study groups, becoming a member of the learning community, and so on.

Experience in developing a community of learners

____Defines community of learners.

____Shares strategies for developing a community of learners.

____Discusses the value and importance of a community of learners in relation to learning.

Experience with student teachers, *MAT interns, inservice professional development*

____APT endorsed.

____Discusses the similarities/differences between the MAT program and the undergraduate.

____Explains that the intern is a colleague rather than a student.

____Describes inservice professional presentation.

____Writes/publishes for the profession.

Experience Rating *(Circle one number for each category)*

Diversity of Experience	5	4	3	2	1
Implementing Inquiry	5	4	3	2	1
Alternative Assessment	5	4	3	2	1
Peer Review	5	4	3	2	1
PDS	5	4	3	2	1
Parents	5	4	3	2	1
Community of Leaders	5	4	3	2	1
Student Teachers	5	4	3	2	1

Comments:

Seriousness of Purpose

Questions

1. Why do you want to be a part of the Center for Inquiry?
2. What unique talents or contributions can you make to help the Center become successful?
3. Describe one of the most valuable professional contributions that you have made to our profession.

Components *(Check all that apply)*

Schedule *that will permit planning during spring and summer*

_____Shares an understanding that summer planning will be entailed.

_____Shares a commitment to give whatever time will be required.

Interested in learning

_____Wants to continue to grow as a professional.

_____Describes commitment to children's learning in a democratic society.

_____Describes *contribution* to profession.

_____Articulates strengths and weaknesses.

_____States evidence of successful *grant writing*.

_____Provides evidence of professional *publication*.

_____Provides evidence of professional *presentations*.

Seriousness of Purpose Rating *(Circle one number for each category)*

Planning Schedule	5	4	3	2	1
Interest in Learning	5	4	3	2	1
Professional Contribution	5	4	3	2	1
Grant Writing	5	4	3	2	1
Publication	5	4	3	2	1
Presentation	5	4	3	2	1

Comments:

Communication/Interpersonal Skills

Questions

There is one teacher on staff who is continually critical of your ideas. How do you handle that and why?

There is one teacher who often acts in a manner that you consider unprofessional. How do you handle that?

Components *(Check all that apply)*

_____Has pleasant voice and clear articulation.

_____Expresses confidence.

_____Elicits information.

_____Shows evidence of conflict resolution skills.

_____Smiles.

_____Demonstrates an appropriate sense of humor.

_____Demonstrates positive body language.

_____Has ease with standard English.

_____Gives clear explanations.

_____Maintains appropriate eye contact.

_____Clarifies or extends with personal examples.

_____Communicates enthusiasm.

Communication/Interpersonal Skill Rating *(Circle one number)*

5   4   3   2   1

Comments: